MINORITIES
IN THE
OPEN SOCIETY:
PRISONERS OF AMBIVALENCE

Reports of the Institute of Community Studies

MINORITIES
IN THE
OPEN SOCIETY:
PRISONERS OF AMBIVALENCE

Geoff Dench

ROUTLEDGE & KEGAN PAUL
LONDON AND NEW YORK

First published in 1986 by
Routledge & Kegan Paul plc
11 New Fetter Lane, London EC4P 4EE

Published in the USA by
Routledge & Kegan Paul Inc.
in association with Methuen Inc.
29 West 35th Street, New York, NY 10001

Set in 10/12 pt Sabon
and printed in Great Britain by
Butler & Tanner Ltd
Frome and London

Library of Congress Cataloging in Publication Data

Dench, Geoff.
Minorities in the open society.

(Reports of the Institute of Community Studies)
Bibliography: p.
Includes index.
1. Minorities——Civil rights.   2. Ethnic groups——Civil
rights.   3. Ethnicity.   4. Ethnic relations.   I. Title.
II. Series.
JF1061.D46   1986   323.1   86–4872

British Library CIP Data also available
ISBN 0–7102–0898–7

CONTENTS

ACKNOWLEDGMENTS vii
PREFACE AND SUMMARY 1
  Summary of argument 8

Part I THE AMBIVALENT STATE

1 TWO FACES OF MODERN NATIONALISM 15
   An issue fudged 15
   Coming to terms with duality 31

2 SERVING TWO MASTERS 42
   Props to the economy 46
   Reservoirs of extraordinary patriotism 53
   Keepers of the faith 58

Part II CAPTIVE LEADERS

3 PIERRE TRUDEAU IN THRALL TO CANADIAN INTEGRITY 67
   In bondage to a higher destiny 67
   Trudeau's advocacy of federalism 69

4 THE RED TSAR AS A PAWN OF GREAT RUSSIAN CHAUVINISM 78
   Patrons in need of a client 79
   The Georgian Affair 87

5 JFK: MESSENGER FOR SECOND RECONSTRUCTION 91
   A nation requiring redemption 91
   Playing the minority card 95

6 DISRAELI'S TRIBUTE TO BRITISH IMPERIALISM 101
   Sponsorship and dependence 102
   The Bonapartist moment 106

Contents

Part III TORMENTS IN CAPTIVITY

7 THE TREADMILL OF ETHNIC HONOUR 113
   Social control in closed communities 117
   The degradation in emancipation 121
   Onto the treadmill 126

8 ON THE RACK OF DEMOCRATIC POLITICS 135
   Bonds of multiple fealty 136
   Pulled between rival patrons 142
   Taking the strain 148

9 TRIALS OF COMMITMENT 156
   The objective test of culture 157
   Weighing up the evidence of roots 161
   Arrested in the lobby 166

Part IV THE FRAMEWORK OF
           CONTAINMENT

10 THE POWER OF COMMUNALISM 177
    The fraternal imperative 180
    Communalism and class 190

11 MINORITY RIGHTS AND NATIONAL STRATEGIES 202
    The utopian period 205
    Vehicles in collision: 1848–1918 210
    Dismantling the Old World: 1918–40 218
    The postwar era – A golden age of decolonization 224

12 DISCRIMINATION AND THE LIBERAL SOCIAL ORDER 228
    Keeping an orderly house 230
    Masquerades of class action 239

    CONCLUSION: THE ROLE FOR SOCIAL THEORY 251
    Theory as exhortation 252
    Taking the pressure off 257
    REFERENCES 262
    INDEX 269

ACKNOWLEDGMENTS

This book develops out of and extends the analysis of an investigation carried out several years ago at the Institute of Community Studies. The further work entailed in this new study was not really part of the current Institute programme. But members of the Institute, especially Michael Young, have played a key part in bringing it to fruition, and I am extremely grateful for this.

A number of people have given me particular support in this venture. From early on in the project, Philip Gould has provided much valuable counsel. Sasha Moorsom has been a source of constant encouragement and stimulus; and Peter Willmott, with characteristic generosity, has made very detailed and helpful comments on drafts. I am also indebted to Greg Andrusz, Georgina Baker, Sean Hawkins, Mary Higgs, John Lea, John Peterson and David Smith for specific criticisms and suggestions, which I have tried to meet.

Finally, at the production stage, Jessica Gould typed the manuscript to a very exacting timetable and my mother, Isabel Dench, liberated me, as she has before, from the main burden of proof-reading.

PREFACE AND SUMMARY

Members of national minorities in modern states are subjected to powerful contradictions. On the one hand they are regaled with promises of free and equal participation in society for all individuals – if not perhaps at once, then in a little while. On the other they are faced with a continuing reality of communalism, among themselves as well as in national majorities, whereby groups identifying themselves in terms of common origin, race or culture tend to stick together. This discrepancy creates tremendous dilemmas for them, and throws up moral and political issues for society as a whole.

It is because of social concern about these problems that sociological theories about race and ethnic relations exist at all. Most of this theory has been reluctant, however, to move beyond conventional public definitions of what actually constitutes the problem. It is this timidity I think, which underlies the general failure to come up with any truly convincing accounts of this area of social behaviour.

The mistake that most analyses make lies in accepting an over-idealistic conception of the basic issues. Current public and conventional idealism in the West holds that the pursuit of individual freedom is a central imperative in the modern world. Communalist behaviours defying it are regarded as intrinsically threatening to social order. Dominant majorities which discriminate against minorities are thus seen as storing up trouble for themselves.

These sentiments may be fine as a political platform. They lead to all sorts of difficulties, though, when taken as a point of departure for an explanatory theory. In the real world liberal creeds and communalistic activities co-exist perfectly well in the same states without appearing to entail instability. Accounts premised on their incompatibility are obliged to call very heavily on paradoxes, special cases and impending transformations in order to sustain any sort of validity.

We can arrive at a clearer understanding of community relations if we avoid the temptation to see the area as a battleground between

I

heroic and demonic forces, and fall back on earthy commonsense instead. There is, in particular, little justification for going along with the conventional piety that official creeds repudiating discrimination are in any true sense antithetical to it. It would be more to the point to see these creeds as an expression of a more refined style of communalism.

In the current international system, it is very much in the interests of a nation – and especially of a dominant national majority – to display some commitment to progressive values. A nation which condemns discrimination enhances its standing among its peer nations, and forestalls external interference on behalf of its minority groups. This is no triumph for individualism. It is just communalism engaging in protective concealment and self-deception. There are no awesome paradoxes here, only the systematic promotion and rewarding of hypocrisy.

Behind the morality-play of a struggle between universalist ideas and communalism, which responsible public opinion manages to conjure up, there is I believe an interplay between an assortment of communalist impulses. These vary mainly in their explicitness. What I have tried to do in this book is to sketch out an approach to ethnicity and race which takes this, rather than the usual proprieties, as its starting point. The outcome is less immediately palatable than are most of the available models in this area. It reveals no easy solutions to minority tribulations. It does, however, lead to more credible explanations. Also I think it is more consonant with minority experience, as it embraces a consideration of the confusing effects on them of the optimistic sermonizing and propaganda which so many commentators are happy to reiterate and compound.

The model outlined here originates in an attempt to overcome certain limitations in theory which suggested themselves to me some years ago, when I was making a study of the Maltese community in Britain. At that time I was chiefly interested in carrying out a limited empirical investigation, and was not greatly bothered by the general state of theory. But I could hardly fail to be disappointed by the inability of prevailing ideas to illuminate my findings more than they did.

What I felt specifically was that most analysts, both those aligned with the political establishment and those following an oppositional tack, seemed keener to preach solutions to minorities, and to demonstrate their own commitment to progressive causes, than to try to understand the ideas held by minorities and respect these as rational attempts to cope with the demands of their situation. Above all, they appeared quite unable to give serious attention to something which seemed crucial in the Maltese case, namely the contribution that public idealism might itself be making to the confinement of minorities. Several years elapsed before I took up this issue again in this present enterprise. In many respects, though, this is really a delayed continuation and extension of that earlier work.

Revisiting the Maltese

When I began on the Maltese study the prevailing, liberal approach to minority problems was still to hold up individual 'assimilation' as the panacea; and the view taken about the Maltese in responsible political and academic circles was that they were exemplary assimilators, quietly going about their business of learning how to be good Britons. Some of them, it was conceded, had managed to find themselves in trouble with the police here. This was, however, seen to be a marginal phenomenon, affecting very few. It was, moreover, one which should not be given too much attention, for fear of hindering the earnest efforts of the vast majority who were integrating successfully.

I was unable to keep my own analyses within this framework. As soon as I embarked on practical fieldwork I found that the troubles hinted at were much more disturbing and injurious to members of the community than the usual account chose to relate. More significantly, and running counter to conventional perspectives on them, the troubles appeared to be intimately tied up with the desire of the Maltese to assimilate. As the study proceeded I came to feel not only was Maltese involvement in crime, as several libertarian commentators feared, hindering attempts at integration, but it also appeared that this criminality was a major stimulant towards assimilation. Moreover, and even harder to stomach, it seemed that assimilation itself strongly reinforced the tendency towards criminality. The overall situation seemed very complex. One thing, however, that soon became clear was that the pursuit of assimilation was not the simple road to personal freedom that it seemed.

Early in my investigations I discovered that the disreputable conduct which some members of the community were engaged in was at the heart of the experience of all Maltese living here. It was a focal point for a sharp duality of treatment from the British public they lived among. Many Maltese informants impressed on me that they felt themselves caught between contradictory pressures from different sectors of British society, over the matter of whether their community should see itself as having a collective duty to control its members. After a while I began to see that the dilemmas and sense of injustice and impotence flowing from this discrepancy in their experience were central to their social relations – not just with non-Maltese people, but among themselves as well. So I decided at a fairly early stage in the project to organize my inquiry around questions related to this. How far did this apparent contradiction exist outside their own anxious and sensitized minds? How much of the life and structure of the community could be understood as a response to it?

Surveys I carried out among non-Maltese people in contact with Maltese immigrants soon confirmed the reality of my informants' dilemma. Formally the Maltese were defined as free individuals like any other British citizens. They were seen as personally accountable only for their own acts. They even came under some pressure from official agencies to discard any ethnic consciousness which they did retain. I found that several government departments were inclined to regard the Maltese 'community' as itself a barrier to orderly settlement. It was seen as more likely to aggravate than bring under control problems within it, and thus as something from which its members needed to be liberated. For example, throughout the period of my investigation the Ministry of Labour gave strong preference to those applications for work vouchers which related to jobs in areas where there were few other Maltese settled. Similarly, a number of local authority housing departments brought forward environmental redevelopments in order to break up supposedly criminogenic Maltese ghettoes, and hasten individual assimilation.

What I also found, however, was that alongside this official emphasis on individualized treatment there co-existed a deep reserve of popular communalism. Large sections of the populace, abetted by the tabloid press, extended moral liability for any deviant behaviour among Maltese to the ethnic group as a whole. Such people deemed it appropriate to apply informal, extra-legal sanctions for this behaviour to any person identifiable as Maltese. Neighbours and work-mates regularly indicated to known Maltese associates that they could not fully accept them as fellow citizens so long as they permitted wayward compatriots to carry on as they did. The message conveyed by their hosts' private behaviour was clear. All Maltese possessed an additional and logically prior civic obligation to stick together in mutually regulating networks, until they had cleaned up their collective performance and reputation.

Not all British people regarded the Maltese in this way, of course. Many private individuals expressed views consistent with public policy. But enough communalist attitudes and treatment occurred to compromise seriously the formal rights of Maltese to live peacefully as free and self-interested British citizens. The more information I collected, the clearer it became to me that this split imperative issuing from different manifestations of the host nation must set a major obstacle to the Maltese escaping from their marginal and insecure position as recent immigrants. They were the simultaneous subjects of incompatible régimes. It was difficult therefore to see how they might become generally accepted. They inhabited more than one Britain. Whichever set of rules they might decide to follow, they were bound to incur the displeasure of some part of the host community.

Those willing to take part in ethnic community controls over their wilder compatriots were liable to find themselves designated as perpetuating the bonds, customs or relationships in which the deviance was presumed to be grounded. On the other hand, those trying to integrate as law-abiding citizens free from the ties of ethnic solidarity were plagued by criticisms from other quarters for walking out on their communal obligations. There was no way that any of them could hope to satisfy all of the groups in the majority capable of inflicting some form of punishment on them. They were effectively all caught together in a pincer. Any effort to disengage from one prong only led to greater impalement on another

I found little in existing theory to help me to develop these ideas. The literature contained many concrete studies showing the enduring vulnerability of particular minorities to oppression. But the theoretical models generalizing from them seemed to prefer to emphasize that only small and unrepresentative sectors of a host community had any real stake in supremacist behaviour. Many even managed to identify benign, historically ascendant forces within national majorities with which minorities could safely be advised to make a progressive alliance.

None of this had much pertinence in the Maltese case. My findings gave little support to the presumption that national majorities and minorities have an overriding common cause in getting rid of ethnic stratification. The British majority seemed to be able to impose dilemmas on the Maltese with impunity to itself. This indicated a serious and obvious divergence of interests. There was little reason to believe that exclusive behaviour towards the Maltese came only from an insignificant or deviant sector of the British majority. Nor was there any evidence that it was having any harmful effects on wider British society.

In fact the general drift of my findings pulled strongly towards the conclusion that the ostensibly disparate and contradictory elements of British treatment of the Maltese worked in the same direction, and were much more intertwined than they seemed. They could perhaps even be seen as complementary aspects of an unspoken and only half-conscious majority strategy for keeping them subordinate by keeping them confused.

Communalist bullying undermined Maltese personal rights and freedom. Meanwhile confident declarations about the inevitable processes of integration encouraged them to believe that if they left it all to their hosts and masters then everything would turn out alright in the end. The combined effect of these contrasting modes seemed to be to allow the British to carry on excluding the Maltese from national life without revealing themselves along the way as outright supremacists. It enabled them to insulate themselves morally and politically from the problems that Maltese had in accommodating to their lives here. As long as the British could tell each other and concerned opinion abroad that most Maltese were happily making good progress towards assimilation, they felt justified in pursuing a policy of benign neglect towards the real difficulties. British liberals dreamed sweetly of peaceful integration, and of Albion's vanguard role in the creation of the multi-racial society of the future. Meanwhile Maltese dilemmas remained largely invisible; unexplored and unresolved.

From minority dilemma to majority bind

Before very long I was forced to decide that bland faith in the power of assimilation was not merely displaced. It was itself a major factor sustaining Maltese troubles. The vision it held out of the gradual dawning of an individualist utopia might not have been a root cause of their predicament. But it certainly aggravated it. It neither succeeded in countering British hostility, nor permitted the Maltese to perceive and face up to it realistically. By sublimely ignoring the strength of ethnocentric currents among the majority, and treating their intolerance as something that would simply go away if right-thinking folk repudiated it, such confidence ended up by allowing supremacist forces a sort of indirect licence – almost colluding in them. Then, by closing its eyes to all the signs of its own failure of analysis, it exacerbated the

6

tendencies towards disorganization within the Maltese settlement, which held them in impotence.

The outcome of exposure to ambiguity, and punishment for whatever they did, was demoralization of the whole ethnic group. It became trapped in a cycle of disorderly behaviour and majority intervention and victimization. No single response to the group's problems was adequate. So none could enjoy the undisputed acceptance of all members. The settlement was plagued by a pervasive factionalism which drained energy away from collective endeavours to make sense of and come to terms with their situation, channelling it instead into a multiplicity of hopeful alliances with well-meaning patrons in the host society.

These alliances in turn helped to open up internal community divisions and tensions. The policies of different factions were inevitably in direct competition with each other. So the limitations of each scheme for tackling anything tended to be blamed on the immediate and evident factors of rival compatriots' wrongheadedness and treachery – over which the group could still hope to exercise some influence – rather than on duplicity or obstruction on the part of British patrons. Maltese were pitted even more firmly against one another.

Self-congratulatory British commentaries set great store by the desire of Maltese for rapid absorption into British society. This dream, however, was largely an unfulfilled aspiration. And behind it lay an agonized rejection of a community immobilized by contradictory pressures from outside, then poisoned by mutual suspicions and recriminations within.

The feeling I came away from that investigation with, and which has hardened since with further reading, is that prevailing perspectives on race and ethnicity lie far too close to governing ideologies. This also includes 'critical' commentaries on the left. They are all too suffused with hopeful bluff and promise to be able to put up convincing explanations of how communal relations really do operate. There is a body of idealistic premises commonly detectable beneath conventional accounts – such as belief in the tractability and intrinsic goodness of human nature, or in the power of values to transform society, in a 'harmony of natural interests' and so on – which seem strangely at odds with the aim of clarifying how things actually work. What they do seem tailor-made to do is to help keep minorities docile, by boosting confidence in the progressive character of the national communities controlling their destinies.

The presence of such beliefs inhibits consideration of the part played by optimistic prognoses in diverting minorities from realizing their true prospects. It is this inability of conventional theories to operate reflexively which is their most serious analytic defect. It prevents them from even admitting, let alone explaining, the fact which otherwise would be self-evident, and which is the natural starting-point for a proper theory of ethnicity and race. This is that national majorities which are prominent in upholding liberal creeds are often the most successful practitioners of discrimination. Hypocrisy is the norm.

No account of ethnic relations can carry much weight if it fails to explore how integrative ideologies and exclusivist behaviour can operate, in effect, as a double act in favour of majorities. Because of their subjection to this ambiguous treatment, minorities are obliged to adopt a highly ambivalent attitude towards the national majority and the state machine it controls. These figure together as the source both of promises of freedom and equality, and of the obstacles to their attainment. In the last analysis I think it is this ambivalence which does most to keep minorities quietly in their place in modern societies, and to prolong ethnic hierarchies without obliging majority groups to display the full force of their communalism.

SUMMARY OF ARGUMENT

The ambivalent state

Part I of the book looks briefly at the dual character of modern states. Formally they are committed to progressive, 'universalist' values. But they still operate through traditional 'national' vehicles tied to the destiny of particular communities. The ambiguity inherent in this is no great problem to dominant majorities, who can interpret universalist prescriptions in partisan ways that suit their own needs. But this works at the expense of weaker communities lacking the power to turn the contradictions in their favour.

The behaviour of minorities in 'open' societies can best be understood as attempts to minimize punishment from the majority. They need to act in ways which satisfy both communalist demands from the masses as well as the integrationist expectations of the national *élite*. The best way of doing this lies in turning a blind eye to their patrons' abuse of the system and accepting more or less at face value the progressive claims the host state makes for its policies and practices. Acquiescence in a sanitized account of what goes on is at the same time an act of communal submission. Thus minorities are recruited to loyal clientship or tutelage. They are keen to display their faith in the system and their future, but are ready to wait before receiving the reward of equal participation and achievement. In this capacity they become a valuable natural resource for deployment by the sovereign whim of the majority. They provide willing hands to prop up the national economy, super-patriots to promote the nation's vision and destiny, and high priests at the universalist altars from which host nations ultimately receive their mandate and legitimacy.

Captive leaders

The second section explores in more detail one of the key services that minority clients perform on behalf of their national masters, namely the exercise of integrative leadership during periods of political crisis and change. Such individuals are well placed to retain the confidence of minority groups even when carrying out measures patently geared to majority interests. This gives them a 'Bonapartist' ability to unite a deeply divided society. In the same way, simply by holding office they can boost the credit a nation enjoys in the international community – imparting a universalist quality to actions which would appear as grossly nationalist if performed by a member of the dominant community.

Several cases are examined. Pierre Trudeau, a self-confessed agent of Anglophone supremacy, has recently reintegrated Canadian society around a centralized consolidation of individual rights which effectively suppresses French Canadian identity. Stalin, Lenin's most important protégé, was ideally suited as one of its colonial subjects to take a key role in modernizing and reviving the Russian empire under the banner of universal proletarian solidarity. Kennedy enhanced America's wavering claim to primacy in the liberal world at a critical moment, by successfully launching a Yankee bid to reassert hegemony over a reactionary Dixie. Finally Disraeli can be seen as having nationalized British political life, without besmirching the liberal credentials of its native establishment, during a transitional period when simple devotion to *laissez-faire* and international trading was no longer sufficient to uphold British interests.

Torments in captivity

Part III develops the theme that although the ambiguities of minority status can create special types of opportunity for ambitious individuals, in general they result in dilemmas which members of dominant communities can exploit in order to underline their supremacy.

This is clearly the case in relation to the allocation of responsibility for criminal or anti-social behaviour. One implication of integrative creeds is to weaken the controls that minority communities can exert over their members. But any resulting deviance is then blamed back by popular nationalist opinion onto these communities themselves. This is used to justify reprisals against any group members, thereby severely undermining the citizenship rights of even the most law-abiding members.

Similar practices compromise participation in the political realm. Minority individuals are pressed by universalists to join in national political movements. But they are then held back from using this system to do something about their specific collective grievances, by nationalist definitions of which political interests are and are not legitimate. The typical outcome is that minority politicians can survive only so long as they express majority concerns. Equally, minority interests are only treated seriously when voiced and reinterpreted by members of the controlling majority. Thus the main political role for minorities is to serve as ballot-fodder and cheer-leaders for parties which ignore their own special needs.

A third area of entanglement between contrary demands which is considered here has to do with 'culture'. Culture is officially regarded in progressive states as a matter of personal choice and expression. Most people, however, use it as an emblem to indicate group membership, and thus as a medium for testing loyalties and asserting communal hierarchies.

Members of minorities who elect to adopt a majority culture are liable to teasing by hard-line communalists as imitators, or even saboteurs. Those who decide to cherish their own cultural heritage are variously open to condemnation as clannish, as agents of an alien and colonizing state, or even reactionary devotees of barbaric practices. The many traps in this area may make it very difficult to construct a stable and satisfactory personal identity.

The framework of containment

The focus changes in the final section. It takes up some questions raised in the first chapter, about the nature of the forces in modern society which impinge on minorities, and concerning the implications for a host state of containing oppressed groups. The argument developed is that communalist values giving moral priority to groups over individuals are in reality a major force in modern states. The action of class groups often appears more salient. But this arises partly because communalism has an incentive to disguise itself *as* class action, to render itself more compatible with ruling progressive morality. Humanist ideas have a capacity to provide a dignified cloak for communalist designs. It may only be because of this that creeds and constitutions embodying these values have been formally adopted at all in modern nations.

This even applies in relation to those ideals concerned very specifically with the rights of minorities. The only principles reliably acted on are those suiting the foreign policy requirements of leading nations. The minorities most likely to enjoy these rights are those currently serving as pawns in a leading nation's global design.

The conclusion this must lead to is that discrimination against minorities is not in itself a great threat to the social order. On the contrary it would appear to be an integral part of the modern world system. It furnishes liberal *élites* with strategies for asserting their superiority, both domestically and in the international arena. Modern régimes maximize their legitimacy and support in the community of nations by keeping up the appearances of an 'open' society.

This task is much easier in powerful states. These can provide their members – even the second-class citizens – with a better living than they could enjoy elsewhere. Citizens of such nations have little incentive to spoil the show by revealing the extent to which national performance falls short of declared standards. Ruling *élites* can steer dissidents among both minorities and the majority masses into phrasing their discontent along class lines. These conflicts are both relatively shallow, and do not offend international morality.

Weaker states do not have the same chance to seal off their domestic affairs from international criticism and intervention. The conflicts within them over limited resources are inevitably sharper and more desperate, and more likely to open up deep communal fissures. So it is among peripheral and vassal states that discrimination against minorities is most obvious. It is here, too, that the international system can exact punishments for it.

In the Conclusion there is a short discussion of the role played by social theory itself in facilitating the confinement of minorities by echoing official promises. Many theorists are afraid that if they admit the strength of communalism they will encourage majorities in oppression. The opposite effect seems equally likely. Through conspiring to overlook the obstacles to full incorporation of minorities, and endorsing the universalist claims of political activists, they flatter them into dreams that cannot be fulfilled. This helps to maintain the duality in minority experience that keeps them confused and dependent.

Commentators who cared less about their own or their nations' progressive images would be more cautious in declaring the imminence or historical necessity of racial equality. This might allow subjugated groups more latitude to interpret for themselves the situations they are in.

PART I
THE AMBIVALENT STATE

CHAPTER 1

TWO FACES OF MODERN NATIONALISM

> The state in theory extends its benefits and protection equally to all its citizens and all equally participate in it; but the inherent personal-community element of the nation works to limit the full participation in the state to those who can establish their national acceptability.
>
> (Rupert Emerson, 1960, p. 111)

It is a commonplace that minorities lose out because of contrary impulses within the modern state. All constitutions with any pretence to civilized status embody some variant of the humanist creed, proclaiming the equal worth and civil estate of every member. But the states licensed by these creeds are controlled by particular and partisan national communities. So there is, as Minogue (1967) put it, a discrepancy between political association based on the rational consent of individuals, and solidarity arising out of involuntary ties of birth and descent. This duality is woven deeply into the fabric of the state system.

This contradiction is not, however, the curse and problem for all concerned which it is so often portrayed to be. It is obviously a curse for minority groups. Few would seriously dispute that. I cannot believe, though, that it is much of a problem for majorities. Universalist and nationalist ideas can prove remarkably complementary when spun together in the service of a powerful community. Public declarations of their irreconcilability have to be seen as part of an establishment's ruling bluff.

AN ISSUE FUDGED

Analyses of race relations in specific settings often remark on the hypocritical nature of official idealism. Thomas Blair (1977, p. 4) opens his account of white-black relations in the US in this vein.

15

(America's) rise to greatness is based in large part on a special blend of materialism and imperfect idealism, low cunning and high-mindedness ... There is an air of pious fraudulence in a nation that still remains the beloved community of white Anglo-Saxon Protestants, of Emerson, Thoreau, Melville, Twain, James, and others, and where the essential social levers of opportunity – education, jobs, housing and political power – are kept out of the reach of the masses of black citizens.

This interpretation is not given much prominence in generalized accounts. Most theories about community relations resolutely fudge the issue. They declare that any co-existence of different principles of association cannot last very long, as it offends against the requirement that social systems possess internal consistency. Nationalist exclusion of minorities from full participation in national life is not just morally repugnant. It is also harmful to the whole of society. Toleration of discrimination gives the lie to universalist promises made by the system; and this must in the end undermine the legitimacy of even those rights enjoyed by members of the majority themselves.

Discrimination is so corrosive of legitimate social order that it threatens the welfare and unity of the whole realm. Majorities and minority groups share an overriding common interest in working to narrow the gaps between liberatory promises and actual national performance.

The consensualist foundation

Propositions like these have been common ground for progressive political thinkers and virtually all social theorists for the last hundred years or more. They were laid down again, very explicitly and forcefully, by the influential generation including Robert MacIver and Robin Williams during that classic period of sociology at the end of the second world war, when the US was establishing the moral basis of its new hegemony.

Discriminatory practices are sustained by narrow interests and are accepted by a large public that remains unconscious of their more profound import ... The frustrated groups unable to share in and contribute to the community life develop their quotas of racketeers, black market operators, gangsters and so forth, and though these form only a small minority of such groups they suffice to confirm the prejudice of which they themselves are a product ... All disparaged groups tend to become disaffected, and when the range of discrimination is so great as it is in the United States the resulting loss to the solidarity of the national life, to its healthful vigor and strength of purpose, must be considerable.

(Robert MacIver, 1948, pp. 244–5)

It is important to notice that such affirmations of the need for a truly open society come both from those with an interest in upholding an existing social order, and from those opposed to it. A ruling, liberal approach proposing that individualism can and will break down group barriers offers the simpler model. But Marx and his followers have expressed opinions on discrimination that are remarkably similar to those of Acton and his ilk.

The socialist variant of the argument differs by interposing an element of class conflict, which must be played out before social justice and individual freedom are accessible to all, and which in the meantime permeates all social life. Socialists therefore insist on pointing out how discrimination is a refraction or displacement of class conflict, and cannot be eliminated independently of it. But they are not blind to the problems that discrimination itself creates in the meantime. They take a similar view to liberals of its likely consequences for national unity and stability.

To a significant extent, universalists of all hues are in agreement on race and ethnic relations. All share in what might be called a 'consensualist' idea of society, which regards continuing tension between universalist and nationalist values as a source of political weakness and instability. Moreover, most of them are optimistic about the future. They tend to see history, or specifically 'modernization', as working inexorably to weaken communalist bonds.

In passing it might be added that the third major political orientation towards race and ethnicity, namely overt Nationalism, does itself appear to rest on a sort of inverted consensualism. Nationalism is hardly represented at all now in academic social theory. Its ideas are therefore rarely expressed systematically. However, right-wing Jeremiahs prophesying the imminence or inevitability of racial strife do seem to be driven by fear that the whole social order may be collapsing. Their calls for purification of nations through the removal of alien elements imply an assumption that societies need to be based clearly on one set of agreed principles. What makes them different, and deviant in modern contexts, is that it is the communalist principle which they regard as valid, with integrative creeds as the irritant requiring elimination.

Consensualism in its inclusive, universalist forms has dominated conventional thinking in this area for generations now. And it is highly practised in playing down the significance of nationalist aspects of a state. Wherever we look we can see nations failing to provide full citizenship for their minorities. But such observations are easily neutralized and turned into grist for the consensualist mill. This is done by treating them merely as evidence of the aberrant or still imperfect nature of the particular societies under scrutiny – sure signs that they are about to collapse from their own internal contradictions.

The trick lies in taking an idealized model of the state as the operational norm. Commentators confronted by the dual nature of states avoid awkward questions by invoking the spirit of Acton and divining a distinction between 'universal' states as they ought to be – and which also happens to be logical and comprehensible to the libertarian mind and nice to theorize about – and 'national' states which, although admittedly only too abundant on the ground, are monstrosities defying serious consideration. The latter can best be dealt with by being shunted into anomalous categories outside of the main lines of history and theory. Their inability to live up to expectations can then be turned into confirmation of harmless, subsidiary hypotheses.

This device was used a great deal by those who laboured to produce Pax Americana's supporting mythology. Wagley and Harris (1958), in their comparative study of minorities in the New World, felt impelled to conclude that the national character of all the states they had looked at in their inquiry rendered them 'transitional' between the ideal-types of traditional and modern. They were new vessels indeed, but were still occupied and moved by pre-modern national communities. So it was necessary to regard them as hybrids or mixed types. Handled in this way they created no problems for idealistic concepts of the modern state. Their internal contradictions surely presaged either transformation or speedy extinction. So it was excusable to forego interpretation of them in their own right, and to treat them instead as heralds of the fully modernized article.

A similar equation of inconsistency with instability, coupled with a sterner emphasis on the need to purge would-be modern states of all their traditionalist residues, was made by Parsons (1960). He warned that no further delay was possible in extending full citizenship to blacks in the US. Otherwise the survival of those areas of rational political organization that were already in operation among whites would be endangered. Failure to move forward decisively into a contemporary, post-discriminatory world must mean slipping back into a feudalistic past.

Honouring creeds in the breach

The aroma of sophistry hangs over all such endeavours. What they cannot conceal – merely rendering paradoxical – is that in the most modern of societies ethnocentric practices clearly do survive perfectly well alongside value-systems proscribing them.

How could discrimination remain so prevalent in the most successful states in the world system if it really were so detrimental to national unity and purpose? Clearly the burden cannot be too crippling. Indeed, might not the regular concurrence of these values and practices invite a different and more down to earth interpretation, in which human selfishness, duplicity, and the self-serving nature of morality play some part?

It is possible to come close to yielding this point without leaving the consensualist fold. Wagley and Harris, for example, admit minorities' continuing exclusion from national life in all the states surveyed. They manage, nevertheless, to draw the conclusion that in spite of this, liberal creeds do operate on their behalf, by providing official validation for their aspirations.

> ... it is the Brazilian creed that provides the basis for the idealistic policies and efforts of the Brazilian Indian Service ... (and) the very presence of the American creed has had a profound influence in the arena of competition for Negroes and Whites in the United States by providing a legal and moral basis for the Negroes' struggle.
>
> (1958, pp. 280, 284)

A hint of scepticism does, however, find its way into their final sentence.

> Although it is often honoured only in the breach, an idealistic creed favourable to minorities has been a common factor present in all of the minority-majority situations studied in this book.
>
> (p. 285)

'Honoured only in the breach'! It is difficult to say how much deliberate irony there is in this parting shot. What does emerge clearly, though, is that consensualists are disposed to lay down their tools just as the analysis is getting interesting. There are some things they cannot afford to contemplate, for fear of losing their faith.

Uncomplicated belief in the transient nature of communalism is difficult to maintain over an extended period. It has come under increasing strain over the last fifteen years or so. Throughout the western world ethnic minorities have gone through a period of growing assertiveness – challenging ruling myths about integration, and drawing attention to continuing oppression by national majorities.

Some theorists have clung to consensualism by eschewing optimism and taking on a Cassandra role. John Rex has forebodings about a New Dark Age (1974), or at the very least mounting violence and instability (1979), if colonial minorities continue to be excluded from soi-disant 'open' societies. This stance seems very widespread at the moment.

It is not, however, the only development. In order to accommodate the increasing visibility of communalist phenomena, theory has branched out in several directions. Three main trends are discernible. Each takes a rather different line on the duality of minority experience. All retain serious limitations.

The sociobiological impetus

One school of thought removes communalism from the province of social theory. This is the orientation usually known as 'primordialism', taking its name from Clifford Geertz's references to communal solidarity as a 'primordial' sentiment.

The general position taken by primordialists is that ethnic solidarities are always with us, and have a biological, non-calculative basis in the human need to bond in inward-looking groups. It is admitted that this drive can have socially undesirable results. To deny its existence because of this, however, is seen as throwing away any chance to understand and control it. During the 1940s and 1950s there was ideological pressure to overlook communal sentiments. This did, however, not make them go away. The apparent resurgence in ethnicity since the 1960s can, it is argued, be seen as in part a consequence of this denial, as public opinion and academic commentators together have been obliged to see the error of integrationist prognoses. A convert to sociobiology, Van den Berghe (1981) insists that only through recognizing the vitality and true nature of ethnic cohesiveness can society hope to come to terms with it.

I do not intend to rehearse here all of the arguments against primordialism. On the Left it is seen as the very essence of neo-Conservatism. There are, therefore, plenty of critical commentaries around already, such as Martin Barker's (1981).

What I must do, though, is point out that methodologically it is a weak instrument for handling the duality in social treatment of minorities. The first article of sociological practice is that it is important to look for social causes of social phenomena. If some social behaviour is allowed to be explained in non-social terms, it becomes difficult to see the interconnectedness of the whole social system. We are liable to end up only bothering to explain that which it is congenial or convenient to explain. There may well be biological drives that coincide with exclusive forms of social behaviour. But equally there may also be biological imperatives promoting universalist behaviour. We hear little about these from primordialists, who contrive to suggest that it is only the desire to belong to small, exclusive groups which is at root non-rational.

Their accounts are therefore lop-sided. The discrepancy between communalism and universalism in modern society is effectively reduced to the Old Adam factor – the tension between Nature and Society. Whatever labels its opponents may have attached to it, primordialism is at bottom idealist. It believes in the power of social institutions to confront and subdue obdurate biological forces. Culture and social organization are represented as rational and integrative; human nature as regressive, stubborn, and posing endless problems for the guardians of social order.

Preoccupation with this type of duality diverts attention away from what is sociologically more interesting – that is the tension between opposed social values and modes of action, and the interplay between these. It is at this level of analysis that a coherent and convincing account of race and ethnic relations must be constructed.

New Left consensualism

For capital requires racism not for racism's sake but for the sake of capital. Hence at a certain level of economic activity (witness the colonies) it finds it more profitable to abandon the idea of superiority of race in order to promote the idea of the superiority of capital. Racism dies in order that capital might survive.

(Sivanandan, 1976, p. 367)

The most vigorous trend in recent theorizing on race and ethnicity in Britain and most other western European countries consists of an updating of socialist ideas to give a more prominent place to ethnic and nationalist sentiments. Traditional Marxism discounts communalism as false consciousness. Where communal solidarity happens to coincide with the needs of the class struggle, then its existence can be played on strategically. But it is not to be taken seriously as a rational impulse in its own right.

This position has come under great pressure with the decolonization of European overseas empires and the growth instead of internal empires in the metropolitan heartlands. Minority communities have become a visible and highly significant feature of northern European societies. Traditional working-class organization has been reluctant to incorporate them. Their political and emotional ties with their countries of origin have remained strong. All this has strained the credibility of old-fashioned notions of the pre-eminence of class solidarity.

The modern Left has accordingly cultivated those elements of doctrine most capable of embracing the recent unfolding of ethnic consciousness. This has usually involved resurrecting Leninist propositions about Imperialism. The general argument put forward is that because capitalism has been going through a stage in which its main social feature has been colonialism, then class conflict is complicated by communal considerations. These do currently have some realistic basis and content.

Under this revised schema it is possible to take ethnicity much more seriously – even to give it a moral priority that the old Left denied it. Full class consciousness is now seen as unattainable until the struggle against oppressive nationalism – including that of the metropolitan masses – has been won. This revision significantly alters the agenda for revolution. It puts minorities in the vanguard of the class movement for the immediate future, and defines minority consciousness as inherently progressive rather than an annoying irrelevance. This is good integrative campaigning stuff. It feeds eagerly on post-imperial guilt among idealists in the national majority. It also meets minorities' need for allies in the majority who will allow legitimacy to their aggrieved feelings. Oppressors and oppressed can unite with renewed hope, as together they sweep away their shared imperial past.

However, it needs to be appreciated that this position marks less of a departure from traditional socialist ideas than it at first appears. Communal sentiments are allowed temporal priority. But class is still the more important principle, and the moral source of the legitimacy which is given to communal consciousness. Only those manifestations of communalism that can be squared with class analysis are treated seriously. The possibility that national consciousness follows a different logic of its own, with properties and dynamics at variance with class, is rarely touched on.

This hanging on to the pre-eminence of class is very understandable. Class analysis does not just conjure up a more appealing future. Also, in the real world of here and now, it is more palatable to prevailing ideological tastes than is communalism. For class consciousness is not incompatible with the high valuation given by all universalists to individual freedom. It is the oppositional or group protest mode of the humanist idiom.

Although class doctrines are collectivist in format, they do allow for personal choice in group alignment and re-alignment in a way that communal identities cannot. Communalist values in general, as I show in chapter ten, revolve around group memberships and obligations from which there is in principle no escape. The involuntary aspect of this is all the sharper for minorities. Group membership is ascribed by powerful collectivities, onto weaker, with little regard for whether there is a subjective basis for the identities delineated. The category 'Asian' in British society reflects a whim of the majority. It has little meaning outside its local usage. Other labels, like 'Chinese' or 'Cypriot' are not much better. Many hyphenated identities in the US, such as Polish- or Italian-American, which today seem relatively innocuous, were equally insensitive and coercive in their origin.

In class terms, however, such individuals are not denied personal control over collective identification and allegiance. It is up to themselves to decide whether to regard themselves as members of the working class, of a fraction of it, or perhaps as part of an unwaged underclass, or as following an entrepreneurial road and so on. They can then make political alliances accordingly. Class groups only exist insofar as their members are convinced that it is in their interests to belong to them. No doubt duress is sometimes applied to those seen by others as class traitors or scabs. But this is foreign to the principles on which solidarity is declared.

All this makes the pre-eminence of class a good political platform. As an analytic stance, however, it leads us eventually back to one-sided, consensualist reflexes, in which the duality of minority consciousness is liable to get defined away. For the new Left, communal oppression is in practice liable to become played down to the level of a transient difficulty that the political algebra of class fractioning and capital formation will resolve. The cries of trampled minorities are all part of the noise of class battle. Everything leads towards the same ultimate struggle; so there is only one true consciousness and rationality.

This is evident in the remarkably sanguine appraisal made of decolonization, which seems to be regarded as entirely governed by the internal logic of capitalist development. This is all very questionable. There are good grounds for supposing that decolonization normally takes place when a competing, and rising imperialism allies itself with subjugated groups against their current masters. The collapse of European overseas empires this century surely cannot be understood without looking at the global aspirations and strategies of the USA. Decolonization cannot just be treated as the triumph of universalizing ideas or the working through of an impersonal logic. It entails a displacement of one paramount national community by another.

The new Left is no more inclined to see this than was the old. They are always happy to disclose class interests underlying communalism. But they resolutely avoid detecting communalist interests behind 'class'. If they admit a Yankee imperialist hand underneath recent decolonizations, then they are quick to point out that beyond this is the arm of Capital. Their aim may be to explore and explain imperialism, but from the outset only certain types of explanation are admissible – that is, those in which capital and class are the independent and dynamic factors.

The inability of these accounts to confront the autonomy and distinctiveness of communalist sentiments limits their credibility to all except those committed to retaining a socialist viewpoint. Even those who can accept them at this level find them difficult to apply in the building of stable, cross-community alliances. Centrality of class keeps pulling back towards a traditional socialist portrayal of nationalist struggles as a distraction or, at best, a side-show.

The basic tactic for incorporating communalism to class action lies in declaring those minority actions which can be approved of to be 'aspects' of the working-class struggle. The problem, of course, is how to decide which behaviour can be condoned and dressed up in this way. If the net is cast too narrowly, to leave out unruly or unpatriotic behaviour that the majority working class are disdainful of, then the procedure will not satisfy the desires of minorities. The potential virtue of the new Left's position is that it promises minorities some specific legitimacy for their grievances and reactions. Unless their special experiences and needs are recognized and incorporated to the concept of class action, they will hesitate to surrender their autonomy and allow their destiny to become defined in class terms.

If, on the other hand, class struggle is defined too broadly, socialists in the majority will end up with some very strange bedfellows. When these are eventually repulsed, they are likely to be even more bitter than if they had not been given fraternal encouragement in the first place.

Recently, for example, some socialist theorists working in the area of race relations (Lea and Young, 1984) have opened up a fierce dispute by doubting whether black crime can be designated as in the vanguard of resistance to the oppressive state. Young (1983) has also portrayed Black Vanguard claims as culturally hegemonic. The sharpness of the debate they have unleashed reveals the difficulty that socialism has in encompassing minority sentiments.

An alliance built on the idea that minority cultures of resistance are concordant with class revolution is precarious. So long as class principles are used to universalize minority protests, and co-opt them into broader democratic protests, then communal sentiments are bound to remain marginal and incompletely represented. Consensualist enterprises which set out to reduce the duality of minority experience to a single dimension sooner or later encounter phenomena they cannot encompass.

Ethnopolitical realism

The third major strand in recent thinking about communalism is found among libertarians on the centre-Right of the political spectrum. It is often referred to as 'instrumentalism'. This is because its defining feature is an emphasis on seeing ethnicity not just as a sentimental association (i.e. primordialism), but as a framework for a rational and goal-oriented mobilization of group consciousness. This approach is more popular in the US, where there is a long tradition to be drawn on of regarding ethnic communities as the natural organs for articulating protest and resistance. Joseph Rothschild (1981) provides a good summary of the field.

Instrumentalism overlaps in its interests with modern socialists, especially in relation to structures of colonialism. But its central concern with 'ethnopolitics' leads it into almost directly opposed interpretations. Socialists see class as the paramount dimension of consciousness, and ethnicity as dependent and ultimately dispensable. For instrumentalists it is the other way round, with ethnicity dominant.

The keynote in instrumentalist accounts is the idea that centralized states declaring universalist beliefs have tended to operate on behalf of dominant communities controlling the central *élite* and state machine. Ruling ideologies about modernization, and oppositional movements focused on the idea of class, have both contributed to this centralist domination. This epoch, however, has now come to a close. With the gradual extension of effective democracy, communities that had become submerged and marginalized have been able to rethink their position. Consequently they are organizing themselves along the regional and ethnic lines which realistically correspond to their exclusion from equal participation. Since the middle of this century, lobbies openly agitating for direct redress of ethnic injustices have become increasingly salient.

Ethnicity is thus revealed as the true axis for collective action and mobilization in the modern world. It is suggested that states containing self-conscious minorities have been obliged to adopt new conventions of political legitimacy and bargaining which admit the validity of ethnic claims. As a result of this flowering of ethnic solidarities, ethnicity is becoming an established and effective mode of political protest. Meanwhile class ideology is a fading illusion.

Ethnopolitical analysis is clearly a potentially very valuable analytic tool. Its particular strength lies in its ability to debunk class theory by demonstrating how this has itself traditionally played a part in colonizing minority groups. Socialists old and new are adept at sniffing out the class interests concealed behind ethnicity. It is a useful corrective to this to have accounts which reveal how class movements can serve communalist purposes. This provides a good starting point for identifying the differential moral bases and mobilizing properties of these alternative modes of collective consciousness, and for investigating the ways in which they interact.

But ethnopolitical analysis also contains tendencies which limit its own power to give a balanced account of the interpenetration of these contrasting principles. It is itself prone to placing undue emphasis on one dimension of solidarity – in this case communalism – at the expense of the other. In particular it fails to attach enough significance to the continuing moral superiority of universalist values and ideologies in the modern world system. Consequently it vastly overrates the liberating capacity of ethnic lobbies. These various points require some elaboration.

In their eagerness to write obituaries for class action, instrumentalists have been too ready to see the new wave of ethnic assertiveness as being consonant with modern state institutions and political values. Take the Welsh as an example. Until it revived during the middle of this century, Welsh political nationalism had been firmly subsumed to class identity for several generations. Under leaders like Nye Bevan, the Welsh had maintained a strong allegiance to the Labour Party. Conventional social theory up to the late 1960s regarded them as having become well integrated to a unitary British class system.

Instrumentalists take issue with this view. They prefer to see the Welsh as a group which the English, under cover of policies of 'modernization', had succeeded in marginalizing and collectively proletarianizing. English control of the British state during the nineteenth century ensured that investment in Wales remained low, and occurred in less profitable industries. The free market rhetoric of the business classes concealed English supremacist designs.

As class politics developed in Britain, the Welsh joined in centralized oppositional movements, seeing them as the best available means of securing benefits for Wales. But there was always a sense of being Welsh which lay behind and mediated loyalty to party, and which even English workers transposed to Wales came to share. In recent decades this feeling has grown as it has become increasingly evident that class action was not delivering the goods, and that even the Labour Party was dominated by English working-class concerns. The Labour Movement has not given high priority to resisting this process. Welsh protest has therefore become more explicitly nationalistic, in order to fight for true representation of those regional needs which have been neglected since Union.

There are many useful features in this new model. It is not, however, a fully rounded account. What instrumentalists also need to concede, and rarely do, is that the resurgence of Welsh nationalism that has accompanied exposure of internal colonialism in Britain has itself been helped along by the continuing attachment of many Welsh to class ideology. As we have already seen, the language of class is morally superior to that of ethnicity and communalism, as it does not ascribe identity and impose exclusive loyalties on group members. Instrumentalists are rather slow to appreciate this, and are too quick to dismiss class ideology as merely a smokescreen for majority community interests. What they significantly neglect is that in so far as class ideology has provided a smokescreen, this is because it offers a moral cover which is consistent with universalist values. Furthermore, this is no less true even now that ethnic interests are being pressed more openly than in the past.

Consider the Welsh case again. The Welsh community contains many who still prefer to see themselves as bonded by class interests, and who contribute to everyday collective activities in this spirit. Socialists, it must be remembered, are a powerful group even within Plaid Cymru. The existence of such people is very important in preventing universalist ideologues – whether radical individualists or old-fashioned socialists – from being able to condemn the Welsh as inward-looking separatists and historical throw-backs.

If anyone tries to accuse the Welsh of these vices, there will be many Welshmen and observers of Welsh ways who can respond that 'really', at root, Welsh solidarity is that of an oppressed class. Maybe it does have a regional quality or edge to it. This, however, is a reaction to the Englishness of the capitalist class that has attempted to subdue them.

This ability to take cover under a protective class mantle is most important. Without it Welsh nationalism would have had a much tougher job in avoiding portrayal as a negative and retrograde phenomenon. It is not proved that Wales has received benefits as a result of making explicitly nationalist demands. If it has, though, this is surely only because class loyalties, including the Labour Party, have worked in tandem with the nationalist lobby, to keep it respectable.

The emergence of a communalist angle to Welsh protests does not represent an abandonment of class feelings. It is more to the point to see the growth of an ethnic lobby as tied up with the shift within modern socialism itself towards a sympathetic accommodation of anti-colonial sentiments. To the newer Left, Welsh nationalism is not a betrayal of class. It is a stage to be recognized in the emergence of a viable class movement. In practice the new ethnopolitics has thus worked alongside and arguably given an extra edge to traditional class loyalties and action.

How is it, one may ask, that students of ethnopolitics have managed to underrate the continuing vitality of universalist values, and their role in supporting ethnic lobbies? The answer is partly that most instrumentalist theories are American, and class has yet to make a significant entry into American politics. There is a universalist ruling ideology in the US – that is, individualism. But there is no oppositional variant of this. Protests are phrased mainly in communalist terms – and are politically weaker for it. Americans seeing the emergence of apparently successful ethnic lobbies in Europe can be forgiven for thinking that at last the idiom was becoming acceptable in its own right.

What is probably more important than this, though, is that the ethnic movements which have stepped into the open in recent decades, stimulating the analysis of politicized ethnicity, are phenomena which in practice can all enjoy the tacit approval of most universalist thinkers. The struggles of Basques, Bretons, Kurds, Walloons, Ulster Catholics and their like are articulated in communalist terms. But like the Welsh they are all able if necessary to pass responsibility for the communal structuring of their consciousness onto others. They are all relatively weak groups that are attempting to resist the bullying of stronger ones. Liberals can accept their mobilization as an appropriate collective strategy for removing collective disabilities. Socialists, as we have seen, can define their lobbies as legitimate fragments of the class struggle.

Thus the ethnicity that instrumentalists study usually refers in practice to anti-colonial or 'reactive' movements that enjoy indirect universalist legitimacy. This *de facto* legitimacy has perhaps lulled those deeply immersed in detailed studies of the ethnic trend into overlooking its underlying discrepancy with modern ruling values. Academics inspired by the revival of submerged nationalities, or the new pride of humble immigrant communities, must find it easy to confuse the new political confidence of these groups with official approval of communalist demands.

What in reality seems more likely is that minority lobbies are condonable because they are a negation of something much worse -- the nationalism or imperialism of powerful groups. Ethnicity has little independent, inherent virtue. It gets support out of sympathy with its resistance to oppression. States responding to ethnic claims are not thereby allowing direct legitimacy to communalism. Basically they are just trying not to appear to have any truck with majority communalism.

Instrumentalists who become too fascinated by the current trend towards overt ethnicity in under-privileged communities make two related mistakes. In the first place they forget that these open expressions of communalism are only able to be open because they are consistent with the dominant body of universalist values. Second, and by the same token, they give less attention than they should to the covert communalism of powerful groups.

National majorities need to operate covertly, because communalist action they engage in overtly is bound to appear oppressive and so not condonable in universalist terms. At the same time they do enjoy excellent opportunities for covering their communalist tracks. Their central position controlling state institutions and policies gives them plenty of chances to refer to universalist goals to defend and disguise the *status quo*.

It is surprising that instrumentalists tend to overlook this. A basic tenet of this genre is that powerful communities can subvert both liberal 'modernization' programmes and class protests to legitimize their own privileges. To follow the Welsh example, it was, after all, the marginalization by the English of their Celtic cousins under the banner of *laissez-faire* which is seen by instrumentalists as the basis of their modern communal problems.

The reason for failing to see that such malpractices still go on must be that most theorists are looking for happy endings. By playing down the continuing superiority of universalist values, instrumentalists manage to convey a misleading impression that powerful communities no longer possess the weapons they once had. We live, they suggest, in an Age of Redress. Minorities are now fighting back. Ethnopolitics implicitly shifts the balance of advantage away from the centralizing tricks of majorities towards the determined quest by their former victims for liberation and group justice.

These implications need to be resisted. Ethnic action that is covert, by being hidden from most people's view behind the pursuit of acceptable universal goals, is still more likely to be effective than overtly ethnicized actions. The rise of direct ethnic protest is not necessarily a sign that it works. All it really shows is that class action has failed them.

Ethnopolitical analysts interpret the changing form of protests since the last world war, from a class to a communal axis, as movement into a dimension where the oppressed can at last realistically confront their oppressors. It is not as easy as this. Movement into the open can just as well be seen as a gesture of weakness and despair. Dominant communities, as is manifest in Israel at the moment (Bernstein and Swirski, 1982), do still exploit the rhetoric of progress and modernization to their advantage. The relative lack of interest in this by instrumentalists is a source of imbalance in their work. It leads to a one-sidedness analogous to that of the new Left. In this case it is the importance and legitimacy of ethnicity which is grossly played up instead. Oppressive communalism and the universalist values that shield it receive far too little attention.

To sum up the argument, the world has changed less than ethnic instrumentalists would like to imagine. Current states still embody a strong tension between communalist and universalist principles. Moreover, it is dominant groups who still hold the best cards. They can easily dissemble in order to exploit ambiguities to their own advantage. Where lines of conflict are kept complex and confused, the *status quo* is more readily maintained.

Ambiguity, then, is surely a key factor in keeping minorities immobilized and marginal. This is perhaps not a problem for individuals who are prepared and able to break loose from their communities and to forget their obligations to other members. These may escape its dilemmas and find their way into individual assimilation. But for the bulk of group members excluded from full participation there will be no clear path for making claims on the state.

Protests by minorities are almost by definition divided between two dimensions of group consciousness. The Welsh, as we have seen, cannot be wholeheartedly nationalist in their solidarity, as this would lose them their universalist legitimacy. Nor can they commit themselves absolutely to a universalized class struggle. To do this would risk subordinating their specific needs to the interests of the dominant English working-class movement.

The fate of minority communities is to be suspended between two principles of collectivism – and to have muddled consciousness imposed on them. The partial and confused solidarity they display – half in and half out of the nation – suits a dominant majority rather well, by keeping them marginal and dependent. Ethnopolitical analysis which is not realistic enough to see the role of progressive ideology in helping trap minorities in this way, and which neglects the benefits which this still gives a ruling majority, does not represent much of an advance on pristine consensualism.

COMING TO TERMS WITH DUALITY

None of these developments in race theory escapes from the consensualist premise that a double system of political mobilization must eventually resolve into one. As a result none can offer an adequate interpretation of the persistence of duality in stable and successful states. An understanding of this requires willingness to see that the different principles can serve compatible ends.

The key element missing in consensualist analysis is some awareness that the uttering of empty promises to minorities maximizes the interests of a dominant community. For this way its credit is kept up in the society of nations, without any loss of domestic supremacy.

I am not proposing that a majority group as a whole will conspire to deceive its minorities. To begin with, of course, national majorities do not exist as clear groupings in modern society. A majority is, in a sense, simply what is left after you have mentally subtracted those members of a population who are most likely to experience communalist obstacles to full citizenship. Even if national majorities did exist as coherent entities, it does not make sense to envisage them deliberately attempting such massive deceptions. Hypocrisy on this scale is only effective if it operates below conscious level – through the bland overlooking of possible hidden relations between different aspects of behaviour.

A nation is engaged all the time in the pursuit of a variety of ends, which not all elements in it will value equally. In so far as conflicts between objectives cause difficulties for powerful groups in the nation, then public attention is given to them, and explicit resolutions sought. This does not occur where contradictions cause suffering only to weaker groups. So long as the dominant community is successful in maintaining its general position *vis-à-vis* others, and in minimizing its own perceived problems, there is little incentive for its members to explore too critically the precise connections between its various activities and proclamations.

There must be many individuals within majorities who have some inkling of the net effect of their diverse practices on minorities. And it is to be expected that they will play on this knowledge to their own advantage. The common denominator in all this is majority supremacy; and the sum of such behaviour amounts to a degree of collaboration against minorities. But this still falls short of a conscious group strategy of duplicity.

The importance of international legitimacy

Consensualists do go part of the way towards recognizing that a declaration of values may serve a diplomatic function. The latent implication of Wagley and Harris's depiction of liberal creeds as 'honoured only in the breach' is surely just this – that these creeds are less effective as weapons against the maltreatment of minorities than as shibboleths which, if paid due lip service, impart a protective legitimacy to régimes upholding them.

This is never admitted directly. But it is often implicit. Immediately after the passage cited earlier, MacIver goes on to add:

> Not only does discrimination generate disunity and a masked caste system wholly alien to the faiths and loyalties in the strength of which America has become a distinctive nation, ... it has a further consequence of particular moment at a time when the United States is thrust [sic] into a position of world leadership. It diminishes our influence in world affairs and tends to discredit the more far-reaching programmes of our statesmen.

It is significant that this further consideration should typically be thrown in as an apparent afterthought. For it is important to the upholding of consensual mythology that this is not accorded the same weight as the argument preceding it. The goal of stability and harmony is a universal good. Majorities and minorities alike share it. The goal of keeping up appearances and legitimacy among other states is by contrast mainly a benefit to the national majority. What it is really about is preventing external interference on behalf of downtrodden minorities.

If we follow up this further objective it soon becomes hard to see it as of only secondary importance. In the arena of the international politics of human rights, there are very genuine dangers to the stability of a state – ranging from minor diplomatic unpleasantness to forceful intervention – which may follow from the practice of discrimination against minorities. In recent history, concern over the alleged oppression by a national majority of its minority groups has been a very popular pretext for violating its sovereignty. This is without doubt a potent factor influencing current official attitudes and credoes.

It is probably the dominant factor for most régimes. The reason for such coyness among social theorists in referring to it must be – except where they are secret nationalists using liberal morality to cloak their real concerns – that it brings them too close to an uncomfortable realization of the impotence of their own values. Once we move into the level of international relations, where even quite weak communities may possess a state machine with enough autonomy to be capable of constructing and publicizing their own interpretations of events, it becomes much easier to discern the subservience of moral values to the pursuit by the powerful of their own dominion and glory.

Consensualists venturing into this inhospitable area find it very hard to uphold the bluff that discrimination is inherently disruptive. It is abundantly clear that what activates external pressures on behalf of vulnerable groups is not the degree of oppression they experience. It is the relative power of the states involved.

For example, when Turkey invaded Cyprus in 1974 to liberate the Turkish minority there, Greece did not join in as it was clear that Turkey commanded the greater force. Similarly, India was able to intervene successfully on behalf of Bengalis in Pakistan, bringing about the creation of Bangladesh. This was because India was generally stronger than Pakistan, and the logistics of defending a geographically divided territory created tremendous military difficulties for Pakistan. It is probably worth adding that India – ever fearful herself of being destabilized – was apparently aiming to increase her domination of the sub-continent through this exercise. By the same logic, if she were now to intervene in Sri Lanka, she would further boost her own power, and help to overcome separatist feeling among her own Tamil insurgents.

Miscalculations do occur of course, especially when a powerful neighbouring state is temporarily weakened. Somalia supported an uprising in Ethiopia among fellow-ethnics in the Ogaden, in the belief that Ethiopia was at the time too weak to resist. In the event the Ethiopian empire repulsed the attack. It is now Somalia that is in crisis as a result – burdened with refugees and bitterly divided over future strategy.

All these cases illustrate the same basic rule. Discrimination itself generally does little more than to provide a charter for actions whose likelihood and outcome are governed by military and economic factors.

Several instrumentalist commentaries make frequent reference to this international dimension. They tend, however, to interpret any action on behalf of minorities as responses to, and governed by, minority ethnic demands. This becomes further proof for them of the strength and effective legitimacy of ethnicity in the modern world system. This is a brave attempt to keep up some of the old consensualist spirit. But, just like the new Left's idealization of decolonization, it requires turning a blind eye to the powerful communalisms prompting and orchestrating minority demands.

If there has been an explosion of ethnic assertiveness in recent decades then the main reason for this is the use by the US of an anti-imperialist crusade to help secure its own mandate for world domination. Not only does the outcome of discrimination depend on the relative power of interested parties. How discrimination actually gets defined is in large part determined by the strategic needs of leading world powers of the moment.

Locating the treatment of minorities in a framework of human rights politics, where idealistic holy wars are so manifestly part of the struggle for power, inevitably influences one's view of the dual character of states. We are soon forced to abandon the idea that discrimination is intrinsically destabilizing for states that practice it. In fact, in view of the phenomenal spread and persistence of hybrid 'nationalist' states in the modern world, we have to acknowledge that it is a creature capable of surviving very well – a viable system in its own right. Duality is not weakness, but strength.

Up to a point consensualism is valid, of course. Discrimination certainly does have alienating and polarizing consequences which may spread throughout the whole of society. Blatant withholding of promised opportunities must lead to frustrations and disaffection, and can foster a lack of commitment among marginal groups to the host régime. This in turn will furnish the more exclusivist elements in the majority with the justifications they seek for resisting equal rights. A vicious circle of mutual repulsion may be set in motion which would appear to lead all too readily to insurrection, reprisals, expulsions and pogroms.

Where these accounts lose conviction is in their simplistic assessment of the role of official creeds in forestalling this process. The argument usually advanced is that only active and vigorous implementation of an inclusive public morality will halt descent into communal strife. But this is obviously untrue. The existence of a progressive creed and movement may well have the effect of preventing an escalation of distrust. But this does not necessarily, or even normally, mean that an actual reduction in majority bullying takes place. The mere affirmation of humanist ideals by a governing class can have a unifying influence. What it does is to alter the significance that victims of offensive practices attach to their experience, and set the scene for progressive alliances with interest groups in the majority.

Exclusion and exploitation are surely less likely to lead to complete alienation when accompanied by strong public denunciations from prestigious Verlighte voices. Reports like those of Kerner and Scarman condemning discrimination and calling for renewed attacks on it help to create a mood in which present difficulties are seen as but temporary delays on a road of converging destinies.

Nationalist doctrines are divisive in the modern world. When they are proclaimed as official state ideologies they invite destabilization from foreign powers. But this does not follow where ethnocentric behaviour by a majority is qualified and offset by the simultaneous promulgation of a universalist national creed, periodically reaffirmed through the launching of a New Deal or opening up of New Frontiers. In these circumstances groups at the receiving end of discrimination can be lulled into seeing a worthwhile future in the nation. They will put up with an astonishing amount of injustice in the here and now. In this way, publicly upheld liberalism and covert exclusion can merge in a virtually unassailable package. Together they smother and resist the demands of minorities, without dividing the nation in the process.

Two dimensions of legitimacy

There is available to us, therefore, a simple and common-sense way of understanding how states survive and flourish while containing radically opposed principles of national identity and political association. It lies in appreciating that they are subject to more than one type of demand on them, each of which may need responding to at the same time. We should expect states to have mixed characters. Those which do not are liable to be unstable.

Contrasting aspects of state policy and practice should not be seen as antithetical forces battling for monopolistic control. They are interdependent expressions of a broader quest, whose common underlying element is nationalism. The different faces this adopts are determined by the particular challenges being responded to.

In very broad terms there are two major types of challenge to its authority which a régime in command of a state needs to meet and which are pertinent to its treatment of minority groups. There are pressures from other states, which may result in forceful international sanctions or intervention. And there are claims issuing from the 'masses'; that is from large sectors of the domestic population occupying only subordinate positions in society and relatively excluded from control over the state machine, but who are numerous enough to back their demands with threats of insubordination, disruption, or violent insurrection. The fundamental duality in modern states is an outcome of the need to cope simultaneously with this two-dimensional threat to integrity and sovereignty – signified respectively by the mob in the streets, and by foreign gunboats off the coast or armies at the gates.

The universal aspect of a state relates primarily to its attempts to maximize legitimacy within the international community. By playing down its links with and dependence on a particular national group, and visibly championing values and causes regarded as serving the shared interests of humanity at large, an incumbent government can seek to avert punitive intervention and to rally support for its own actions against rival states. In the same way, the more directly national-ist component has to do with securing adequate internal support for the régime among the masses. What this entails in practice is making sure – whatever postures need to be struck for the sake of world opinion – that the dominant community inhabiting the territory under its jurisdiction, and holding the balance of street power, is accorded special privileges within the state.

The two sets of political principles that get called out for these purposes are obviously poles apart in most respects. They are, however, not so utterly irreconcilable as they may initially appear. This is because they are deployed in different dimensions, which are not of equal moment.

In public situations the emphasis must clearly be given to the uni-versalist principles. An international system is not sustainable at all unless states participating in it give formal priority to the supranational values bound up with it. So in their official pronouncements, at the very least, states looking for a legitimate place in the community of nations need to present their universalist aspirations as their highest political objective.

For most of history, world religions have provided unifying ideol-ogies above nationalism. In the present age their place has been taken by an attachment to the idea of the sovereignty of the individual. The chief distinguishing feature of modern societies is a wide-ranging recognition of the primacy of the individual citizen over the state. The basic moral conviction of humanism is that social groups are subordinate to the individuals comprising them. And the principal mutual obligation laid on national states by it is to judge each other in terms of their capacity to respond to and serve their citizens' wishes.

Over the last century and a half this liberal philosophy has come to occupy a virtually unchallenged place as the highest political mandate. It is central to international relations, where it gives *élites* in dominant states a convenient idiom for conducting their external affairs and consolidating their global positions.

This does not mean that its values have equally entered the hearts of common people. Individualist notions lend themselves all too easily to the defence of élitist privileges. The sort of moral system that most ordinary people feel the need for is one which ensures for them some entitlement to rewards and respect, regardless of the importance of their own specific role in the division of labour. This entitlement is best provided by fraternalistic principles of distribution, turning on the obligation of the rich and successful to look after the poor and weak.

These issues are explored further in chapter 10. The important point to draw attention to at this stage is that fraternalism logically involves a prioritizing of groups over individuals. This is potentially divisive between nations, and between communities within nations. It is therefore not appropriate as a ruling mandate. Nevertheless fraternalist values do possess an integrative capacity of their own. This is highly complementary to that of liberalism. It can therefore play an important role in moderating an official cult of individualism.

Synthesis in universalizing nationalism

Liberal creeds, through their emphasis on universal goals, are very effective in bringing together the aspirations of diverse tribal, kinship, sectarian and territorial communities. The trouble with them is that they also give a mandate for class inequality. This makes them alienating between hierarchically differentiated groups.

Fraternalism by contrast embodies a relativistic calculus which is horizontally divisive between parallel communities. But it can help to bind society vertically by serving as a charter for redistribution between classes within communities. If both moralities can be woven together into a single fabric, this generates an extremely resilient ideological structure, capable of recognizing both an authority structure, and restraints on it. By doing so it provides for rewards in the same system for social groupings with divergent interests and values.

It is in this light that we should look at those modern doctrines of enlightened nationalism which have grown up in the post-feudal world. What is significant about them is that they embrace both universalist and communalist concerns. Politically, therefore, they represent meeting-points at which the new humanist *élites* have been able to make a compact with fraternal sentiments. This rounds out their régimes' popular appeal by implicitly drawing on the patriotism of the historical communities which they inherited.

The basic format of these doctrines is very simple. It all hinges on the idea that a national community may lift itself above collective selfishness, and become a champion or guardian of universal values in the world. This is achieved by identifying the nation's own destiny with the creation and defence of a social order from which humanity as a whole can benefit. Modern American patriots, for example, do not see themselves as activated by self interest. America has a mission to the world, to fight for mankind's freedom. Any exercise of national power to this end will be vigorously defended as being in humanity's best interests.

The neatness of the progressive nation formula lies in the way that it gives licence to collectivist sentiments without requiring *élites* to compromise themselves or their constitutions by direct acquiescence in fraternalist propositions. All that is needed for a compact to be made with the masses is an effective decision to work through traditional national groupings in order to achieve the desired utopia.

I suggest later on that this merging of moralities in progressive nationalism was a necessary condition for the historical emergence of régimes committed to humanist values. The synthesis has an inherent ambiguity which allows the major parties to it – cosmopolitan *élites* and ethnocentric masses – each to interpret state actions in ways consistent with their own moral preferences.

This was illustrated recently in the debate at Westminster over the proposal to insert a clause in the Police Bill making racial discrimination a specific offence in the Force. The argument which appears to have clinched its acceptance in the Lords was that some such measure was necessary in order to convince other countries that Britain is genuinely committed to racial equality.

Phrasing the legislation's aim in this way opens it up to two entirely contradictory interpretations. Opposed purposes can thus be served at the same time. Libertarians can read the legislation as a victory for fairness, and a step towards an integrated society. Nationalists can go along with it as a gesture needed to placate and confuse foreign critics, and thereby stop them interfering in Britain's domestic affairs. From diametrically opposed premises, but united by a desire to advance Britain's interests, both groups can agree on the same policy. This epitomizes the character of enlightened nationalism.

The ambivalent state

The rewards of hypocrisy

The mixed and ambiguous nature of progressive nationalist ideas serves as the basis for a mutually beneficial trade-off between the main groups in contention within the modern state. Governing classes can increase popular acceptance of their authority and privileges, by tacitly conforming to communalist expectations and steering the state machine in directions which mainly reward the dominant community inhabitating its territory. For their part, the masses can hope for a reasonable share of the spoils, provided they fall in with the universalist rhetoric called on to dignify these exploits in the eyes of the outside world.

This trade-off and resulting compact depend ultimately on an *élite*'s ability to deliver the inducements needed to bribe the masses into endorsing an official creed at odds with their own sentiments. Provided it can respond materially to fraternalist claims, then its inability to admit them formally does not matter.

The chances of resolving the contradictory values held by *élite* and masses into a coherent and politically viable synthesis are much greater within powerful nations that are in a position to carve out a leading role for their members in world affairs. The more opportunities generated for pursuing national interests in a dignified matter, the less need there is for any members to spoil the show by expressing blatant ethnocentrism.

From time to time leading states may be so successful in attaching their own concerns to a supra-national cause that they can plausibly claim to have approached the ideal of the 'universal' state. France in the First Empire; Britain during the great age of *laissez-faire*; Russia briefly under Lenin, before the nationalizing of socialism; and the United States in the middle part of this century, as the eager standard-bearer of anti-colonialism. At such times and places, the very close identification that particular and powerful communities are actually able to make with internationalist aspirations blurs the distinction between universal and national behaviour. For a while libertarian idealists, especially those who belong to the vanguard nation and who therefore have a patriotic incentive as well, can claim with confidence that they are pushing back the frontiers of national consciousness.

Inside nations, especially again the more powerful ones, the mixed value system plays similarly into the hands of *élite* groups – thereby giving some personal compensations to consciences troubled by the compact with nationalism. It is a mistake, made all too often, to

40

suppose that the main advantages from any toleration of popular communalism must go to the exclusive, nativist sectors of a majority. Nothing could be further from the truth. There are a variety of ways in which non-discriminating members of a dominant group can benefit from the existence of hostile treatment of minorities.

This is not least because of the occasion it provides for asserting their own superiority over the uncouth King Mob practising it. Liberal values may be honoured mainly in the breach. But they *are* honoured. And this is a sure source of private advantage for their advocates.

In particular, liberal creeds and equivalent codes in socialist societies serve as a most convenient device for regulating admission to responsible office in the state. It cannot be a coincidence that it was just at the historical juncture when the masses were becoming admitted to participation in the state that the leprosy of racialism and xenophobia should have been diagnosed amongst them. It has defiled all it touched, and rendered them incapable of fully exercising their newly acquired political muscle. Consequently, even movements ostensibly serving the masses need *élite* sponsorship and leadership in order to achieve respectability.

All members of a national majority receive some benefits as a result of a state's tacit receptivity to communalist demands. It is, however, the *élite*, who are above overt voicing of such demands, who come out of the compact best. For it is they who can exploit the inherent tension between progressive nationalism's constituent principles to their own profit.

Meanwhile the chief cost of it all is borne by those groups of citizens excluded by the dominant community's definition of itself, and lacking the power to work the ambiguity in state practices in their own favour. The compact with nationalism does give humanist values a home. But this is at the expense of national minorities. These have difficulty obtaining nationalist legitimacy from the masses, and are too small to be able to threaten force to back up their pleas for fairer treatment. Their adjustment to this situation is examined in the next chapter.

CHAPTER 2

SERVING TWO MASTERS

To sanguine observers, the subscription of modern states to humanistic values appears to temper the power of nationalistic elements over minority groups. But this is illusory. In practice the interaction of opposed moralities enhances the responsiveness of minorities to their hosts' 'national interests'. For although the humanist world order promises equal participation in public affairs for all citizens, the principal agents operating the system are national governments. All that humanist ideology can do to support members of weaker communities is to furnish an idiom of natural rights in terms of which these governments may seek to achieve merit in each others' eyes by easing the lot of the downtrodden.

There is little that is new or truly liberating in this. The weapons it gives minorities are ones which are liable to multiply their problems, by making them a source of international embarrassment for their national masters. They cannot assert their rights without appearing a threat to national security. This is bound to alienate them further from the ethnocentric masses. The urge to correct impressions of disloyalty, in order to become admitted to full membership of the nation, makes minority groups all the more amenable to nationalist vetoes over their behaviour.

Pressed into service – the patronage bind
The only way that minorities can back up claims against a majority refusing them social justice is by looking for external patrons who are willing to intervene on their behalf. This is a very hazardous business. Foreign powers are reluctant to take this sort of thing on unless there is a clear advantage in it for them. Activities which do take place in the name of minority rights rarely have them as their sole or main objective. The moral obligation that humanism puts on the world community to look after minorities tends to result in their being cast as pawns in transactions between rival powers, who have little concern

for their clients' interests. Kurdish rebels in Iraq were let down badly by the Shah of Iran in 1975. Many minorities, for example the Catalans in Spain, are reluctant to court assistance from sympathetic neighbouring states – in this instance France – for fear of exploitation and betrayal.

Historically, those minorities that have been most able to articulate and assert their rights have been the protégés of stronger nations with imperialist designs on their host state. Between the wars, the minorities who fared best in central Europe were German communities encouraged and backed by an expansionist fatherland. This breaks the consensualist rules, as it means that the degree of active concern for the rights of a minority is in most cases a measure of the fundamental dissonance of its interests with those of its national majority.

This has a corollary which minorities cannot afford to forget. Any criticisms they venture to make of their masters are liable to be construed by anxious members of the majority as treacherous alignment with enemy states. The capacity that 'progressive nationalist' syntheses give to majorities to deal in double-standards is very evident here. Their members can exploit the ambiguity of the synthetic ideology to give a progressive interpretation to their own behaviour. Self-serving adventures are readily dignified as manifest destiny, white man's burden, and 'missions civilatrices', etc. – and thus as of greater benefit to humanity as a whole than the imperial nation itself. This universalizing rhetoric is commonplace. What the synthesis also permits is the discrediting of minorities by majorities, through the imposition of communalist interpretations on their behaviour. Minorities expressing grievances which may be entirely justifiable in strict universalist terms are easily accused by their hosts of trying to pull the house down. The main support that minorities can hope for lies outside their host state. This fact plays into majority hands. To the nationalist mind, refusal to knuckle under is obviously not just a matter of seeking universalist justice. It must be inspired by a particularistic alliance with the expansionary aspirations of a competing patron.

Not all Russian Jews who protest against unjust treatment are necessarily in league with the US and its European lackeys. But Russians can nevertheless de-legitimize – even criminalize – their dissent by ascribing this intent to them. There is a self-fulfilling aspect to this. Minorities are more likely to risk forfeiting popular credit in the state they profess to hold primary allegiance to, and to invite majority suspicions of them as fifth-columns, where they do actually harbour subversive aims.

Most national minorities have little to gain from putting themselves under the protection of foreign allies. It might help to consolidate or enhance their legal rights. But this would be at the expense of legitimacy among the nationalistic masses, which is the source of their longer-term security. The more that aggrieved minority individuals complain to the world community about the partiality of their host state, the more that they set themselves up for de-universalization by an embattled majority, and collective assignment to the status of an alien, subversive, or even colonizing presence.

External sponsorship is only worth having in certain circumstances. It needs to come from states which have a good reason of their own to support that cause, and are decidedly more powerful than the current host. In such cases the existing patron's cries of destabilization, irredentism, revanchism or whatever may be well founded; but will be made in vain.

Within a reasonably strong state there is a lot to be said for assuming that the current national masters are the best patrons available. There is no point in sticking your neck out by siding with adventures or interference that may not succeed. And in a powerful state there may also be material comforts, even for second-class citizens, which are not to be found elsewhere. These sweeten the experience of minority status.

The greater facilities offered by a powerful nation may even impart a plausibly 'voluntary' aspect to minority status within it. O. C. Cox, himself no sycophantic admirer of the American system, has written:

> From my personal experience in Africa and the West Indies, it seems possible to conclude that if the movement of black people were reciprocally free, we should expect that for every black American who voluntarily leaves the United States for Africa, in order to find opportunities for community service and self-improvement, there will be scores of Africans ready and happy to move permanently in the opposite direction into the United States.
>
> (1976, p. 298)

If this was true in 1976 – and there is no reason to doubt it – then how much more true it is likely to be today. While the third world staggers from crisis to disaster, America moves into even higher gears of growth.

Reconciling contrary demands

Within a secure state there is little to be won by grumbling about injustice or inconsistency. Discomfort is minimized by looking for a way of accommodating simultaneously to the different demands made by the main sections of the host community.

Broadly speaking, the politically responsible classes offer full membership of the nation. What they expect in return for this is some demonstration of belief in the fairness of their system. The national masses for their part will require submission to their collective supremacy. Minorities refusing to acknowledge it will not be allowed proper enjoyment of the universal entitlements formally accorded them.

Optimal fulfilment of these commandments lies in accepting at its face value the state's official interpretation of the dominant community's intentions. Most members of minority groups keep faith publicly in conventional, idealistic proclamations about equality – real or impending. This is not necessarily because they believe them. Some may do. But that is largely irrelevant. In terms of intergroup relations, upholding this faith constitutes a collective affirmation of loyalty to their hosts.

Thus the key to accommodation is an act of communal submission. Instead of haranguing their hosts with evidence of failed promises, and producing ammunition for enemies of the state, they will try to placate and flatter them by praising their national institutions, and paying tribute to their generosity as patrons. In this way, by swallowing grudges and treating the 'progressive nationalism' of their hosts as a genuinely inclusive and progressive article, they can serve both masters – enlightened *élite* and xenophobic masses – at the same time.

Little is lost by this compromise. By tacitly accepting an inferior or pupillary partnership with their national masters, minorities can boost their nationalist legitimacy and increase their real chances of participating in national life. This strategy of not rocking the boat may be rationalized by accepting the nationalist argument that an incumbent majority has already made a great contribution to national progress. Other groups hoping to join in must work a collective passage of dedicated national service, to arrive at full citizenship. Subject communities that quietly go along with this view may thereby purchase some hope for liberation in the future.

This is probably an optimal solution for a vulnerable minority in a strong state. It is, however, even more advantageous for the host community. Minorities' apprenticeships may well turn out to be pro-longed, and become the prelude to a new style of collective bondage. For it is while they are excluded from full membership and privileges, that they remain of most value to their masters. The rhetoric of freedom has awakened and fuelled ambition in them. But so long as a nationalist presumption of disloyalty is kept hanging over their heads, which they must constantly strive to overcome, this ambition is channelled into a fierce dedication to the national purpose. It takes the form of an urgent need to contribute to the wider community. This is typical of newly – or shall we say nearly – emancipated underdogs.

And so minorities postpone their personal claims to equal rights and rewards, and project aspirations onto later generations. By doing this they render themselves into a reserve of compliant and malleable energy. Without this the custodians of open societies would find it much harder to sustain such smooth-running national machines.

PROPS TO THE ECONOMY

The most obvious and concrete manifestations of this underpinning role occur in the economic realm. The desire to accumulate nationalist legitimacy steers minority workers into those jobs least attractive to the dominant community. This produces a marked tendency towards a split or dual labour market in which an ethnic underclass concentrates itself in menial, dirty, arduous or risky occupations, or those requiring the utmost devotion and self-sacrifice. In turn this releases an additional 'surplus labour value' for providing enhanced rewards and prospects for majority workers, and giving an investment holiday to their bosses. (Bonacich, 1972)

Roles analogous to this have been played by client groups through-out history (Holmes, 1978, Robinson, 1979, Lunn, 1980). But tra-ditionally their performance has been entailed by formalized collective dependence or servitude. These underlabouring tasks take on an extra dimension in the context of humanist creeds, where all labour is supposedly entered into voluntarily and according to merit. So in present-day conditions the supportive economic activities of marginal workers operate also as an ideological prop, helping to obscure serious deficiencies in the open society's official account and understanding of how it functions.

The received model of the liberal system does not give a credible

explanation of how 'free' labour can be recruited to the least prestigious jobs in society. Most rhetoricians of incentivism are content to
reiterate the need to give generous rewards to talent. This is after all
what counts at that end of the market in which its philosophers and
their paymasters have a personal interest. Meanwhile the rest of the
system is largely ignored, on a Rawlsian assumption that untalented
'losers' will acquiesce in their own failure, without need for further
persuasion or coercion.

Some of us find it hard to understand how individuals possessing
full political rights can be expected to accept designation as losers
without crying foul. But the question gets postponed for practical
purposes so long as there are less-than-free participants prepared to
step into the gap. This is where migrants and ethnic minorities come
in. Super-patriots hungry for recognition and security will always take
on undesirable jobs, while stifling latent discontents at doing so. In so
doing they become a solid bargain basement of good losers, whose
presence holds up the whole meritocratic house of cards.

Creation of an ethnic underclass permits the survival of inequality
in modern societies without visible compulsion or conscription. The
whole process depends on the ambiguity inherent in the minority
experience. It is through the 'voluntary' balancing of contrary pressures, rather than in deference to any explicit directives, that they
come to be recruited to the economic roles they occupy. If minority
individuals are too ambitious and industrious, they will be resented as
pushy by those who fear displacement by them. If on the other hand
they are too easy going, they will be regarded as idlers or parasites,
spurning or not deserving the opportunities graciously held out to
them by their hosts.

The best way to meet both of these demands at once, and maximize
acceptance in the workforce, is to confine their main efforts to activities
where their endeavours complement those which the dominant community prefers to engage in. They labour hard and enthusiastically.
But they avoid jobs where they pose threats to the majority by duplicat-
ing their exact productive roles.

This division of productive effort is integrative in a Durkheimian
sense. Carving out specialized and distinctive niches in the market
place (Wallman, 1979) helps to transform a potential conflict between
communities into a degree of economic interdependence. Some virtue
is made out of the ascription of group status, by using it as the basis
for an organic binding into the fabric of wider society. This is better

47

than relying for integration on the merely mechanical solidarity of shared class position which, as I argue in later chapters, is liable to be withheld unilaterally from members of weaker communities.

A common theme running through this avoidance of competition, and which signifies the asymmetric nature of the accommodation being made, is an orientation towards catering for the personal needs of members of a wider society. Entertainers, including certain types of sportsmen, domestic servants, preparers and adorners of food, and traders distributing exotic goods which would not otherwise be obtainable by the host community, are occupations with many minority practitioners. All draw on special skills and resources in order to increase the range of delights and gratifications on offer. It is also the case that all are governed by the whim of the sovereign consumer. They survive and prosper only so long as they are able to meet the demand for novelty, flattery and excitement.

The life is not always too bad. Some entertainers may become rich and famous. Many change their names, whether to escape ethnic identification, or – and as part of their act – to flatter the national majority. Baltzell quotes from Harper's magazine to show how many Hollywood heroes were playing at being Anglo-Saxons.

A sample of the *Warner Brothers* stable of stars included Doris Kapplehoff, Larry Skikne, Bernie Schwartz, Mladen Sekulovich, Marie Tomlinson Krebs, Frances Gumm and Arthur Gelien; among the famous at *20th Century Fox* were Max Showalter, Virginia McMath, Mitzi Gerber, Balla Wegier, Claudette Chauchoin and Ethel Zimmerman; at *MGM* were Vito Farinol, Joseph Meibes, Tula Finklea and Spengler Arlington Brough; stars at *Columbia* included Dianne Laruska, Judy Tuvim, Gwyllyn Ford, Margarita Carmen Cansino, Aldo Da Re and Vincent Zoino; while Zalma Hedrick, Donna Mullenger, Sarah Fulks, Ella Geisman, Issur Danielovitch, Daniel Kaminsky, Dino Crocetti and Joseph Levitch were among the leaders at *Paramount*.* ... *The assumed names of the stars, in the order listed above, were as follows: *Warner Brothers*: Doris Day, Lawrence Harvey, Tony Curtis, Karl Malden, Marjorie Main, Judy Garland and Tab Hunter; *20th Century Fox*: Casey Adams, Ginger Rogers, Mitzi Gaynor, Bella Darvi, Claudette Colbert and Ethel Merman; *MGM*: Vic Damone, John Ericson, Cyd Charisse and Robert Taylor; *Columbia*: Dianne Foster, Judy Holliday, Glenn Ford,

Rita Hayworth, Aldo Ray and Vince Edwards; *Paramount*: Kathryn Grayson, Donna Reed, Jane Wyman, June Allyson, Kirk Douglas, Danny Kaye, Dean Martin and Jerry Lewis.

(Baltzell, 1970, p. 324)

Some of these individuals may by passing cease to be publicly recognizable as outsiders. But most are probably impelled by the same anxieties. Certainly they are subject to the same occupational insecurity.

The benefits that these service workers traffic in are largely inessentials, which their recipients could manage without, or furnish themselves if necessary. Trade may be lucrative in the short run, but tastes change without warning, and in a slump this sector is among the first to suffer. It is an area that involves little risk of allowing outsiders to gain a secure foothold in the economy. So it can be safely left open to all comers and all talents.

Moreover, in many cases, it is not just individual labourers who are brought into service. The nature of the enterprise often requires that larger groups are involved to some extent. Service industries are intensive consumers of labour, drawing in whole families, and mobilizing ties throughout an ethnic community. This intensity of input and effort highlights the inferiority of the providers. And this sort of industry would often not be viable at all unless groups already deemed inferior, prior to and regardless of taking on those occupations, actually existed.

Taxing success

Between them, these various underlabouring and servicing reflexes greatly reduce the competitiveness of minorities. But no response can fully meet the complex stipulations erected by a modern majority, so that there are some unresolvable hazards constantly threatening accommodation. To start with, exclusion from the main opportunity structure may simply act as a spur to success by a back door route. Minority groups, especially diaspora communities that fall back on their own transnational ties for a living, are well placed to build up successful trading empires. Middlemen groups such as Jews, Chinese, Lebanese and Greeks have built many prominent commercial houses. (Lehman-Wilzig, 1978)

Similarly, the struggle to discover unmet needs and untried methods, when combined with a relative freedom from the conventional restraints of the established trade associations from which they are excluded, imparts an innovative quality to minority enterprises. These are then, as high risk ventures, inclined to pay off high profits as well. The pioneering exploits of Huguenots and Jews and their like are legendary. 'Enterprise' is one of the eternal virtues of marginal groups which periodically receives the admiration of grateful national leaders.

The populations urged to emulate them are rarely so appreciative. This sort of 'success' may well be seen by the majority more generally as a challenge to its own supremacy. Hostility may be generated towards its executors unless they pay a stiff super-tax of loyalty. This can be settled through donations to majority political parties and charities, or patronage of the arts. Or it may involve taking steps to ensure that the lion's share of employment created and credit earned end up in majority hands. Prosperous or skilled minorities – such as diaspora trading groups or refugees like the Flemings and Huguenots – may be required to share their expertise by teaching members of the dominant majority their trades. To attempt to maintain a profitable monopoly is to forget one's place as a client.

Great care is needed here. It is, for example, typically at moments when they have ceased to regard themselves as living in Babylon, and so neglect to pay homage to their political masters, that Jews have found themselves forcibly reminded through pogroms and expulsions of their conditions of sufferance. Jewish communities accordingly always seem to contain some who see their role as cautioning against false confidence.

This brings us right back to the nub of the problem, which is that there is no uniform majoritarian body to which minorities can bind themselves in clientship. There is any number of different groupings, to which different accommodations are appropriate. What seems like diligence and enterprise to one patron, looks like unfair competition and the embodiment of amoral *laissez-faire* to another. The more gratifying a minority's behaviour is to one faction in the majority, the greater that group's risk of becoming caught up in a domestic dispute within the majority itself.

Thus it is only in a generalized sense that the tendency of minority labour to move into the least profitable areas actually reduces competition. For in detail it does, of course, focus and maximize conflict with those particular sections of the majority who do depend on work in that field. To these people the penetration of this sector by marginal men represents an undercutting and further reduction of profit margins. Whether you regard the Asian corner shop operation as rescuing a local service rendered uneconomic by supermarket chains, and already being abandoned by the indigenous workforce, or as family sweatshops squeezing local workers out, depends above all on whether you want to be a shopkeeper yourself.

The greater the initiative displayed by minorities, the more they may have to pay in terms of loss of popular toleration. Except under conditions of very rapid expansion, there is a limit to the extent to which minorities can become drawn into an economy without being taken up by bosses as a stick to beat the backs of 'lazy' indigenous workers. Wherever unions are powerful enough, sweated labour is bound to be proscribed. Weaker groups of workers will then be induced to move into areas of self-employment when the state cannot hope to regulate them. Some ways of avoiding competition, such as acceptance of poor working conditions – not to mention the evasion of welfare legislation that small companies can often get away with – are morally indefensible to many in the democratic majority, who are quick to interpret it as a betrayal by aliens of the people's hard won progress.

Crime as service

Sweating is by no means the greatest of these problems. People in marginal positions are prone to become drawn into areas of enterprise which the formal economy refuses to handle altogether. The public demands governing minority labour are heterogeneous. Therefore it is only to be expected that many of the livelihoods available to them are in fact vacant precisely because they are of contentious morality. Risky and dirty work shades imperceptibly through that of dubious legality into the outrightly criminal.

Minority individuals have a lot of factors pulling them into economic crimes. There are, to start with, only limited alternative opportunities open to them which do not entail serious and direct competition with the majority. Second, the activities in question may not be illegal in the homeland culture of the minority, so that members of the community are, or may be thought to be, experts in it. Third – and I think most significantly as it helps to illustrate that minority criminality is very often a compliant option – they are in a far weaker position to resist that public demand to which certain types of crime are a response. A good deal of the crime of minorities centres on rackets, like fixing illegal production and trading, or organizing vice, gambling and supplying drugs. These ventures, in addition to creating a living for those engaged in them, must also be seen as providing services. They are prohibited because powerful groups or the balance of public opinion are against them. Nevertheless, they are desired by a considerable number of people.

A great deal of minority crime is not predatory. Sometimes, no doubt, it is entered into in a spirit of truculence and fatalism. Its perpetrators know that whatever they do will be condemned by some. Therefore there is no great point in holding back from financially rewarding possibilities. But more often, and especially in the earlier stages of criminal careers, it has to be seen as the extension of the 'servicing' reflex up to and beyond the margins of legality. Involvement in it forms part of the broader search for an accepted role in society. One excellent way of becoming tolerated among those sections of the host community that they are in contact with, who are, moreover, often the very people who would be arch rivals in the straight economy, is by taking the risk of providing for those needs which the distant state machine and *élite* – a common enemy uniting them with their customers – refuses to countenance.

This is, of course, a thankless road to follow. The purveyors of these services get blamed by non-users in the national community for the existence of the demand they meet. In addition, and as part of the service provided, they must not expect any public support from their customers. Too great a need to please can then lead into an acquiescence in pariah status. This can only prolong further the passage to full and honourable citizenship.

A logical corollary of the avoidance of competition may then be a willingness to accommodate on terms that inhibit fuller entry into society. In a sense, therefore, the ultimate contribution of minorities to the economy lies in remaining a dispensable resource. Many young blacks in Britain, for example, are reluctant either to take a job which deprives a white brother of work, or to live on charity at their expense. Blacks in the US were among the first to move back to the South when the industrial centres of the North went into decline. When times are hard the only solution is to travel on somewhere else, taking the true scapegoat role of serving as sacrificial victim for the sake of a superior being.

It is salutory to remember that in the modern world a large proportion of immigrants are moving from as well as to minority ethnic positions. This year's hopefuls are the children and grandchildren of settlers who have failed to break into a stable and worthwhile role in their last nation. Migration in the pre-industrial age led fairly rapidly to fixed patterns of group subordination. That in the 'open' society of today creates an invisible fifth world of dispossessed people. Its inhabitants are flushed around by the ebbs and flows of economic fluctuations, ever looking for a safe anchorage to settle down, and all the time available as stop-gap labour and eager cheerleaders for whoever will offer them a temporary haven.

RESERVOIRS OF EXTRAORDINARY PATRIOTISM

The part played by minorities in giving invisible support to economies is readily appreciated, and given plenty of attention in contemporary theory. But this role is really only one dimension of a much broader and more enduring condition, of heightened attachment to the 'national interest'. The need of identifiable members of minority groups to achieve nationalist legitimacy elicits an intensely patriotic reaction among many of them. This is a resource that the majority can use in a variety of ways. There are many areas where expression of wholehearted devotion to the common good is called for – as in war, sporting contests, and even upholding 'national values' or pushing oneself to meritorious scientific achievements and so on. In all these minority groups seem to come forward with more than their quota of volunteers, eager to prove their allegiance through heroic deeds of self-sacrifice and ordeals of application.

It is not merely as cannon-fodder that they serve. Their calling can be at the highest level. The special character of their patriotism also equips minority individuals to exercise strong political leadership in certain circumstances. What makes their allegiance to the state and nation special is that it clearly implies a denial or renunciation of a lesser or competing group loyalty. It rests discernibly on a conscious and deliberate act of personal will. This brings it far closer than the automatic patriotism of the majority to the enlightenment ideal of elective association. As a result it can both reflect more credit on the state evoking it, and serve as an exemplar of dedication for the rest of its citizens.

What this means in political terms is that minority patriots, rather like the slaves and eunuchs who administered public affairs in classical antiquity, can make an unusually close identification with the central and general interests of a nation. This is not true of leaders originating within the majority. These start with an assured fund of nationalist legitimacy at their disposal. They can attempt to exercise power on behalf of their own private cliques or factions, without much fear of being accused of disloyalty to the nation. As a result they are freer to be partisan and divisive in their programmes.

Those from minority backgrounds, on the other hand, cannot afford to display partiality to their own groups of origin. These by definition are not legitimate sectional interests in nationalist terms. In order to achieve any nationalist acceptability at all they are obliged to rise above sectarianism and aim at the widest possible political appeal. This has the effect of making them extremely integrative leaders. They are especially useful when the nation is strongly divided against itself, or established institutions and authorities appear incapable of holding it on course.

Bonapartist integrators

This is the point of departure for Bonapartist styles of leadership, wherein a nation in travail puts itself into the hands of a charismatic saviour from outside its ruling community. A recent exponent is Chairman Mengistu of Ethiopia. Such a leader cannot share any blame for the errors and internal wrangles which have helped to bring about the previous régimes' crises of integration or legitimation. He therefore stands a better chance of laying down a new social order around which the people can reunite and rediscover confidence in their common destiny.

Leaders from minority backgrounds have played major parts in both of the climacteric progressive revolutions in recent European history, featuring radical alterations in codes of civil conduct, dismantling of traditional social divisions, and insistence on higher levels of individual loyalty to the state. The eponymous Little Corsican stabilized the French revolution, instigated modern centralist reforms, created a new *élite* and revived national pride. Likewise it was a little Georgian, born into a barely conquered nationality, who converted socialism into a system for national government and emerged as the patriarchal figurehead for the modernization and reconstruction of the Russian empire.

It is tempting to suppose with Weber that this capacity of modern nationalism to find a central place for adoptive patriots vindicates its claims to be open and elective. Weber remarked that 'It goes without saying that "national affiliation" need not be based upon common blood. Indeed, everywhere the especially radical "nationalists" are of foreign descent.' (Gerth and Mills, 1957, p. 173)

This view fails to observe the distinction between objective and subjective affiliation. It does not penetrate the progressive nationalist smokescreen. In reality, voluntary patriots are valued and honoured because they are highly amenable to majority public opinion and guidance.

A captive leader can expect a large measure of tolerance from libertarian pockets within the majority. Their more refined communalism is flattered by the implied vindication of their national institutions. The nationalist sees it otherwise. Voluntary allegiance is an unnatural and therefore questionable phenomenon. It suggests tactical or mercenary calculations, and seems capable of being withdrawn as readily as it was offered in the first place. Leaders from minority origins are therefore subjected to constant surveillance by loyalists, to make sure that they do not fail to serve dominant group purposes. This point would not be lost on Andrew Young, who survived in office only very briefly after announcing that he was no token nigger.

Bonapartist popularity is as shallow as it is wide. Napoleon himself came to power by satisfying French thirst for military glory. He soon lost his position when expansion ceased and the nation was once again confined by its traditional rivals.

Members of oppressed groups are all born with progressive credibility. Minority leaders enjoy the greatest integrative power when using this patrimony to impart a universal style to their masters' national causes. Both of the major revolutions referred to were fought out in unyieldingly egalitarian terms. The real achievement of both Bonapartes lay in reconciling the new ideology with prevailing national interests, thereby enabling the dominant community to accept the new credo they needed. French expansion was licensed as the pursuit of human liberation. Russian imperialism was renewed and extended in the name of fraternal proletarian internationalism. Each was more plausible under the chairmanship of a voluntary patriot.

Dirty political workers

The assets possessed by a captive leader go well beyond the mere standing outside internal national ruptures. For by virtue of their recently oppressed status, such persons retain a benefit of doubt in progressive eyes. This enables them to transform tasks which would be deemed objectionable if performed by their overlords, into condonable acts. By publicly patriating their birthright of progressive credit within the destiny of their host nation, they can do a lot to help cleanse and universalize the nation itself.

At all levels of society we can see politically dirty work being laundered through the handling of a voluntary patriot. Black Americans in the front line in Vietnam were not just there to stop the bullets. They also, just through choosing to be there, stood as symbols of the anti-imperialist nature of US involvement.

Minorities who pledge their own legitimacy too uncritically to their patrons may reduce it in the eyes of the outside world. Eldridge Cleaver commented bitterly:

> Some people think that America's point in sending 16 per cent black troops to Vietnam is to kill off the cream of black youth. But it has another important result. By turning her black troops into butchers of the Vietnamese people, America is spreading hate against the black race throughout Asia. Even black Africans find it hard not to hate black Americans for being so stupid as to allow themselves to be used to slaughter another people who are fighting to be free. Black Americans are considered the world's biggest fools to go to another country to fight for something they don't have for themselves.
>
> (1969, p. 127)

It takes more than pointing this out, to liberate minorities from it. For it is an old problem. Franklin shows how Germany during the first world war put out propaganda making this very point – namely that Black American servicemen were fighting to secure for others what they did not possess themselves (1974, p. 343). The soldiers resisted the argument and fought with distinction against the Germans. They then returned home to find the Ku Klux Klan proving the Germans' case, in the 'Red Summer' of 1919.

The patriotic urge is very strong. The gentlemen of the Cheka, and other executioners and party henchmen throughout the communist *bloc*, have been heavily drawn (Leggett, 1981) from outside national majorities. They exhibit the ethnically liberative aspects of the new régimes they serve at the same time as demonstrating their devotion to the national cause. It was likewise a Jewish judge, and Jewish prosecutor, who convicted the Rosenbergs. Quislings and Judenraten everywhere help marvellously to blur the lines of oppression and forestall foreign criticism.

At the highest levels of political responsibility and representation, where nationalist vetoes are an ever present influence, this laundering role inevitably assumes even greater importance. Careers of successful captive leaders are likely to encompass a number of key testing points at which the sponsoring community demands clear affirmation that loyalty to them is greater than attachment to the identity of origin.

A typical test, embracing a good amount of dirty work, consists of taking initiatives to stifle resistance to majority supremacy, and leading restive minorities into periods of renewed captivity. No one can perform this service so effectively as a tame super-patriot, whose colleagues in marginality are never quite able to convince themselves that he would really sell them out. The need for such an operation is one of the most common considerations prompting the admission of such an individual to high office in the first place.

Actually carrying out dirty work is by no means the end of the ordeal. Eventually it becomes impossible to deny the reactionary aspect of Bonapartist achievements. When this happens the rising cohorts of progressive opinion will sooner or later try to dissociate the nation from the less savoury tasks carried out on their behalf. They do this by resurrecting stereotypes prejudicial to their former national darling. Minority patriotism, they tell each other plaintively, is a funny thing. Sometimes it goes over the top and turns into rampant chauvinism. There may be no finer dedication than that of the new recruit; but there is also none fiercer.

Napoleon and Stalin danced too readily to the call of populist sentiments and carried their revolutions into nationalistic excesses. In the end both were reduced in the mind of the next generation to caricatures of their most philistine hosts. They were only just able to escape being deemed to have destroyed the gains so painfully made by the nation. They achieved this with the sacrifice of their own political reputations – a loss necessarily shared to some degree by all in their communities of origin. This is the final stage in the laundering process.

Reassessment of the revolutionary task does not take place until the more polluting activities have already been completed on the nation's behalf. So for the dominant community the cycle of decline, brutalizing upheaval and gradual regeneration is gone through with a minimum of moral cost. When things settle down afterwards it may be considered necessary to denounce some of the means by which national unity and sense of purpose have been revived. But the majority group can avoid the main blame for them. To some, its main fault may seem to lie in having been too open-hearted in giving minority individuals a chance to exercise power. This is a virtuous failing, for which it need not greatly reproach itself. In any case it only helps to refurbish the moral indebtedness and inferiority of its marginal and super-patriotic communities.

KEEPERS OF THE FAITH

If there was a Promethian humanism in Marx and in the Marxist vision, there was, to an even greater degree, the messianic hunger for justice, the prophetic obsession with a kingdom of equity on earth, which is central to Judaism. If there was 'Asiatic' tyranny in Lenin and Stalin, there was also the murderous paradox that so many of those who had brought this tyranny to office and who had now to be eliminated, from Trotsky onward, were Jews and Jewish intellectuals.

(George Steiner, 1978)

Modern nations cannot survive on patriotism alone. This will turn to dust in the mouth unless regularly refreshed by the currents of humanist idealism. And it is at the ideological level, as high priests at the altars of progress, and guardians over the springs of hope and inspiration from which nations replenish belief in their own redeemability, that minorities find their most fundamental and enigmatic roles.

Moreover, the will and capacity to perform these services are not incidental. They, too, are generated by the cross-currents of minority experience, which stimulate a strong impulse towards the adoption of utopian political orientations.

Servitude in the open society is made tolerable by the belief, which progressive nationalism inculcates, that loyal service will eventually be rewarded by the granting of full citizenship. But as the frontiers fail to get any nearer, some passengers on the journey to the promised land of integration are bound to ask themselves sometimes whether they are, after all, going anywhere. There are, broadly speaking, three ways of attempting to cope with this ever-pending disappointment. These are related to the main ways that progressive nationalism itself can be viewed.

Those who are chiefly impressed by the nationalistic character of their hosts' behaviour are likely to conclude that their liberators are frauds. They will then abandon the venture, turning instead to reactive or introspective communalisms of their own. Those, on the other hand, who see progressive nationalism as an indivisible package will usually decide that their patrons are doing the best that can be hoped for. These will continue to submit to their hosts' grand design, and postpone their aspirations yet further.

The third possibility lies in concentrating attention on the universal destination announced by the controlling community, and looking for ways of hastening arrival. This is in some respects the most constructive response, as it can be conciliatory in its assessment of the national majority, without grovelling before it. It combines criticism of a current system and régime with an idealistic belief in the perfectability of man and society. This focuses discussion onto what sort of institutions are needed to achieve the ideals the nation is supposed to be pursuing, and makes it possible to side with one's host without adopting their nationalism.

This is the basis of the appeal of consensualist utopian ideals to minority individuals. Such beliefs may appear escapist or messianic to many people. From the point of view of minorities, though, they can be seen as a thoroughly this-worldly means of making some common cause with their national masters. Devising revolutionary schemas for joining with the suffering masses, to bring down the walls of Babylon and rebuild a new world, makes political sense for minorities. It is a way to immerse themselves harmoniously in the mainstream of social evolution, alongside their captors, and together wash away the stigmata of oppression they both bear.

Thus the experience of servitude makes minority groups fertile breeding grounds for integrative reveries. Particular visions and fancies may only enjoy short working lives. Marginal individuals are, however, always beavering away in the shadows to produce new ones. It is consequently almost impossible to imagine how the humanist tradition could have taken off and retained its momentum and vitality without their passionate involvement.

Jews in the priestly role

Pride of place here obviously goes to Jews. Their own culture has been tuned by millennia of dispersion and exile into a highly sensitive instrument for picking up and broadcasting radical vibrations. Attitudes cultivated originally in Babylon and codified in the Talmud have been intimately involved in the fashioning of the modern world order, right from its first glimmerings.

It was Jews who generalized the struggle against Roman rule and disseminated the ideas about a Universal Father. These ideas then became reworked within the ruins of that empire into an integrative religion binding its remnants into an international community. Reformist Judaism of the late medieval period, developing alongside the new commercial cosmopolitanism, collaborated with gentile rationalism in undermining the decaying Holy Empire itself.

The major contribution has been since Napoleonic emancipation. Jews more than any other group have discovered a special affinity to utopian political ventures, and found a role for themselves as producers and purveyors of radical humanist ideas, above all communism.

> To a people conscious of centuries of constriction, the ghetto, the Pale, there was a breezy openness to Communism. They were members of a new order, on a par with others, equals, or rather more than equal, for they were charter members, each a minor Moses leading not merely a people, but Mankind, into a promised land ... And the Jewish Communist who combined his creed with a sense of Jewish history could even tell himself that he was making the vision of the prophets manifest on earth, for there was hardly a humane sentiment among the slogans of Communism which had not received its first utterance in Scripture.
>
> (Chaim Bermant, 1978, p. 215)

Many people in other minority groups also steer their dissent and energy into socialist and communist movements. But apart from a few, like Gramsci, they tend to be much more practical in their orientations, taking up radical ideas in order to universalize and broaden the struggles they are engaged in. Not many show an inclination to labour as temple guardians at the sources of progressive faith. It is predominantly Jews, from Saint-Simon through to Marx, and via Frankfurt, to Sartre and the late Parisian Left, who have been the true schoolmen of revolution, spinning webs of impenetrable scholarship to protect the central mysteries from hostile scrutiny, and imparting their liturgical styles of exegesis throughout all adjacent realms of social speculation and investigation.

The significance of this priestly role is that it provides national majorities with ready oracles to consult when they need to confirm their own progressive credibility. It is not seemly for a dominant community to attempt to exonerate itself from the subjugation of the weaker, by proposing that rich and poor, weak and strong, are alike prisoners of an impersonal system which together they may understand

and overcome. Far better that such revelations are made by recipients of their intolerance. If Jews, who have suffered for so long, are able to believe that tinkering with social institutions can alter the hearts of men, then it is churlish, not to mention inopportune, to dispute it too hotly.

How many non-Jewish social scientists truly believe that there is a route for minorities out of their vale of tears? How many, however, are humbled and flattered by the apparent conviction of colleagues from Jewish backgrounds into agreeing with propositions which they could not, in good faith and modesty, put forward themselves? It is obvious that minorities have a burning incentive to persuade themselves that social problems have rational solutions. But this does not seem to detract from the utility of their labours. The mere fact that they are prepared to stand up and declare their confidence in the future is enough to launch victim-led bandwagons of hope and self-deception. It does no harm to members of national majorities to make a friendly gesture by taking the occasional ride on them.

Perhaps it would be better to rephrase this slightly, as 'apparently victim-led'. If it was possible to look behind the hopeful revolutionary countenances we would, I think, discover many anguished spirits trapped into idealistic postures by the sheer weight of obstacles to alternative goals. The optimistic purity of universalist vision which renders them so valuable as ideological labourers does not arise just as spontaneous creation. It is constrained and imposed on them by those who utilize their products.

Rosa Luxemburg – exemplary keeper

We can get some hints at the nature of the pressures inducing congregation at shrines to human consensualism by looking briefly at Rosa Luxemburg. Her life within the socialist movement shows both why Jews should have felt such a strong urge to maintain 'pure' universalist doctrines, and how even in doing this they may end up performing a service for dominant majorities.

Towards the end of the nineteenth century very many Jews in Europe were becoming disillusioned with the slow passage to the liberal promised land. Many did not thrill to the prospect of a retreat into Zion. Nor were they willing to follow those like Disraeli – or in a different milieu Ferdinand Lassalle – who were reclining into adoptive patriotism. Instead they transferred their affiliation to socialism, in the hope of a surer destination. The Second International was, however, itself riven by nationalist suspicions and intrigue. Jews gravitating to the movement found that the dilemmas of identity from which they were trying to escape were often reproduced, albeit more furtively, in their new political relationships.

In some respects they were even intensified. The cosmopolitan aspect of many Jewish identities interacted with the internationalist pretensions of the movement to multiply the suspicions that could be directed at any Jews achieving prominence in it. Rosa Luxemburg herself was variously suspected by German socialists of covertly favouring the Polish cause, by Poles of being an agent of the Russians, by the Russians of having pro-German leanings. To all of them, except to the Zionist Bund, who looked on her as a traitor to her own people, she was also, or even primarily a Jew. And this meant that she was open to the charge of having become a socialist for communalist reasons – a charge which socialist Jews were not beyond making about each other. Even Trotsky held that Jews were not the best party members, having not joined out of class interest.

The only way to survive under such intense fraternal scrutiny lay in maximizing one's consensual identification, through a fierce attachment to the pure Marxist dogma that all national and communal sentiments are mere veils, which reveal universal class interests when drawn fully back. At a time when many around her were losing their faith, Rosa Luxemburg carried on implacably drawing back veils of communalism. She helped thereby to keep the Second International on the rails that bit longer. When the movement did finally crash she managed to salvage a reasonably pure revolutionary doctrine.

During the years running up to the collapse of the International, some of her principal doctrinal antagonists were Russian Bolsheviks who needed to make a tactical manipulation to socialist theory in order to attract the support and membership of minorities in Russia. In particular, it was important to them to allow a principle of national self-determination which was not too rigidly tied to a notion of the priority of class interests and action. The Bolsheviks won this battle and subordinated socialist theory to the dictates of nationalist strategy. But when the tactical need had passed, and the Bolsheviks had become a governing party, they required a de-communalized ruling mandate to fly from their Moscow flagship. They then quickly reverted to the line that Rosa Luxemburg had tended in the meantime, blaming their former deviation from it onto another non-Russian, Stalin.

The generation of oracles that Rosa Luxemburg belonged to did not long survive the end of the Second International and housing of official Marxism in Moscow. Many of them died as Judases to nations presuming to adopt them. Luxemburg herself fell in the Spartacist revolt against German nationalism. And Trotsky, who had tried to support the true line from within the Bolshevik party, was moved on as a troublesome cosmopolitan when the old Russian nation surged back to reoccupy the remandated state apparatus.

Nevertheless, the beliefs that they had striven to uphold survived. These gave fresh hope to the world's struggling peoples, and thereby imparted a new international legitimacy to the Russian state machine, which now saw itself as godfather to all other revolutionary movements. Later generations of socialist idealists have questioned Moscow's right to mandate itself in the name of Marx, as more and more defects in the Soviet system have become evident. But this is all too late to deconsecrate the system, which was amply sanctified at its inception by the deeds and declarations of many authoritative oracles.

The majority of the first Politburo were Jews. This nearly matched the eight out of eleven Commissars of the Hungarian 'Socialist People's Republic', set up briefly in 1919, who were Jewish, including their leader, and friend of Lenin, Bela Kun.

All of them except collaborators were eliminated as the Russian nation regenerated. They had by then, however, already played their part as co-guarantors of the progressive character of the structure for which they were helping lay the foundations.

Rootless minority individuals are moved by an urgent desire to believe in man's ability to build a better world for all. This plays back into the hands of the very national majorities excluding them in the first place. In attempting to free humanity from one type of shackle, they may find themselves helping to forge the chains for a new captivity. Later generations can see this more easily. A community which takes on the role of formulating progressive and liberating programmes over a considerable period is bound to accumulate a bitter legacy of collective self-hatred.

Radical Jews in the nineteenth century took some pride in the part played by their forebears in developing the market system which had freed Europe from Feudalism. But many were nevertheless driven towards dissociation from the Jewish community, because of the collective guilt it now bore for the evils of mature capitalism. Likewise many Jews this century, while fascinated by Marx and Trotsky, revile the system which they helped to establish. Szajkowski quotes a Jewish journalist who wrote:

> The concrete and powerful figure is Leon Trotsky, and next to St Paul, Leon Trotsky is the greatest Jewish figure in Jewish diaspora history. Just as St Paul organized one of the greatest revolutions in the world's history and the Sauls paid for it, so Leon Trotsky is now organizing one of the greatest revolutions in history and the Braunsteins will have to pay for it. This is our tragedy. For the deeds and misdeeds of Leon Trotsky, the next fifty Jewish generations will suffer martyrdom and pain.
>
> (Szajkowski, 1974, p. 203)

The nature of the guilt keeps changing. Yesterday's dreams become tomorrow's nightmares. What carries on is the ambivalence towards one's collective role in sustaining the process. This is one of the hardest chains of all to break.

PART II:
CAPTIVE LEADERS

CHAPTER 3

PIERRE TRUDEAU IN THRALL TO CANADIAN INTEGRITY

IN BONDAGE TO A HIGHER DESTINY

The combination of a degree of group exclusion – in which their overall level of participation and rewards is kept somewhat below that enjoyed by the national majority – with a judicious flow of opportunities for individual enterprise and success, results in a most economical husbanding of minority resources. This way the incentives for patriotic exertion are maintained at a high pitch. Minority communities will tend all the time towards the condition of semi-incorporated appendages to the national body. They become pools of latent energy, from which enthusiastic effort can be drawn off into domestic service for the host community.

Nowhere is this cropping system more striking than in the area of national political leadership. Minority individuals in a self-consciously open society are extremely well placed to accumulate a wide base of political legitimation. This can make them more effective as political brokers and 'integrative' national leaders, than members of the majority itself. This is useful to the host nation, especially when its internationalist credibility needs a boost. At the same time it constitutes a clear enhancement of the individual opportunities available to soldiers of fortune in minority communities, ambitious to make a contribution to national life.

In this group of chapters I examine a few well documented cases of such national leadership. This will enable me to indicate something of the range of situations in which it is called on, while drawing attention to some of the common elements of clientship involved in them all.

A variety of plausible cases can be made concerning the 'real' intentions of these leaders. They are sometimes presented as merely selfish opportunists. Some, however, will see them as having sought high office in the belief that it was indeed possible to promote a genuinely more inclusive society. Yet others, especially perhaps within minority groups, may prefer to think of them as secret labourers for the specific advancement of their own people of origin. Many interpretations are possible. And it is, after all, this uncertainty over their real aims that underpins their broad political appeal.

But even if they knew themselves what they were about, which should not be assumed too readily, it is not available knowledge to the rest of us. Nor does it matter very much. Each was dependent for political selection and survival on the sponsorship of groups located firmly within the dominant community. Moreover, these groups proved only too well aware of how to play along a minority front man for the benefit of their own causes. So in the event none of them was able to make much impact on the prevailing ethnic hierarchies in their respective societies. Any influence they exercised was as trustees for groups they were born outside of. It is accordingly in their recruitment and retention as proxies for the majority that we find the essential common factors in their careers.

The national political account of a minority politician typically does not open until a transaction has occurred within an interest group within the majority, at which point a crucial interchange of legitimacies takes place. An aspirant client must first hand over to his chosen patrons the universalist stock which, as an outsider, he was born with. He does this by endorsing their cause as a credible national or global platform worthy of his dedication, and by dissociating himself from minority criticisms of it.

This moment of appropriation is often documented through the publication by the client of an analysis of the ethnic question, in which his original identity is portrayed as subordinate to that represented by the patrons. This is something that he cannot easily retract. In return for this gesture of commitment, the patron is then able to extend nationalist credit and protection to the client. At this point he becomes adopted as an honorary member of the national majority, in their eyes.

This transaction occurs between members of very unequal groups. While it provides a basis for an accumulation of credits by the individual political entrepreneur, it also entails some cost to the community he springs from. Under the ground rules of ethnic dominance, hardline members of the majority feel free to treat any minority individual as representing that community he can be identified with. When the client gives witness to the progressive aspect of a political programme, he does not merely tie his own hands. He will also be seen by many in the majority associated with his patron as having also effectively disqualified minority colleagues from speaking against that programme. At the very least, he will be regarded within the majoritarian heartland as having accepted the role within his chosen movement of replying to, and condemning, any of his former compatriots who would try to oppose it.

Similarly, the captive leader's personal investment carries one-sided risks. If he fails to live up to the expectations of his backers in the majority, his contractual identity falls apart. Once they cease to trust him, his nationalist capital will be lost without much hope of recovery. He cannot easily make a fresh start with another party. Having bound himself to a favourable view of his adopting patrons, he is thoroughly implicated in their activities. So he cannot hope to extricate his own universalist reputation, and retrieve his original stake. To criticize a mission he had previously paid tribute to would expose him to charges of inconsistency, unreliability and, most of all, ingratitude.

In addition to sacrificing office and the chance to influence national policy from inside the power structure, he will henceforth be regarded as lying on the sectarian and retrogressive flank of minority consciousness. The nationalist legitimacy acquired by a client in the sponsoring transaction is purely conditional and easily forfeited.

By contrast, the original universalist patrimony, once handed over, cannot normally be restored. After he has placed his trust in the gallantry of his patron, there is little that even the most idealistic minority leader could do to escape with dignity. Having contracted in, there is little real option to following a narrow path of subservience to the way revealed by the sponsoring majority. All he can do is hope that it will indeed broaden out ahead as promised. This is why it does not greatly matter what his original purposes actually were.

TRUDEAU'S ADVOCACY OF FEDERALISM

One of the main strengths of a client leader lies in being able to align openly with a nationalist majority, without necessarily appearing to sell out on, and to lose the support of, minority compatriots. Even in the most polarized situation, as when a large, coherent and restive minority is confronting an anxious majority with explicit demands for a greater stake in the system, or for the freedom to opt out altogether, it is possible for a member of that minority to ride into power on an enigma, blur the lines of conflict, and deliver his community into a further, reconstructed era of captivity.

Canadian public life is periodically dominated by a resurgence of francophone nationalism and demands for Quebec autonomy, and provides just such a context. And there is no finer contemporary exponent of the art of using minority charisma to defuse integration crises than Pierre Elliott Trudeau.

It must be admitted at the outset that Trudeau has been assisted in cutting across the cleavage in Canadian society by the small but salient ambiguity within even his own identity as a francophone. His father was a complete French Canadian, and it was as such that Pierre himself was formally brought up. But his mother was half-Scottish, and had transmitted her patronym of Elliott to Pierre. His full name was Joseph Philippe Pierre Yves Elliott, and he was known at school as Pierre-Philippe until his teens.

As an adolescent he found the authoritarianism of Jesuit education too irksome. He was able to loosen the hold of French communalism on him by taking up the name of his anglophone ancestor. During his late teens he established himself as Pierre Elliott in a move which one biographer (Radawanski, 1978, p. 37) has described as '... another gesture apparently designed to taunt the French nationalists around him.'

In this way he projected himself from an early age as a free individual, more authentically Canadian than those preoccupied with the ancient tribal battle against the English, and already sensing a personal calling to work towards creating a more united nation.

Trudeau's personal strategy for surviving adolescence was a logical point of departure for a federalist francophone policy, along the lines successfully adopted by the first French federal Prime Minister Wilfred Laurier. Extrapolating from his own position as a bilingual and liberated 'Québecois', Trudeau formulated the stand that true advancement of French interests did not lie in a defensive retreat into a little Quebec. Such a state would become even more of a pawn to the great power bourgeois interests of their southern neighbour than Canada itself was already. The only way forward was through the fulfilment of the Actonian potential of the existing Canadian constitution. This meant extending and protecting the individual rights of citizens in the nation as a whole. If Canada succeeded in becoming a truly pluralist democracy, in which French culture was nowhere a disability, then there would be no need for francophones to identify so strongly with Quebec and seek to turn it into a French state.

Whatever Trudeau's personal motives in adopting this federalist dream and urging the universalist potential of Canadian society, there can be no doubt that it was a position which made him highly attractive to anglophone politicians. Following the post-war decolonization of European empires, and the related surge of negro self-respect in the US, francophone consciousness in Quebec was steadily growing under leaders like Lesage.

The Anglo-Canadian establishment at Ottawa found itself being pressured by Quebec's calls for provincial autonomy into making ever greater concessions. After the re-election of Lesage in 1962 on a rising tide of French nationalism, the English community began to fear in earnest for the federal union. A Royal Commission on Bilingualism and Biculturalism was appointed to examine the grievances which francophones were expressing more and more forcibly. The federal Liberal Party meanwhile had an eye on the phenomenal popularity of Kennedy south of the border. They decided to offset the centrifugal effect of men like Lévesque by inviting several prominent moderate – i.e. federalist – francophones to stand for election to Ottawa on their ticket. Trudeau was not at the time a Liberal. But he recognized the opportunity this sponsorship offered. He joined the federal parliament on this basis with one or two francophone colleagues in 1965 (McNaught, 1976 (ed.), chs 19 and 20).

In return for this majoritarian dispensation, Trudeau was soon expected to take on the job of party spokesman on constitutional issues. These were now becoming critical. In 1966 Lesage had lost power in Quebec to an even more strident 'Union Nationale' admin- istration, and Lévesque had formed his 'Parti Québecois'. In 1967, reports of the Royal Commission started appearing which documented the disadvantages of francophones. Fuel had been added to the move- ment with de Gaulle's famous call at Expo 67 in Montreal for a 'Québec Libre'.

Trudeau was projected into national prominence early in 1968 as Ottawa's federalist champion. He rebutted 'Québecois' insistence on rewriting the British North America Act to give Quebec greater powers. Instead he advocated the insertion of a Bill of Rights to the existing constitution, to guarantee French language and educational rights throughout the federal union.

During the public debate on this, Trudeau was able to demonstrate his enormous integrative potential. English Canadians were impressed by his ability and willingness to stand up against fellow francophones. In addition, their progressive consciences were flattered by his argument that the whole of Canada, not just Quebec, could realistically be seen by French Canadians as a homeland in which they could find social justice. In a book on the Canada Question published in the same year, Trudeau clearly indicated to anglophones that he regarded British culture and institutions as a sound basis for a tolerant democracy.

French Canadians for their part listened to the federal case more carefully than if it had been put to them by an anglophone. Trudeau could not seriously, at this stage, be charged by his compatriots with selling them out. He was putting forward a reasoned programme of reform which he could be presumed to believe in, since it was embodied in his own career. And there is every reason to suppose that it held a genuine appeal for the individualistic element in minority experience, which was not yet submerged.

In tapping the individualist current in the French community which found the closeness of minority solidarity cloying, Trudeau was in some respects feeding off the authoritarian aspects of Lévesque's mobilization of the community, just as Laurier had done off the communalist politics of Henri Bourassa. (Basham, 1978, ch. 7)

At the collectivist level, and in spite of occasional carping references to his not entirely French background, he was on the whole regarded as genuinely committed to the best interests of francophones. So he enjoyed an insider's licence to tell the French a few home truths about themselves.

Radawanski notes:

And, as a French Canadian, he can talk to Qúebecois in terms that would be foreclosed to an anglophone, speaking about the dangers of independence and the advantages of Confederation with a brutal frankness that would be perceived as patronizing if it came from an outsider.

(1978, p. 343)

Purveyor of home truths

Trudeau's lack of inhibition in doing just this has been extraordinary. In his 1968 book, for example, he repeated several quite savage condemnations of French tendencies towards parochialism and authoritarianism. These would have scandalized francophones had he not seen himself as a product of the very traditions he was criticizing. He opens his case disarmingly by suggesting that his rejection of sectarianism can perhaps be seen as the quirk of a natural dissenter.

> The only constant factor to be found in my thinking over the years has been opposition to accepted opinion ... I chose to apply it to politics, and it led me to power – a result I had not really desired, or even expected.
>
> (Trudeau, 1968, xix)

His attachment to the Canada Act, and sense of the absurdity of 'Québecois' pretensions, thus stems from the instinctive reaction felt by any free spirit to the constraints of a repressive group.

> (And so) I get fed up when I hear our nationalist brood calling itself revolutionary. Quebec's revolution, if it had taken place, would first have consisted in freeing men from collective coercions; freeing the citizens brutalized by reactionary and arbitrary governments, freeing consciences bullied by a clericalized and obscurantist Church; freeing workers exploited by an oligarchic capitalism; freeing men crushed by authoritarian and outmoded traditions. Quebec's revolution would have consisted in the triumph of the freedoms of the human being as inalienable rights, over and above capital, the nation, tradition, the Church, and even the State.
>
> (ibid., p. 205)

This physiological reflex towards dissent happily coincides with what is politically desirable in the modern world. Trudeau appeals to Acton as a suitably Catholic authority for allowing due credit to non-Catholic constitutions for their ability to rise above the claims of particular cultures and sectional interests. He feels that English culture is the better medium for distilling liberal values and institutions, on which an integrative pluralism can be built. It is this, in the last analysis, which leads him to support the anglophone federalist case.

> In 1960, everything was becoming possible in Quebec, even revolution. A whole generation was free at last to apply all its creative energies to bringing this backward province up to date ... Thanks to English and Jewish lawyers (ah, yes!), thanks to the Supreme Court in Ottawa, personal freedom had at last

triumphed over the obscurantism of Quebec's legislators and the authoritarianism of our courts.

(ibid., p. 209)

Trudeau was again following in Laurier's footsteps here. According to Basham (1978, p. 203) Laurier had

... gained support from English Canada and was brought to power largely through his frequent indications that French Canadians owed their religious and cultural existence to British institutions, surviving under the British flag, which 'floats tonight over our heads without a single English soldier in the country to defend it, its sole defense resting in the gratitude which we owe it for our freedom and the security which we have found under its folds'.

By comparison, French assertiveness is derided by Trudeau, in language teasingly borrowed from Fanon, as stubborn, petty-minded reaction.

Several years ago ... I tried to show that the devotees of the nationalist school of thought among French Canadians, despite their good intentions and courage, were for all practical purposes trying to swim upstream against the course of progress. ... The truth is that the separatist counter-culture is the work of a powerless petit-bourgeois minority afraid of being left behind by the twentieth century revolution. Rather than carving themselves out a place in it by ability, they want to make the whole tribe return to the wigwam by declaring its independence.

(ibid., pp. 168, 211)

His advocacy of federalism on behalf of the Liberals made inroads into French support for communal extremists in spite of these cutting attacks on French communalism. Or perhaps it was because of them. He may have persuaded compatriots of the dangers of collective introspection.

Either way, the integrative appeal exercised by this new Canadian Kennedy was remarkable. So much so that the premier, Pearson, who felt unable to withstand Quebec's demands himself, retired in his favour. This allowed Trudeau to lead the Liberals into a new election, and enabled the party to reap the benefit from the fervour he was arousing.

The 1968 election which followed shortly, marked the high tide of millennial Trudeaumania in Canada. His call for One Nation drew strong support in Quebec, where he was thought to be basically on the side of the French and – since he stood on the verge of office – worth giving a chance. It also proved extremely reassuring to anglophones, capturing many habitual Conservative voters.

His conservative rival, Stanfield, was completely wrong-footed by Trudeau's campaign. In trying to undercut Trudeau's implicit appeal to francophone voters, he adopted a 'Deux Nations' platform, courting the French with explicit promises of further concessions on autonomy for Quebec. This strategy failed to carry any conviction among the Québecois. It succeeded, however, in alienating many diehard anglophones, in Trudeau's favour. The Liberals were returned to power with their first clear majority for fifteen years. Basham's verdict was that: 'Clearly all Canada sensed the need for a national politician of French Canadian extraction who could hold the nation together.' (1978, p. 218)

Trudeau's magic evaporated under the rigours of administration. In 1969 he embarked on the Liberal programme of pluralist reform with an Official Languages Act, scheduling bilingualism in the civil service, as recommended by the Royal Commission. This did not go nearly far enough to satisfy francophone aspirations for equal opportunities. At the same time it sowed seeds of anglophone discontent, particularly in the monolingual western states. In the 1972 election he lost his overall majority, and only just held onto office.

Growing scepticism in Quebec about Liberal policy, not to mention a system of electoral representation which seriously devalued the francophone vote, sparked off a round of separatist violence. In the short term the disturbances served to discredit the separatist case; and firm anti-terrorist measures by Trudeau's federal government re-united the nation. But by the mid-1970s the fissures were once more apparent. Quebec's sensitivity to unresolved cultural disadvantages had resurfaced. This first forced the provincial Liberal party to draw closer to Lévesque. Then, in 1976, it gave power to Lévesque's own 'Parti Québecois'. Provincial Bills aimed at turning Quebec into a unilingual French state persuaded many anglophones in the province to get out. Meanwhile anglophone opinion in the country as a whole, having already pressured Trudeau into modifying even the minimal existing government implementation of bilingualism, was hardening around the conclusion that it might be better to let Quebec go its own way after all.

With his federalist strategy falling apart, Trudeau lost both the anglophone support that his office depended on, and even the apparent will to go on striving. The provincial governments in the oil rich West were also becoming hostile to the encroachments by Ottawa which Trudeau's federalist powers entailed. In a mood of general disenchantment and weakening national unity, a listless Trudeau was voted out of power in 1979, and started to speak of an early retirement.

The retaming of Quebec

But this departure revealed just how strong a binding force Trudeau still was. A few months of anglophone Conservative administration brought the nation even closer to break up. When this government fell during 1980 over an inept and contentious budget, the Liberals pressed Trudeau to lead them again in the ensuing election. In the event he managed to recapture some of the mood of expectancy of his presidential-style 1968 campaign.

Having bounced himself back into office with recharged vigour and mandate, Trudeau immediately took up again his task of retaining Canadian integrity. He campaigned strongly for a 'No' vote in the Quebec referendum on independence, or 'Sovereignty-Association'; and he probably played a decisive part in defeating the proposition, through his portrayal of the separatist movement as petty and inherently racist. He was able to capitalize heavily on a blunder by Lévesque, calling Trudeau's authenticity as a 'Québecois' in question, on the eve of polling.

Lévesque's mistake lay in declaring that 'Elliott' was not a Quebec name. Trudeau had, however, played the role throughout that campaign of the defender of small minorities. These had been alarmed by Lévesque's Bill 101, enforcing the use of the French language. Trudeau now adroitly played on these fears. By pointing out that his British ancestors had lived in Quebec for two hundred years, he drew attention to the potentially oppressive tendencies latent in francophone nationalism. This severely weakened its claim to be a progressive movement.

French opinion was temporarily demoralized and divided by the defeat of this bid for independence. Trudeau seized the opportunity to launch a programme for longer-term containment, knitting Quebec more tightly into a centralized federation. A major plank in the Liberal 'No' campaign in the referendum had been a promise, instead, to patriate the British North American Act – regarded by many of the French as a symbol of national vassalage and a prop for anglo supremacy – and to enact a new Canadian constitution enshrining full rights for francophones throughout the union. Trudeau used the result of the referendum as a mandate to pursue this. He laboured throughout 1981 putting together a new constitution promoting individual rights. This, as it took shape, clearly involved the curtailment of provincial powers like those of Lévesque's Quebec.

Lévesque was bitterly angry at what he saw as Trudeau's betrayal of French interests. The proposed Charter of Rights directly undermined his own provincial unilingual legislation – Bill 101. Trudeau's new constitution only received the required level of approval after it had been amended to give provinces the right to opt out and override the charter on certain issues.

This, however, seems unlikely to happen – certainly for the foreseeable future – as the steam has definitely been taken out of the separatist movement. The new federal rights created for francophones go well beyond those provided in the 1969 Act. Having failed to get a majority vote for independence before the existence of these rights, Lévesque and his successors can hardly expect to obtain support for opting out of the system now. It will take many years for francophones to give the new institutions a trial and feel out their inadequacies, before clear grievances emerge for communalist reaction to coalesce around. In the meantime, by confusing French aspirations, Trudeau has averted the most serious challenge that has yet arisen to the unity of Canada. He has also gone some way towards fulfilling his ambition of boosting the prestige of the Canadian system as a whole, and giving the nation a leading mission to humanity.

(If British and French Canadians) will collaborate at the hub of a truly pluralistic state, Canada could become the envied seat of a form of federation that belongs to tomorrow's world. Better than the American melting-pot, Canada could offer an example to all those new Asian and African states ... who must discover how to govern their polyethnic populations with proper regard for justice and liberty. What better reason for cold-shouldering the lure of annexation to the United States? Canadian federalism is an experiment of major proportions; it could become a brilliant prototype for the moulding of tomorrow's civilization.

(1968, p. 211)

CHAPTER 4

THE RED TSAR AS A PAWN OF GREAT
RUSSIAN CHAUVINISM

The career of Joseph Stalin offers an illuminating example of captive leadership. It shows clearly the transactions whereby a political movement within a demoralized nation extends communalist legitimacy to a minority individual, who can then revitalize that nation. Also it reveals the symbiotic quality of the relationships entailed between ambitious clients and their patrons in the majority.

Stalin was very much the creature of Lenin. It was Lenin who plucked him from relative obscurity, and turned him almost overnight into an important national figure. But the benefits were mutual. Lenin and the interests he stood for would have been hard pressed to carry through a successful revolution without access to the internationalist credit they unlocked by sponsoring this 'splendid Georgian'. It is perhaps not going too far to suggest that Lenin's astute selection and cultivation of this protégé was the single most important contribution he made to his party and fatherland.

The centrality of Stalin in securing Lenin's revolution has been obscured by the latter's supposed death-bed renunciation of his disciple. Since Stalin's fall from grace this has been conventionally regarded as evidence of an emerging contrast in dispositions and aims. It is assumed that this would have quickly brought about the eclipse of the coarse Georgian if Lenin had survived long enough to see it through. One should not, however, attach too much significance to this repudiation. For one thing, the received account of the affair owes a good deal to the testimony and interpretation of Trotsky; and he had personal reasons for wanting Stalin out of the way. But more pertinently, Lenin's apparent condemnation of Stalin bears all the marks of a ritualized and bogus dissociation, which is part and parcel of any long term patronage relationship.

The heavy handed behaviour that Stalin was slated for can hardly have come as much of a surprise to Lenin. It was, after all, entirely in line with his knowledge of Stalin's character, and with his own expressed ideas about how assimilated non-Russians could be expected to operate. Lenin could not of course give open support to Stalin without damaging his own progressive credentials, and with them those of Russians and the party generally. But it is difficult to believe that some such proclivity towards over-zealous reactions was not in fact written into the role for which Stalin had been selected. This does not of course rule out the possibility that Stalin had completed the main tasks for which he had been groomed, so that Lenin was, indeed, by this stage prepared to abandon him.

In the event, Lenin's early death opened the way for Stalin to become an open Russophile and transfer his loyalty from Lenin and the party, direct to Mother Russia herself. But even this shift in orientation was well underway while Lenin still retained his powers. It is, moreover, quite consistent with the general task Lenin seems to have had in mind for Stalin. This was to help secure continuity in the Russian empire. It was a project which patriots with a wide range of political orientations were agreed was essential if modernization was to take place, in whatever form, without turning Russia herself into a colony of the more advanced West.

PATRONS IN NEED OF A CLIENT

Because of her position on the edge of Europe, Russia had been able to resist the penetration of secular ideas for longer than most European powers. For several generations she had seen herself as defender of the Christian faith against the new barbarism. But as humanism moved into a more explicitly communalist phase on the continent, during the second part of the nineteenth century, it was perforce taken up by Russia herself to support Slav minorities in central Europe.

This inevitably laid Russia open to an application of the same principles internally, among her own suppressed nationalities. Democratic fraternalism is not a safe weapon to be wielded by a heavily imperial structure, in which more than half of the population are minorities, and where much of the aristocracy are foreign transplants too. Consequently, through the final quarter of the century the holy empire was rapidly falling prey to western interventionism. Enlightened patriots of all hues were casting around desperately for a new mandate for their imperial hegemony.

Socialist ideas naturally figured prominently in this quest for a new order. In addition to imparting a radical cachet which many Russians felt their country to be lacking, these theories articulated fears of subjection to western capitalist domination, and made a direct appeal to a population still moved by traditionalist *gemeinschaft* values.

But in the crucial matter of addressing the problems of minorities, even this cast of thought needed careful local adaptation before it could be acceptable either to Russians or their colonial subjects. Mainstream socialist theory had responded to the sharpening national consciousness of the late nineteenth century by taking a greater interest in imperialism, and in the corresponding desire of oppressed nationalities for liberation. It had developed its own internal debate over the conditions in which liberation movements were to be deemed conducive to proletarian internationalism, and merited tactical support.

The basic socialist strategy of giving conditional support to the idea of minority rights strongly favoured a people like the Germans – especially the Prussians – who were in an expansionary phase. Most liberation movements in Europe at that time had a fairly bourgeois complexion. But as Marxist theory argued that it was necessary to go through a capitalist stage, some formula could usually be devised to ally with these movements when they appeared to coincide with the imperatives of German expansion. At the end of the day, if Marx should prove wrong and capitalism failed to collapse, the expanding nation would at least have the compensation of having acquired a new empire.

Conditions were very different in Russia. It was a dying nation if ever there was one. In this context a tactical admission of minority self-determination did not provide a scenario around which a united socialist movement could hope to develop. To many metropolitan Russians, however penitent they might feel about the Tsarist legacy, the theory spelt imperial dismemberment. For some it presaged the overrunning of the Russian heartland itself by western colonialism. Few Russians had any illusions that German socialists, quite apart from the rest of the Teutonic hordes, would put international brotherhood before Fatherland if it came to the test. Even revolutionaries with a strong faith in proletarian unity preferred the idea of running their own affair, from the security of their own empire, rather than risk becoming a side-show to someone else's.

To the subject nationalities in the empire, on the other hand, the Marxist line did not go nearly far enough. Its portrayal of support for minority secession as a tactic for moving towards complete restructuring of the social order sounded to many of them dangerously like closet imperialism. Nationalist movements seeking independence wanted a genuine autonomy. They were not interested in deployment as disposable pawns in someone else's power game – least of all a proletarian power game.

As anti-imperial sentiments intensified, it became evident to many socialists in Russia that the movement could not hope to secure the trust and co-operation of smaller nationalities, without a theory more responsive to their sensibilities. In particular they needed to disavow the suggestion that minority self-determination was to be seen merely as a convenient step towards more important goals. After the 1905 uprising had shown the strength of anti-Russian feelings in the empire, Lenin and his colleagues were left in no doubt that the outcome of the Bolshevik programme would turn on the attitude towards it of the smaller nationalities. (Horace Davis, 1967, pp. 195ff.)

The reconciliation of these competing anxieties called for a softer and more discreet approach towards the harnessing of minority energies than was offered by existing theory. Lenin's 'two-stage' strategy achieved this balance brilliantly. It consisted of allowing a virtually free rein to secessionist aspirations, while issuing minorities with a fraternal invitation to reassociate later with the metropolis if they wished. This contained just enough constructive ambiguity to gain support across the lines of mutual nationalist suspicions. It served as the official policy of the Russian Social Democratic Party during the critical period before and during the main revolution.

Lenin's insistence that 'enlightened Great Russians' like himself should atone for their collective imperial guilt by being more responsive to the feelings of oppressed peoples served a multiple purpose. It acted as a prompt for unreconstructed chauvinists who had yet to appreciate the need to make concessions to the minority spirit. It also went some way in alleviating minorities' fears about imperialism re-emerging in a new guise.

At the same time, that part of the theory which went on to suggest that freed minorities would soon discover that it was in their interests to reassociate voluntarily with Russia carried just enough hints about possible 'fraternal persuasion' to reassure Russians, without causing undue alarm among minorities.

What, however, clinched the credibility, and political usefulness, of this partisan revision of Marxism was that part of Lenin's strategy expressed in practical example rather than mere precept. This was his giving a prominent role in the process to a minority individual. Lenin seems to have been well aware that the value of a revolutionary theory could be greatly enhanced by careful stage-management of who appeared to be the prime mover of key policies. He realized that his own status disqualified him from playing the leading role in relation to nationalities. When he felt that it was now imperative for the party to endorse his strong line on 'unconditional' self-determination, he recruited a non-European individual to be his mouthpiece, and to visibly identify the policy with its supposed beneficiaries.

Stalin had all the right characteristics for this job. Lenin recognized this, and sponsored his rapid promotion to a central position in the party. He also closely guided his hand in the publication of a treatise on the nationalities problem which backed his own line. Having thereby imparted an authenticity to his sensitive strategy of giving strong support for secessionist movements, Lenin was himself freed to develop the issue further in subsequent articles and pronouncements under his own name. This holding on to a theoretician's role probably in turn helped further to reassure backwoods Russian opinion by hinting that they were still in control.

By this deft piece of ethnic politics, Lenin effectively forestalled the aggressive use of minority rights doctrines against the Russian empire. He forged the concept instead into a weapon of defence, with which the Bolsheviks might hope to retain it.

Elevation of 'this splendid Georgian'

The event which actually forced Lenin's hand in this matter was a tangible sliding among RSPD members during 1912. Their main drift was towards the strategy of 'cultural autonomy' proposed by Otto Bauer for minorities in the similar, though less critical, situation in the Hapsburg empire. This policy provided for recognition of formalized group identities, but without any effective group powers. In Lenin's opinion this was crypto-imperialist humbug. If the RSPD adopted it, this would finally undermine the confidence of non-Russians in the party.

To halt this slide it was essential to give the appearance of genuine concern for oppressed peoples. The virtue of Stalin was that he combined manifest qualifications to do this, with personal dispositions which made it highly unlikely that he would get carried away by his own rhetoric into actually believing in real self-determination.

When he was taken up by Lenin, Stalin already encapsulated in his personal experience both the anguished dilemmas of an ailing imperialism, and the seeds of hope for a new and constructive proletarian order. He had been born into a serf background in Georgia, and had succeeded in winning his way into a Russian seminary. There, after and in some degree no doubt as part of a process of Russification, he turned against Tsarist rule and adopted the name of Koba and persona of Georgian nationalist.

As he became more active politically he was caught up in the affairs of the wider Caucasian area. The region was bedevilled by ethnic particularisms. Stalin soon learnt to avoid those by moving beyond local nationalism in favour of proletarian internationalism. It was as the strong man of Baku, an activist who, while retaining his patriotic Georgian title, was vigorously working to unite the labouring classes of different communities, that he impressed himself on Lenin's attention as a suitable person to man the front line on the national question.

If anyone embodied the right mix of basic ingredients for making a unifying appeal to the disintegrating communities of Russia, it was Koba. He enjoyed explicit minority, and through this internationalist, legitimacy. In addition he was highly eligible for adoption as a proxy Russian nationalist. Unlike most RSPD members, he could not be dismissed as a mere philosophizing cosmopolitan. Many revolutionaries were living in exile, fascinated by the events of central Europe. Most were bourgeois in origin. Not a few – including virtually the entire Menshevik faction – were Jews. So it was not easy for the party to convince the Russian masses of their real commitment to Russian problems.

Stalin, however, for all his fierce hostility to Tsarist domination, was working assiduously and with some success inside Russia. The cause he served was not incompatible with the integrity of the old empire. Nor, for that matter need it rule out continuing seniority of Russia within it. In fact his very effectiveness in trampling over complex ethnic divisions, as only a minority individual could do without being regarded as utterly insensitive, was thoroughly in line with the traditional role given to ambitious outsiders in the old Tsarist system.

> The Czarist regime selected its leaders from all the national groups without distinction, provided that they identified themselves with the dominant ideas of the Russian Empire – autocracy, Greek orthodoxy, and Russian nationalism.
>
> (Jacob Robinson, 1944, p. 193)

If there was an inherent defect in his political make-up, which might hold him back from extending his appeal and advancement, it surely lay in this direction. As an adopting Russian, Stalin had surmounted his own ethnic sentiments. This was liable to make him insufficiently patient with the defensive communalism of others.

This was, however, a deficiency that the association with Lenin could overcome. In the first phase in their double act, Stalin was brought out as a sort of native oracle to sanctify Lenin's line inside the party. This phase can at the same time be seen as putting the final touches to the disciple's own public image, by grooming him in the essential manners of deference to petty bourgeois minority sensibilities.

During 1912 Koba was co-opted in Prague to the party Central Committee, as organizer of underground preparations for revolution inside Russia. He was then dispatched to Petersburg as editor of *Pravda*. Shortly afterwards he was invited out again by Lenin, and primed to write a treatise on the nationalities question. This appeared in 1913 and bears the unmistakeable imprint of his master's hand.

In this analysis Stalin, using that name for the first time, attacked the Austrian cultural autonomy school as a spurious and divisive sop to minorities. This was a line he might have been expected to take on the basis of his track record as a proletarian organizer. But he also makes a case for Bolshevik support for genuine independence. This is quite unlike the short statements on workers' solidarity that Koba had previously put out. It carried overtones of majoritarian repentence that cannot have flowed unprompted from Stalin's pen. This was, moreover, the only thing ever written by Stalin of such length and detail. It is hardly conceivable that Lenin did not aid the project.

Whatever its academic or journalistic merits, this construction nicely balanced the theoretical and political needs of the movement. It also sealed the mutual transfer of legitimacy between patron and client. Lenin became licensed by this publicized concurrence of his client to mobilize party support for self-determination. A letter to Gorky from Lenin in 1913, expressing his alarm at new waves of militant nationalism, and Tsarist repression of them, contained the reassuring observation that he had recruited a 'splendid Georgian' to work on the problem for them. According to Trotsky (1947, p. 154) this patronizing reference to Stalin's ethnicity was the only occasion on which Lenin ever referred to a Russian subject by his nationality. So it obviously was a significant consideration for him at that moment.

For his part, Stalin was henceforth marked out as the focal point in the party of progressive, consensual nationalism. In the October Revolution he was the obvious nominee for the crucial position of Commissar of Nationalities. Later he was co-signatory with Lenin of the Declaration of the Rights of the Peoples of Russia, that patriotic revamping of enlightenment thought that formed the charter for the Bolshevik strategy for preventing the complete breakaway of colonial territories. Stalin's participation (Payne, 1966, p. 215) served to underline the voluntary nature of the international union that the Bolsheviks sought.

The personal indebtedness of Stalin to Lenin and the Bolsheviks became more pronounced as the faction moved into active revolutionary government. Up to that point he had served as a sort of anti-imperialist figurehead, promoting the cause simply by being there. As a member of government his position changed. He was thrust into a position of direct and personal responsibility for nationality policy, to a party fighting desperately to stabilize its position. His minority status could still be manipulated to party advantage in the country at large. But inside the party it could no longer prevent him from being made the fall guy if the strategy he stood by should fail.

His first test arrived very quickly. Immediately after the October Revolution, Stalin was sent to Helsinki, where he made that historic and symbolic offer of independence which launched the Bolshevik imperial gamble. Students of the symbolism of granting independence (see chapter 8 below) will notice the spuriousness of the message to the Finns. This is made unmistakable by the use of a minority representative to communicate the offer. Stalin himself was presumably aware of it.

As early as December he was already beginning to suspect that the venture would fail. Bolshevik-backed forces were supposed to engineer a reintegrative coup. But they were meeting stiff resistance from Mensheviks, who were finally to forestall it by collaboration with occupying Germans in June 1918. Throughout the Baltic region, western intervention was helping bourgeois elements to retain the upper hand in independence movements. The whole strategy of Bolshevik support for liberal self-determination was thrown into confusion. Stalin, the reluctant advocate of the programme, was unavoidably exposed in the front line.

The wisdom of Stalin's appointment now becomes evident. For he did in fact find room for back-tracking on soft pre-revolutionary pronouncements. Indeed he was one of the first to do so. A colonial subject strongly identified throughout the empire with anti-imperialist sentiments could in fact go further in advocating fraternal intervention against bourgeois secessionism than any Russian could, without being suspected of harbouring chauvinist designs.

Moreover, as a celebrated pragmatist, none too hot on the finer points of theory, he could afford to muddle through situations that would have unsettled more refined minds. So he didn't experience any great difficulty in getting the Bolshevik policy revoked in the 1919 Congress. He simply pointed out that the Leninist doctrine was proving impossible, and opening the door to foreign adventurers. Accordingly he proposed a return to the harder, orthodox line of subordinating independence movements completely to the class struggle. If minorities did prove to have any special needs these could always, he suggested, be met through a system of federation.

So Stalin had no problem reversing his patron's line in the heat of action. But maybe that is something which had been allowed for all along in Lenin's master plan – a key element in their partnership. Hingley takes the view that Stalin was able right from the outset to take a harder line than Lenin on the right of minorities to self-determination.

> But however authentically Marxist this posture might be, it could all too easily appear as that of a Russian chauvinist. How advantageous, therefore, to have seemingly russocentric sentiments expressed by a tame 'native' from an alien corner of the Empire – himself the representative of a minority nationality, but one who had long abandoned any lingering romantic Georgian patriotism of his youth and was becoming a Russian nationalist by adoption. In 1913 a Dzhugashvili from Gori could voice views on the nationalities question which might have been suspect had they come from an Ulyanov of Simbirsk.
>
> (Hingley, 1974, p. 72)

Although Stalin could change direction comparatively easily, it was loaded with longer-term danger to his own reputation. Lenin was now obliged by the logic of events to go along with the modification of strategy put forward by his protégé. But he could do it with reluctance and dignity. Stalin, however, was pressed by the vulnerability of his position into leading the retreat from the policy of voluntary internationalism of the revolution. Thereby he was already being forced to expose the ungentlemanly and over-zealous side of his character which was eventually to earn him Lenin's famous rebuke.

THE GEORGIAN AFFAIR

The crucial test for Stalin was to come, appropriately enough, in relation to the land of his birth. The amended strategy of subordinating national liberation to proletarian revolution, and openly sending in the Red Army to help set up Bolshevik régimes, soon proved effective in halting the collapse of empire. Under the exigencies of civil disorder and foreign intrusions, intervention by the Red Army was not invariably regarded by the local people as a process of recolonization. So local support was often forthcoming.

But progress was less sure in the Caucasus region. Here the multiplicity of nationalities and political factions feeding off them made it particularly susceptible to foreign intrigue and interference. All this led towards a dilemma on which Stalin could hardly fail to impale himself. Any reluctance on his part to take a firm line in securing revolution in that area would have been seen as a condoning of reactionary behaviour among his fellow countrymen. It is also conceivable that one factor encouraging Caucasians, and Georgians in particular, to offer stronger resistance to Soviet centralism, and to remain a major stronghold of Menshevik forces, was the parallel calculation among them that they might enjoy the covert sympathy of their powerful compatriot, and get special treatment.

In truth, of course, quite the opposite applied. There was no risk of his being too soft. All the evidence points to Stalin's having long since abandoned petty nationalism, in favour of the grander sort. But more pertinently, in reality he needed to take a harder line in the area than would any non-Georgian. This was necessary to confirm his commitment in Russian eyes to the general good. His real problem was that in doing so he was bound to give the impression to more sensitive observers of overdoing it.

During 1920 and 1921 Stalin played a part in setting up and operating a Caucasian Bureau, headed by his fellow Georgian and ally Ordzhanikidze. The Bureau had the special task of speeding up the process of revolution. It had an implicit mandate to ride heavily over local feelings where these impeded the setting up of pro-Soviet régimes.

In February 1921 the Menshevik government in Georgia, the last to resist Soviet control, was removed by the Red Army. But that was not the end of the matter. In Georgia even Bolsheviks, after three years of Menshevik rule and autonomy from Moscow, found themselves reluctant to accept that a federal arrangement could provide them with adequate national independence. Only after Stalin had gone down to Georgia himself and, in conventional accounts of the episode, 'settled some old scores' with local patriots, was a régime amenable to membership of a Transcaucasian Federation confirmed in power.

Lenin seems to have been none too happy with these interventionary tactics. He was, however, content to go along with them so long as they were successful and he was not told about the sordid details. But near the end of 1922 aggrieved Georgian patriots wrote to him about their treatment at the hands of Stalin, and he was no longer able to overlook the affair. He dissociated himself at once from his protégé, branding him as guilty of Great Russian chauvinism. He had just started hinting in public that Stalin might have to go, when he died early in 1923.

It is of course impossible to tell whether Lenin's rebuke indicated a real change of heart concerning his disciple, or just marked a new phase in the public relations aspect of a double act. Hingley's rendering of Lenin's complaint makes it clear that he cannot have been greatly surprised by Stalin's behaviour.

Aided by Dzerzhinsky (who had visited Georgia on a commission of inquiry which had whitewashed Muscovite policies), the Soviet Nationalities Commissar had furthered brutal Great Russian nationalist expansion, Lenin said. No matter that neither the Pole Dzerzhinsky nor the Georgian Stalin could possibly claim to be a Russian. 'It is well known (Lenin observes, using a notorious Stalinist phrase) that russified aliens always overdo things when they try to show themselves authentic Russians by adoption.'

(Hingley, 1974, p. 144)

Whether or not Lenin was about to remove Stalin was made irrelevant by his death. Once Lenin was out of the way, Stalin was suddenly left in a very strong position to develop his Bonapartist potential to the full, and concentrate control of the revolution in his own hands.

Inside the party he was already very powerful. He had, as incumbent Party Secretary, forged strong personal ties with the Russian bureaucracy. The only person who could put him in his place was his patron, Lenin, the father of the revolution. Lenin had died without publicly disowning him. So Stalin had little difficulty outpacing fellow members of the Politburo in the race to succeed him.

Once ensconced as leader, he was able to broaden his powerbase in the country as a whole. He increasingly by-passed the party altogether in direct appeals to the masses. Russians saw him as an old-fashioned adopted patriot. But he kept his stock among non-Russians and used it to reformulate the terms of Russian supremacy, in a new fraternal Union.

The form ultimately taken by the empire he rebuilt was remarkably similar, as Trotsky had all along predicted, to the 'cultural autonomy' model linked with the name of Otto Bauer. Stalin had previously denounced this as a sham. But he was also able to get away with this further volte-face. The continuing uncertainty among non-Russians over his real intentions, plus the belief that they were anyway unlikely to get a better deal from anyone else, enabled him to symbolize their aspirations and new-found sense of dignity, even while he was trampling over their efforts to achieve independence.

A Bonaparte can do everything at once. Perhaps he has to, and only stays on top while he does. Certainly the key to Stalin's success in controlling the revolution lay in his ability to keep minorities within the fold while persuading the Russian people to invest their traditional patriotism in the Soviet system (Deutscher, 1961, p. 570).

The most important step in broadening his appeal, and which marked the transfer of his clientship from the party to the Russian people as a whole, lay in his giving priority to the Russian dimension of the struggle. When Lenin died, the programme of the party was still very much geared up to an international day of reckoning. Russia simply happened to be waking up to it earlier than everyone else. Stalin quickly sealed his compact with the Russian masses by the master-stroke – if that is how you are prepared to see it – of defining their revolution as a viable achievement in its own right, whatever might occur elsewhere.

Referring to the assassination of Rosa Luxemburg to justify withdrawal from preparation for world revolution, he fashioned a siege attitude against western penetration. This steered Russian patriots into making sure that their own renewal at least took place. It also had the useful spin-off of taking care of his main party rival Trotsky, who remained an unrepentant cosmopolitan to the end.

This nationalization of revolution was unmistakably the work of a voluntary patriot. It represents the essence of Stalin's contribution to his patron's cause. Only by serving party and nation together, could he be sure of serving either. This was a crucial role. For only when revolutionary energy was concentrated at the national level did it become politically sustainable.

Without this focusing of attention on Russian problems, and consequent tapping of Russian communal sentiments, it is doubtful whether the Bolshevik régime would have survived long enough to build a house for socialist ideals to reside in. The national modernization that this represented confirmed Moscow as a new Rome. At the same time the rehabilitation of Russian heroes over which Stalin presided laid the foundation for the revival of traditional Russian culture.

After his death, and as befits a mere pawn, Stalin was found to be more useful as a scapegoat than a figurehead. In the posthumous division of credit, it is Lenin who is honoured for the benefits that have been won. Lenin gives his name to the acceptable facets of the system. Lenin occupies the Mausoleum.

Poor old Joe, on the other hand, is dismissed as the tyrant and maniac who nearly managed to wreck the whole show. Even in this, he is still performing a service. Through the sacrifice of the reputation of their over-zealous bondsman, the Russian nation rises up again, cleansed and revitalized, and eager to play a leading role in world affairs. Meanwhile Georgians and their like, trapped still in petty squabbles, remain as dependent as ever on Russian tutelage and civilizing missions.

CHAPTER 5

JFK: MESSENGER FOR SECOND RECONSTRUCTION

Few national leaders could possess such contrasting images in the public mind today as the Georgian man of steel, and good king Kennedy. The one is depicted as an anvil on which a hopeful revolution was hammered into a new tyranny. He was feared for most of his lifetime, and dishonoured in death. The other, regardless of the many setbacks to the one major policy identified with him, is everyone's darling liberator and prophet of the new frontier. Some less adulatory biographies have appeared in recent years, such as Garry Wills' (1982). But Kennedy is still mythologized more extravagantly with the arrival of each new president who can be compared with him.

This contrast in reputations is partly a consequence of different personal qualities. Stalin could hardly have been ruder or more intolerant, nor Kennedy more charming. But more important than this is that Kennedy died before he had time to do anything beyond stirring up deep consensual expectations in the American people. He was never really subjected to a test of loyalty within the nation. So he did not have much opportunity to give any real offence to a communal interest. As a result he avoided the grosser pitfalls that await the client leader, and has become an unimpeachable mythical figure, retaining all his Bonapartist appeal even after death.

A NATION REQUIRING REDEMPTION

Kennedy's avoidance of partisan display was made possible by the less urgent nature of the national situation in which his leadership was called on. The condition of the US in 1960, when the Democratic Party successfully nominated him for the presidency, bears very little comparison with pre-revolutionary Russia. The union was not standing on the edge of collapse or imminent dismemberment. It was stronger than it had ever been. Moreover it had never enjoyed greater authority among the community of nations, which it was earnestly and confidently instructing how to become rather more like itself.

But rich and powerful as it undoubtedly was, America did have problems. Its *élite* citizens busily exercising their newly acquired world leadership were finding, as they anxiously passed around copies of *The Ugly American*, that they still hadn't quite won the evangelical battle for the hearts of mankind. There was still a short-fall on the anticipated level of respect and reverence for the virtues of the American Way.

Few thinking Americans had any doubt what the root of the problem was. It lay, as it always had, in their own failure to overcome at home the racial discrimination of which they were so critical in the rest of the world. Whenever Americans had sought to play a leading role on the world stage, racial segregation had been their Achilles heel.

Yankee victory in the Civil War had imposed liberal values and institutions formally on Dixie. But in the longer run this had not greatly changed matters. It might have been better for the North, from a diplomatic point of view, to have relinquished Union and accepted some form of duality, or even outright separation, in order to dissociate itself from the Southern stigma. If a cleaner image or conscience had been the chief aim of the northern states, the war was not a success.

A dominant community can call on a variety of methods for asserting its superiority. It was not long before Jim Crow was encroaching on the reconstructed South. Black servicemen returning from Europe with reinforced beliefs in their own dignity brought down on themselves the fury of a regrouped Ku Klux Klan. Wilsonian idealism crumbled in hubris, and America hastily retreated into moral seclusion to ponder again its own original sin, and to wait for a saviour to rescue its ethnocentric and double-dealing soul.

In the next two decades between the wars several processes helped Americans to raise their morale over the racial issue. A strong Americanization drive was mounted to bring all minorities into a more truly united nation. The Democrats vied with the Republicans to take up the negro's cause, and become the party of renewed reconstruction. Above all, and as outlined in chapter 11, foreign policy manœuvres diverted world attention to the problem of external colonialism. All these factors helped alleviate domestic tensions and anxieties over segregation.

But the optimism this generated soon dissolved at the end of the second world war. America's success in stoking up an anti-colonial movement at the expense of European powers backfired by showing up how comparatively slow and uncertain their own reforms had been. The world headquarters of the UN were set up inside the frontiers of America's own internal black dependency, which between the wars had become a northern phenomenon as well. This brought independent African leaders and American Negroes into direct physical contact. As a result the growth of black consciousness quickened, undermining the ruling Yankee definition of what did and what did not constitute colonialism.

In 1954 the Supreme Court found for Brown and against segregation in schools. This brought increased pressure for new action in the South, both from Blacks and from cosmopolitan interests tuned into world opinion. Eisenhower made a modest start with a Civil Rights Act in 1957. But the limitations of its provisions, plus the fact that even these were openly flouted, rendered it quite inadequate to all but the tamest of negro spokesmen or most amiable of foreign commentators. Something more convincing was needed. By the 1960 presidential campaign leaders in both the main parties were declaring the importance of completing the nation's liberal revolution without further prevarication.

The contribution that Kennedy made to this objective was the formation of a Democratic administration with a mandate to seek racial equality. This may seem a small achievement; less than we think we remember him for. But in the circumstances it was probably crucial.

The Democratic Party was the better vehicle for pursuing this aim at this time. Given the malpractices that prevailed in the political system, no major reform in racial matters could be contemplated without the acquiescence of southern whites. The Grand Old Party was not likely to bring this off. It was still widely regarded in the South as the instrument of Yankee imperialism. If it had stood for election on a clear civil rights platform, it most probably would have lost. Even if it had managed to win it would not have been able to carry the policy out, as this would have precipitated a massive wave of anti-colonial populism among poor Whites.

This was less true for the Democrats. They had long been attentive to the hopes and frustrations of southern whites. They realized that movement towards civil rights met least resistance when accompanied by concern to help poor Whites too, as exemplified in the New Deal. What Roosevelt also discovered, of course, was that this strategy did not necessarily allow a government to commit itself to desegregation.

He was himself held back by the southern veto, couched as usual in terms of the prior need to protect 'national unity', from pursuing outright support of the negro cause.

After Roosevelt the Democrats cooled on the civil rights issue, leaving the Republicans to make the running again. But in Kennedy, at a time when the call throughout the internationalist *élite* for some action on the matter had never been clearer, they found at last someone superbly equipped, by ambiguity of status and orientation, to overcome southern suspicions and unite the party around a progressive racial ticket. In nominating him, the cosmopolitan WASP establishment set in motion a formidable Trojan horse for launching their final moral assault on the innermost strongholds of Dixiecrat bigotry.

Kennedy had already undergone extensive grooming for the role of protagonist on behalf of an *élite* faction of the national majority. His family had been WASP clients for most of his lifetime. The relationship inevitably involved some distancing from the Irish community. Irish-Americans, like other hyphenates, are noted for the fervour with which they combine pride in their roots with patriotism at the national level.

> Among the Irish of the Boston area, for instance, there is a strong sense of community on the basis of Irish nationality as well as of Catholicism and at the same time an above-average incidence of '100 per cent Americanism', as manifested in a generally suspicious attitude towards all 'subversive elements'.
>
> (Parsons, 1942, p. 110)

But mere blending of identities is not an adequate basis for political brokerage. Loyalty to nation that is mediated by loyalty to an ethnic community is not sufficiently amenable to majority control. Before the Kennedy family could acquire majoritarian legitimacy and national prominence, it was necessary to lean rather closer to the centre, and to compromise their full Irishness by subordinating it to the higher destiny of the WASP community.

The key transaction, bringing Irish-Americans into the top political circles for the first time, was made between John's father Joseph, and F. D. Roosevelt. Joseph Kennedy split the Catholic vote by leading many Irish into support for Roosevelt's 1932 presidential candidacy, against the Catholic 'loser' Al Smith. In return for this service he was admitted to the inner political establishment, and rewarded with prestigious public offices.

The timing of this breakthrough into national respectability was a considerable asset to the young JFK. It paved the way for a relatively effortless accumulation of complementary legitimations, in which he could appear all things to all men. Nominally he remained a Catholic. He had, however, attended prominent non-Catholic schools and, through his father's contacts, become assimilated for most practical purposes to the Protestant political *élite*. At the same time, the Kennedy family's political arrival was a recent enough event for minority groups still to identify with John, both vicariously as a symbol, and rationally as a potentially sympathetic leader. His electoral success in 1960 was due in no small measure to his ability to recapture much of the ethnic vote, which had been lost to the Republicans as a result of Roosevelt's overtures to the Negroes.

PLAYING THE MINORITY CARD

In the delicate area of civil rights, Kennedy could encompass in his single person, much as the young Stalin had, a combination of experiences and aspirations, through which he could appeal to a wide spectrum of the American public. What is more he could do this without actually needing to commit himself to specific opinions or proposals, and thus without evident duplicity.

He could for example play a minority card affirmatively, to suggest implicit sympathy for all aggrieved minorities. Even though he had not taken a clear stand on civil rights, he was able to get many blacks to vote for his presidency. He did this simply by standing as someone who had encountered discrimination himself, and who could be presumed to be as antagonistic to segregation as any national leader was ever likely to be. The famous phone call to Coretta King, after the attack on Martin Luther, spoke as eloquently to blacks as the firmest pledge or purest legislative voting record. It achieved its effect without setting up explicit alliances that would hinder him elsewhere.

Similarly, by presenting his minority card obliquely to conservative southern whites, he was able to respond to the duality of their experience as a sort of 'honorary minority' themselves inside the national majority. In the South, reconstruction is widely regarded as an act of imperialism on the part of northerners. Kennedy could treat this southern interpretation with much more fellow-feeling than any Yankee could. He was able to reassure many in the South that he planned no vindictive campaign against them. He may have convinced some that he intended no campaign at all. An Irishman representing a staunchly abolitionist State, who had maintained a decidedly moderate posture during the passage of the 1957 Act, was perhaps to be judged a more reliable defender of Nordic supremacy than those cosmopolitan Democrats from orthodox WASP backgrounds who, unlike Kennedy, could only hope to win minority votes in so far as they actively pursued minority interests.

Meanwhile to such liberals themselves, together with those successful 'new' Americans currently pushing forward the frontiers of detribalization in their own lives, Kennedy could play his minority card yet another way. That is, he wielded it defensively, as a plausible excuse for not proclaiming his own plans and hopes more plainly. As they all understood in their hearts, his aims were at one with theirs. But they had to appreciate his difficulties. Any leader from a minority background was obliged to be circumspect on issues of colour and ethnicity, in order to keep his nationalist credibility. As a Catholic, he had to be especially careful not to antagonize the South. They should, therefore, have faith in him. It was, after all, only by presenting a bland and consensual vision of American society, and avoiding contentious issues, that he could be expected to lull southern whites into electing that democratic administration through which the northern desegregationists could get their hands on the state machine. Acceptance of a moderate platform was a small price to pay for all this.

Through adroit manipulation of complementary readings of his position, Kennedy capitalized on the hopes of intrinsically opposed interest groups. He swept into office on a rising tide of millennial expectations that salutory reforms could be achieved without anyone getting hurt.

This, however, is really all that he managed to do. When he entered office his stock was high. But like Stalin in the Autumn of 1917, his real tests were only just beginning. If he had seriously tried to carry through the programme of reforms his *élite* backers were hoping for, and with which providence has retrospectively credited him, it seems unlikely that he would have been able to find a way of holding the disparate elements of his support together. It was in the end probably only luck that stopped him from being drawn down the disheartening and dishonourable road of outright servility to majority mass opinion.

The most pervasive manifestation of his luck lay in that, unlike Stalin, he was not leading a desperate and beleaguered nation. He could afford to bide his time. The mere fact of his election had already boosted US prestige in the world. So for the time being at any rate, the pressure was taken off. In the longer run this would not have helped Kennedy much. The nation could now argue that by handing over power to a minority individual it had shown its willingness to withdraw from discrimination. So the burden for carrying the movement further now rested very directly with Kennedy himself.

But this responsibility could be postponed a while, and Kennedy's assassination, tragic as it was in a personal sense, must also be seen as politically felicitous. It lifted the burden from him before he could reasonably be deemed to have failed to discharge it.

There is, after all, very little evidence in Kennedy's performance following election that he would have resisted becoming captive to the traditionalist core of the Democratic Party. Of the various interests which supported his candidacy, those southern whites who did so in the belief that an Irishman would be unable to challenge them in Congress perhaps showed the best political judgment.

After taking office, Kennedy did make some response to the calls for action on civil rights. But he moved cautiously and conservatively, declaring a preference for the enlargement of executive action, to the programme of bold and decisive legislation favoured by many in the party, and which was probably needed if changes were to be made.

Draft legislation was eventually recommended to Congress after extensive rioting had taken place, and internal criticisms mounted. But this was not until Kennedy had been in office for two-and-a-half years. By this time mid-term elections had strengthened the segregationist complexion of Congress. Kennedy was himself already starting to court the South and 'national unity', with a view to securing his re-election. At the time of his assassination, passage of the bill was becoming daily less likely, and the prospects for peaceful reconstruction looked distinctly slender.

Success through martyrdom

That any reforms did materialize at all seems to have been due less to Kennedy's own toiling, than to the remarkable and fortuitous circumstances of his death. He was killed in the South. What is more it was in the course of a visit that was widely seen as a last ditch effort to exert moral influence in favour of the projected legislation. He may even have been killed in order to prevent its passage, by agencies regarding themselves as better guardians than he of the nationalist interest.

Politically naïve elements in the South are reported to have rejoiced openly at the news that he was dead.

But if that is indeed what moved his assassination, it proved highly counterproductive. This single act relieved Kennedy of responsibility for delivering civil rights – something which he had shown few signs of being able to do. It placed the buck firmly into the hands of those very people who were the only ones with the real power to see legislation enacted and fulfilled – the southern whites, who now rightly or wrongly were cast as accessories in Kennedy's martyrdom.

The death of a minority president on their own territory greatly increased the moral leverage that could be wielded against southerners. In the eyes of the world community, America's claim to liberal leadership was suddenly reduced again. The incubus of national guilt which had departed after Kennedy's election now revisited with new vigour, and fastened itself more furiously than ever on old Dixie.

Equally fortuitously, the assassination brought to the helm a man supremely qualified and motivated to steer through the legislation to which Kennedy seemed to have been martyred. L. B. Johnson was a southerner, an elder of that morally inferior and obstructive tribal segment. He was ideally equipped both to commune with its members, and to serve as a channel to the larger fraternity in its collective atonement.

He had ample incentive to take on the task. Coming from the background he did, Johnson greatly needed to follow a progressive path in order to become a national statesman. He had taken steps in that direction by supporting Eisenhower's civil rights legislation and had played a decisive part in the passage of that Act. The circumstances of his own accession now gave him the opportunity to become the national saviour for whom many in the South had waited so long.

Johnson would not have made much ground in 1960 as a full presidential candidate. His true intentions would have remained very doubtful to non-WASP voters. He had, for precisely this reason, made a good running mate for Kennedy – reinforcing the appeal to the majority. But then, when thrust by providence into the presidency, his situation changed completely. Johnson became just the man to convince his southern compatriots of the urgent need to change their ways. He was the perfect embodiment of Roosevelt's reconstruction strategy.

There were several arguments that a man like Johnson could use to deliver his community's consent to civil rights. To start with, their acceptance of reform was now essential in order to atone for their historical role in tarnishing the nation's image, and redeem their good name following Kennedy's death. Next, if they didn't allow Johnson to be the agent of reform, they could be sure that the Yankees would impose it themselves, and more roughly. Finally perhaps, if all other arguments failed, there was the simple truth. That is, desegregation did not necessarily spell an end to privilege and supremacy. Reasons would be found for all palates.

The pace of reform was immediately accelerated by the transfer of presidency. Within days Johnson pledged himself to seeing through a far-reaching civil rights bill. This he achieved six months later in 1964, after much wheeling and dealing in Congress to break the southern filibuster. He followed this by calling out the penitent vote for a further term of progressive Democratic government. Then he went on to produce the Voting Rights Act in 1965, and to set the executive context within which the crucial court decision was made in 1967 to the effect that the only school desegregation plan that was constitutional, was one that actually worked. With this redirection towards positive action on racial inequality, the American 'Great Society' was truly on target at last.

There are many, like Franklin (1974, especially chapter 25) and Brauer (1977) who argue that the main contribution to civil rights thus came from Johnson rather than Kennedy. It was Johnson who carried through legislation, activated executive processes and provided armed support for court decisions. And all this was achieved against fierce opposition from hard-line segregationists.

The Kennedy brothers were held by many in government service to be neglectful of true American interests. Because of these suspicions they were constantly facing, they would have had an even harder time in resisting segregationist forces. In the course of rebutting them, they might even have ended up as rabid patriots themselves. It was, after all, Kennedy who stepped up engagement in Vietnam.

Kennedy carried out vital preparatory work for civil rights legislation, in setting up an administration favourable to reform, and above all by his timely martyrdom. But he would not have been able to break the southern white blockade. This task required the unyielding assault of someone whose ultimate commitment to the well-being of the South was above question. When it comes to real decolonization measures, as opposed to pious declarations, a leader from inside the dominant community does hold the stronger cards.

Kennedy, however, seems to be assured of major popular credit for the task for the foreseeable future. This is chiefly because this disposition maximizes the international prestige that Americans collectively can draw from his office. Herein lies the greatest difference with Stalin. Both leaders drew some of their appeal from reflecting creditably on their respective host nations. They showed that their hosts were able to allow minority individuals personal opportunities and success. Stalin's progressive image faded, however, and with it his ability to reflect so favourably on his patrons, as the trials of revolution exposed his uncouth manners, and he slipped for the sake of political survival ever more deeply into illiberal Russophilia.

But Kennedy has been spared this fate. So he retains in death his capacity to serve as an object for national self-congratulation. Even if second reconstruction goes the way of the first, as it shows every sign of doing, and leads to a new type of servitude for blacks, there will be little incentive for Americans to find blame in this for Kennedy. Someone else can carry that one.

Kennedy is far more valuable to the nation's self-esteem if kept as a legend to cherish. Here is a homegrown hero vindicating the American Dream, who surely would have led them the rest of the way to the promised land if only he had been given a sporting chance. He seems secure in popular mythology as one minority leader who never sold out.

CHAPTER 6

DISRAELI'S TRIBUTE TO BRITISH IMPERIALISM

And it is our own fault that we have let the chief power out of the hands of our own order. It was never thought of in the time of your great-grandfather, sir. And if a commoner were for a season permitted to be a nominal Premier to do the detail, there was always a secret committee of great 1688 nobles to give him instructions.

('Lord Monmouth', in Disraeli's novel *Coningsby*)

All minority politicians have at their disposal broadly similar sets of cards to play for accumulating complementary legitimacies. But differences in the structural positions of the groups sponsoring them, and in the national circumstances in which this takes place, lead to considerable variations in the ways in which these assets are realized and deployed.

The three leaders looked at so far all came into prominence at moments of integrative crisis, and in pluralist societies where the issue of communalism was unavoidably central. Each was championed by self-consciously modernizing *élites* urging, especially in the cases of Stalin and Kennedy, the need for wholesale reform. The minority background of these leaders was thus a positive symbol for identifying with the promised new order. It gave them a definite advantage in winning speedy elevation to high office. In each case, too, the acquisition of leadership was rapidly followed by the need to come to terms with a stewardship role on behalf of the groups adopting them.

Benjamin Disraeli followed a very different road to power. The Britain in which he started out on a political career was at the apex of its international prestige. It was communally united, both by virtue of ability to deter outside powers from meddling in its domestic affairs, and through glorious pursuit of dominion overseas. Patrolling and extending empire gave Scots, Welsh, Ulstermen and sundry provincials solace and distraction from their internal subordination. Even the

Jewish community had been found a patriotic role to play in commercial and financial expansionism. Only the Irish remained marginal to the joint adventure; and as they lacked invincible foreign allies they were then a containable group.

Britain in the early middle nineteenth century was internationally very secure. The Chartist movement had Irish, and through this foreign connections: and many of the revolutionary ideas of the era had an alien ring to them. But any crises of control experienced by the political class were easily conceptualized and played out as domestic problems – as merely conflicts between *élite* and masses or rival sectors of the *élite* itself.

This absence of national crisis made Disraeli's political development very different from the other cases. He was not called on to symbolize national regeneration. In fact his principal role was to serve as a counter-revolutionary agent for an effete aristocracy. He was not thrust into power suddenly. On the contrary, he hovered on its margins for an extremely long period. And his minority status did not help him much. In fact its initial trading value was negligible.

Late in Disraeli's life, when Britain's fortunes were flagging, his minority identity acquired more salience and value for his hosts. His introduction of explicit nationalism into party politics, undertaken for party gain, helped move the nation in the more openly communalist direction its reduced circumstances called for. The fact that the helmsman was only an adopted Englishman meant that this shift in course was accomplished with minimal cost to British moral authority in the world. But in his rise to power his minority status played little positive part, and on balance was probably a disability.

SPONSORSHIP AND DEPENDENCE

Most of Disraeli's early political life was dominated by the need to find patronage. It was eventually among aristocratic landowners, who were being forced onto the defensive by the international success of the new trading *élite*, that he located sponsors appreciative of his energy and flair, and with sufficient resources to retain him. After several failures to launch himself as an independent candidate, Disraeli aligned with this laagered agrarian *élite*, and set about forging an identity that would permit him to represent them.

The ambiguity of orientation which followed from being a Jew proved helpful later in the manœuvres which restored his patrons to their accustomed role of being seen to govern. This was, however, only after a protracted apprenticeship in unambiguous dedication to the Country party. It was in service to class interests, as broker in reactionary intrigue, that his political career was grounded.

Representation of the patrician class, a decadent body struggling to hold onto supremacy, and profoundly suspicious of outsiders, required abnegation, not celebration, of minority status. Disraeli did not become acceptable as their leader overnight; but his stance was right from the outset. The baptized son of a lapsed Jewish father, he had played no part in the movement for emancipation popular among Jews of his generation, and appears never to have sought consolation in the expression of communal grievances.

There is some evidence that he was at the receiving end of anti-semitic incidents at school. But if he did find this irksome, he seems to have found adequate relief through his cultivation of an idiosyncratic personal lifestyle. His highly individualistic manner, declared above all in flamboyant dress, avoided alignment with minority consciousness, while equally rejecting direct or slavish aping of the English majority. This can of course be seen as a more subtle way of courting favour with them. For it paid an unspoken tribute to that toleration of eccentricity on which the British ruling class prided itself.

This stance was not enough by itself to afford protection from exclusion. It is the majority which has the ultimate power to define and impose minority identities. Disraeli accordingly could not avoid being seen as a Jew by non-Jews – and this as much for generous as hostile reasons. Some of his appeal to aristocratic patrons lay, inevi-tably, in the chance he offered them of giving a Jew a break – a Jew moreover who, by virtue of his elaborate attempts to escape from the minority strait-jacket, demonstrated worthiness of such support. Disraeli was nothing if not a grateful recipient of favours. As a result, paradoxically, he was to some degree trapped by his patrons into some endorsement of Jewish causes.

Some elements of this sort were almost certainly present in his relationship with Lord George Bentinck, fellow anti-Peelite and foun-der of the Protectionist faction of the Tory Party, and one of Disraeli's most important and timely sponsors. Bentinck's family, which was one of the great 1688 houses Disraeli had anticipated serving, lent him the money to become a landowner. It was this support that gave him the security and dignity of a country seat, from which he could bid for leadership of the Country party.

Bentinck's patronage generated some difficulties for Disraeli. He was not a typical member of that party himself. He probably wouldn't have helped Disraeli if he had been. The Bentinck family had defected from the Whigs in order to fight, from inside the Tory Party, Peel's accommodation with commercial interests, which they believed would be ruinous to them. Their championing of Disraeli took place mainly because they saw in him someone with the parliamentary skill, in which their class was sadly deficient, to lead this fight on their behalf.

An additional factor, however, behind their adoption of Disraeli was undoubtedly that the family retained its attachment to liberal ideals. Lord George Bentinck had been urging the admission of Jews to Parliament since 1830 (Stewart, 1971, p. 122). For him, helping a Jew was a good thing in its own right.

The issue of Jewish emancipation was forced onto Parliament again in the same year that Disraeli – who as an anglicized Jew was not debarred himself – took up his country seat in the house and was admitted to the landowning class. This was brought about by Rothschild becoming elected as Liberal member for the City of London, and then refusing to take an oath to the Church of England. Liberals moved the suspension of the oath. Bentinck voted with them, in spite of the overwhelming hostility of the Protestant party. He declared that he was doing it for the sake of his friend and colleague Disraeli, whom he evidently considered a Jew, even if Disraeli himself preferred not to.

This must have created a very delicate conflict of loyalties for Disraeli. He could not vote with the party without betraying Bentinck's sympathy, and utterly isolating him. But neither could he align with the Liberals without risking his chances of future leadership of the Tories. Bentinck could side with the Jews on purely universalistic moral grounds. But for Disraeli to do so would immediately feed suspicions that he was a closet minority communalist.

Disraeli did manage to satisfy both of the claims on his loyalty. He achieved this by meandering into the imaginary world he had lately created, perhaps for just such an occasion, in his novel *Tancred*, and arguing that Christianity was to be seen as historically and theologically completed Judaism. On this basis he determined that it was illogical for Christians to define themselves in a way that excluded Jews. To do this would be to repudiate their own spiritual ancestry.

The whimsy and apparent irrelevance of his pronouncement, a splendid piece of lateral thinking, astonished the House. But it did enable him to vote with Bentinck and the Liberals without defying the majoritarian values of the Protectionist Party. Politically it was invaluable. Bentinck, now revealed to himself as a Whig at heart, felt impelled to resign his leadership of the party in the Commons. Disraeli's own claim survived the day.

His position may even have been strengthened by this test. The personage which Disraeli had concocted for himself through this bizarre presentation was highly pertinent for minimizing subsequent problems of ascribed minority status. It was an excellent means in these circumstances of assimilating to some degree with the majority, without the abandonment of roots and self-respect. Disraeli made it clear that in his opinion Jews were not an alien community. At the same time it was none too certain whether or not he included himself as a Jew. In this way he both avoided direct association with the Jewish community, while effectively denying that those who did choose to stand up as Jews should be seen as a separate group. Furthermore, his references to the superiority of Anglicanism, as the culmination of that tradition in which Judaism formed a thread, surely humoured his hosts. The implication which Isaiah Berlin (1979, p. 256) has expounded, is that Jews, themselves an 'aristocracy among the nations', would naturally elect to adopt English culture if given the freedom to do so.

Even so, this was barely more than a procedure for survival. Disraeli did soon become undisputed leader of the Protectionist faction of the Tories in the Commons. But his own disability then became a liability for the party as a whole. Because he was regarded with suspicion by so many outside Parliament, he was constrained all the more into zealous dedication to the landed interest at the heart of the party. This narrowness of vision contributed to keeping the Tories divided, and in almost continuous opposition, for the next two decades. During the period national interests virtually coincided with commercial, and the aristocracy came more and more to appear a sectional voice.

A party leader who had not been an outsider would have been freer to act more flexibly in healing the rift with the Conservatives. Such a person would soon have carried a united party into the Peelite alliance, with the new industrial *élite*, which most Tories were coming to feel was unavoidable. Disraeli's over-dependence on landed property helped thwart and delay this process. But in the end he did accomplish a revitalizing alliance for his patrons. And when it came, this was arguably all the more comprehensive and conclusive for having been postponed, and then presided over by a minority leader with Bonapartist magic at his command. It was, moreover, by its nature and timing, to prove highly opportune for the nation as a whole.

THE BONAPARTIST MOMENT

Disraeli served a long and loyal apprenticeship to the patrician cause. He then at last realized an opportunity for broadening his appeal to the benefit of the party, and without alienating its backwoods members. In a masterly performance opening with the Second Reform Bill, he played on uncertainties about his own true allegiance and intentions to blur the lines of class solidarity, and gather wide support for the Tory legislation. This recast the Tories as the party of national unity, with a base in all social classes, and restored his patrons to their accustomed position of being seen to rule.

All this took some improvization. However, it was not an entirely opportunist move on Disraeli's part. He had long been of the opinion that the Tories stood to gain as much from Reform as the Liberals had. From the days of 'Young England' at least, before the hiving off of the Protectionist wing, he had discerned Conservative potential among the urban industrial classes, to whom it was the new liberal *élite* who were now the bosses.

But there were many obstacles to actually pulling off a constructive reform. Not least was the internal party problem that many loyal members were unable to be convinced that the masses' political inclinations could be anything other than revolutionary. Even if they accepted that some sectors of the lower classes could be recruited to their side, there was plenty of room for disagreement in defining who they were. Among the more prosperous artisans there still lay untapped pockets of support for the Liberals. It was important for the Conservatives, while avoiding the presumably Jacobin destitute orders, to make any new franchise wide enough. Otherwise they might simply play into Liberal hands.

Both parties in fact ran some risk of introducing reform that would serve their opponents better. The general atmosphere of bluff and counter-bluff which permeated debates on the franchise did little to allay anxieties of Tories in the country at large, either about the Reform Bill itself, or about Disraeli's leadership altogether.

A minority Tory government had introduced a Reform Bill in 1858 which foundered on these difficulties. Disraeli was obliged to wait nearly a decade before trying again. His chance came when an attempted Reform Bill by the Liberals in 1866 brought that government down in similar fashion. The Liberals were in a generally weakened state. Palmerston had died the previous year. Also their position as the party of the centre, assured of the unsolicited patriotic vote, was becoming undermined as foreign competition eroded the former domination of British free enterprise.

Disraeli at once put forward a similar bill of his own, hoping to capitalize on Liberal embarrassment, and convert the Tories into the broad and popular party of his vision. On this occasion he was finally able to turn the uncertainties of his identity to good effect, in winning cross-party support for his legislation.

Residual Tory scepticism about Disraeli, and the ever-present consideration of his ascribed Jewish status, now emerged as useful levers for breaking the solidarity of the Liberal Party. For, on account of these factors, many Liberals were inclined to regard Disraeli sympathetically as a spiritual confrère and fifth-columnist, patiently biding his time before showing his true colours. His presentation of a bill along the lines of their own played up cunningly to this interpretation of his aims, and succeeded in obtaining a wide measure of Liberal support for the bill.

What is more, it baited the less cautious members of the opposition into proposing amendments which went beyond their own party's original, moderate provisions, and which were to have the effect of enfranchizing those elements of the working class with whom Disraeli sensed that a Tory led, anti-bourgeois alliance was feasible.

Diehard Conservatives remained apprehensive, during all this, about the outcome of Disraeli's leap-frogging strategy. The effectiveness of the operation may even have been enhanced by Liberals seeing them to be so worried. But Disraeli had never, in over thirty years in the Commons, actually betrayed their interests. So he was able to carry enough of them with him to get the bill enacted.

The Tories were not immediately rewarded for this Act. In the country at large it appeared as the product of the Liberals' endeavours, leading as it were from opposition. At the following election it was the Liberals who benefited by being returned. Not until the 1874 government were the aristocracy to receive their reward for trusting Disraeli – in so far as they actually had done.

The extension of franchise had, however, laid the way for the development of mass party organizations. During the years that followed, Disraeli built up the patriotic themes of 'one nation', to cultivate grass roots Conservatism.

This has had tremendous consequences. It has restored the Tories to the position of governing party, from Salisbury to the present day. The Liberals meanwhile, like the Labour Party after them, became subsequently refashioned as an anti-nationalist party. They could only be confident of massive regular electoral backing on the Celtic fringes of British society.

Compact with nationalism

The importance of Disraeli in forging this new ruling alliance for the Tories relates to its nationalist dimension. Nationalism was inevitably a basic ingredient in such a broadly based coalition. But it was not appropriate to let it be too explicit. Disraeli's role lay in standing far enough outside the nation to be able to act as a catalyst in bringing its various parts together.

He did this in the first place by developing a symbolic code for cultivating the patriotism of cosmopolitans. Professional and commercial classes were wooed from Liberalism and brought into a Peelite partnership with the aristocracy by Disraeli's portrayal of the Church and Crown as bastions of Liberty against republican alienation and tyranny. Movement towards more overt nationalism was eased by declaring the British Nation to be the only true friend of Progress.

The labouring classes meanwhile became drawn in through a direct celebration of British imperialism – which more than ever appeared to be underpinning their economic prosperity and prospects. The nation as a whole, through this infusion of popular communalism, was made conscious of the organic interdependence of its parts, and geared up for the competitive nationalism which characterized the last quarter of the century in Europe.

As Rhodes Boyson (1978) has reminded us, the figure of Disraeli as an alien fixer was a valuable factor in pulling the nation together in this way. The suspicions that any one group harboured of him, became further recommendation to their class enemies to trust him. Moreover, because Disraeli was only an honorary Englishman, the groundswell of British fraternalism he stirred up could be passed off as something that was not inherently British.

During the 1870s high-minded moralists delighted in accusing Disraeli of violating British political life with alien practices. The very passion of his attachment to British interests was frequently held up as a distinctly un-British quality. The alleged incompatibility of exercising dominion over a vast empire, with venerable British traditions of fairness and freedom, was rendered explicable by discerning his hand behind it. A satirical biography appeared in 1879 called 'Imperial Ben. A Jew d'Esprit' (Koebner and Schmidt, 1964, p. 158). The morally unacceptable aspects of imperialism were blamed onto Disraeli, both directly and indirectly, for a considerable period.

Thus, even though Victoria's assumption of the title 'Empress of India' took place after her own, repeated request, which Disraeli was hardly in a position to keep denying her, it was he who was blamed for the institutional aberration.

> Disraeli knew that this rather un-English idea would be attributed to the Prime Minister's taste for Oriental tinsel. He made endless attempts to obtain a few years of patience from Her Majesty. But in vain. She was obstinate, and a Bill had to be brought forward.
>
> (Maurois, 1927, p. 244)

Alongside this, and while Disraeli bore the brunt of vilification on its account, the nationalism he unleashed was itself to some extent sanctified by the volunteer status of its high priest. By showing the world that you did not need to be fully British to give assent to the British imperial vocation, he officiated at the birth of that self-righteous jingoism and spuriously reluctant imperialism which came of age under Salisbury's administration.

Disraeli's major achievement of fathering the 'one nation' brand of progressive nationalism did, therefore, in the end involve some of that laundering of communalism for which minority leaders are prized. But this role was not too gross. Britain still possessed immense resources, and did not need to indulge in aggressive displays of ethnocentrism. Also Disraeli had himself followed a long road of class politics before arriving at this nationalist stage. So he was able to carry it off with only minor impairment to his political reputation.

During his parliamentary career his actions had been consistently supportive of majority sentiments. Disraeli needed to break no solemn trusts, slide across no floors, nor sacrifice any integrity, in becoming the spokesman for a more open nationalism when the occasion called for it. As a result, succeeding generations have tended to look back to him affectionately as an essentially honest and honourable statesman.

Progressive Tory democrats disdain popular nationalism. They can nevertheless identify themselves as his legatees, by postulating that it was his concern for matters like factory reform which was the true basis of his success in capturing working-class votes. When his speeches on imperialism refuse to go away, they can resort to the device of referring to this particular enthusiasm as 'Beaconsfieldism', to denote it as a senile aberration. This helps exonerate him, and them as his heirs, from the polluting services he performed on behalf of party and nation.

PART III:
TORMENTS IN CAPTIVITY

CHAPTER 7

THE TREADMILL OF ETHNIC HONOUR

Imposition of collective responsibility
The ambiguities of minority status create special types of opportunities for individualistic people. But for the commonalty they operate as a constraint, not infrequently a crippling one. It is this which is examined in this part of the book. As I mentioned in the preface, I first became conscious of this in relation to the allocation of responsibility for proscribed behaviour. The first chapter here will focus on this topic.

What most impressed and surprised me when I started my study of Maltese immigrants in London was the obsession many had with the idea that criminal activities by some of their compatriots had earned a vicious reputation for them all here. For a while I was not wholly convinced that the community really did labour under the bad name they supposed. In order to check that it was not just a manifestation of some groundless paranoia, I carried out a survey among non-Maltese people to find out what views they held about the Maltese.

The results of this survey were very instructive. They showed that the reputation was indeed widespread. What they also revealed was that it was tied up in prevailing public opinion with the idea that the Maltese community as a whole had some responsibility for controlling its deviant members. This indicated that Maltese feelings of being held accountable for each other were certainly no mere product of their own festering anxieties.

The idea that Maltese people did share some collective liability for each other's behaviour was extremely widespread. Only a quarter of the respondents in my survey, and rather less than a quarter of those who had Maltese friends and neighbours, held contrary views that the community could or should not be involved in restraining its members from anti-social behaviour.

This imputing of collective responsibility to the community appeared to hinge on a desire to enhance social order and control. It was linked with the belief that the wider society could increase its influence over individual Maltese offenders by mobilizing the ethnic group's internal loyalties and relationships, to carry out policing on its behalf.

There seemed to be two considerations informing this policy of indirect control. First there is what might be called the hostage principle. Most people have close personal relationships with others, whose well-being is of concern to them. They are more likely to conform to a required mode of behaviour if they know that these other individuals are in risk of punishment or implication, in addition to themselves, should they fail. Collective responsibility does not, therefore, necessarily negate individual liability. What it does is to channel it through group membership.

> ... collective responsibility can ... be a device used by persons outside a collectivity to force the group that has ultimate face-to-face control of individuals to bring pressure on some particular individual. The outsider may be some other group, an individual, or an administrative superior.
>
> (Sally Moore, 1972, p. 97)

The more widely that this liability is spread among other people, the greater the probability that someone would in fact receive punishment, and also the more of it that can be inflicted.

This leads into the second principle – the amplifier effect of joint liability. Where the fear of reprisals is spread amongst a group of people, many additional influences and sanctions are stimulated against a potential offender, warning and deterring him. Relations inside a group augment as well as transmit threats originating outside it. This increases the chance of punishment being meted out to someone. It also makes it more probable that the 'offender' himself will eventually receive a share of it. In theory, therefore, collective responsibility can enhance the value of punishment by raising its certainty of application.

A necessary assumption underlying the treatment of the Maltese as a jointly liable corporation was that they were a cohesive and close-knit group capable of exercising mutual controls. Most of the non-Maltese respondents in my study did believe this. Those who did not were very hesitant about extending collective responsibility to the community.

But this widespread confidence in their solidarity was misplaced. As I have shown elsewhere (Dench, 1975, ch. 6), the community was weak by almost any criteria, certainly at the time I carried out my own inquiry. Many of its members had come to Britain principally to escape from the more stifling aspects of Maltese society. They had better things to do than reconstruct it here. Most migrants were bachelors, and became pulled further away from their compatriots as they married local, non-Maltese girls. Maltese who arrived as families, and wanted to engage in ethnic socializing, tended to be very disappointed with life here, and to re-migrate quite quickly. So those associations which did exist among members of the settlement were very poorly supported, and there was little enthusiasm for a programme of mutual vigilance and restraint.

Because of this fundamental lack of interest in ethnic relationships, generalized reprisals from the British for 'Maltese crime' could not have their presumed effect of activating internal group sanctions to produce an indirect control of deviants. They had in fact the opposite result of weakening the group still further.

Those Maltese in a position to do so preferred to seek personal salvation by cutting themselves off from compatriots and passing as non-Maltese, rather than concerning themselves with each others' affairs. Those who could not disappear straight into the general community pretended to be Italians or Greeks instead. It was, moreover, the most successful and respectable Maltese who had the greatest incentive to escape in this way. As assumed group leaders, it was they who were most liable to be urged by English associates to do something about their anti-social fellows.

This is how the Maltese gained their reputation among liberal race relations pundits for devotion to the open society. But hence also the greater exposure of the rest of the community to hostile public scrutiny. Dissociation by established settlers deprived the community of those members who would have been most able to exert influence over its wilder element, and to mediate on their behalf with official agencies. This left the unassimilated residue even more vulnerable to the attention of police, press hounds and other instruments of majority antagonism. The net effect was to reinforce the vulgar notion that this visible and reprehensible rump *was* the ethnic group.

It soon became as evident to me as it must have been to most of my Maltese informants that the imputation to them of joint responsibility magnified the tensions and mutual avoidance between them, and weakened their communal life even further. Altogether it placed them in an impossible position. They knew that if they were to unite in response to popular expectations of mutual regulation it would mean turning their backs on the opportunities offered by the open society for full participation. But if they resisted, as most did, the commandment to control their own kind, this inevitably led the community into a vicious circle of majority victimization, increasing disorganization and visible criminality, which perpetuated and compounded the original charges against them.

Those individuals able to fend for themselves might find that they were celebrated by integrationists for their laudable progress in breaking loose. But the rest of the community would become even more brutalized and degraded. All who remained identifiable with it would live in danger of reincorporation into it through majority ascription and reprisals.

The informal application of joint liability within a formally centralized state is thus a clear mark of group subjugation. It necessarily involves a dual allocation of responsibility, under which neither group nor individual justice can be attained. Collectivized liability increases the number of people at risk of punishment for the actions of a particular individual. The total volume of punishment meted out may be far in excess of what any original offence might appear to warrant. A group will only put up with this if it is powerless to prevent it.

Working on the principle of Cui Bono I eventually realized that the ideas about indirect social control which underpinned popular treatment of the Maltese could not be taken at face value. They made most sense as a rationale for group domination.

The consequences of collectivized liability inevitably go beyond social control, if by this term is meant simply the encouragement of behavioural conformity to moral and legal rules binding on all members of a society. What it does, and does very effectively, is to undermine the individual rights of the members of groups to which it is applied. Quite apart from the existence in a society of special legislation aimed at minorities, or biased jurisdictions, or the fact that the basic rules would favour an incumbent majority anyway, the operation of collective responsibility necessarily implies an additional rule for members of minorities – that is that they should concern themselves with each other's moral and legal conformity.

Through the extension of liability for an individual's actions to other members of a group, all the people in it are made multiply accountable for the behaviour of others. They become hostages for each other. Even the most law-abiding person lives in danger of designation as a deviant by association or complicity, whether or not he has any control over those he is being grouped with.

When minority group members do try to exercise mutual control in response to imputed group liability, the main outcome is unlikely to be social control in the narrow sense of greater conformity to universal rules. This may or may not be promoted. What certainly will come about is the domination of that group – that is its collective immobilization or partial exclusion from society as a result of the burdens of extended liability. This is because it is not possible to increase the sanctions operating on deviants or potential deviants within the group without creating extra rules for the rest of the members.

These further liabilities are, however, no guarantee of improved compliance with rules. The regulating procedures within the group may be ineffective. Social control is impossible in this situation without domination. The latter may, however, easily occur without the former. All that is necessary for domination to be promoted is that members of the group should try to operate internal controls. It makes little difference whether they succeed. Indeed if there is any difference it is arguable that domination is served all the better where internal control is not effective. Continuing criminality among members of a subordinate group gives the majority a better charter for further discrimination against all of them.

SOCIAL CONTROL IN CLOSED COMMUNITIES

Collectivized liability only has such a devastating effect in the context of a formally unified social order. In these circumstances there is bound to be confusion among those it is imposed on, over whether they are or are not meant to be an integral part of the wider society.

The principle operates more fairly in an external colony, or even within a less centralized state. Where joint liability is formalized as indirect rule, groups subjected to it are allowed some immunity to discipline their members. This means that they can maintain a workable system of internal policing, and can prevent acts which invite external sanctions against them. This enables them to minimize the compounding of punishments they receive.

Under indirect rule, individual and collective responsibilities are not contradictory. For 'while liability may be collective from the point of view of persons outside a collectivity, there is nevertheless individual legal responsibility for the same act from the perspective of the persons inside the group'. (Sally Moore, 1972, p. 99)

This is the situation which obtained for 'closed' minorities before modern emancipation. The general principles entailed have been documented for medieval Jewish minorities. In feudal Europe, Jewish communities were regarded as fully accountable for the behaviour of their members: 'Christian authorities regarded "the Jews" of any country or city as a single corporate entity. Duties were allotted, taxes imposed, and crimes imputed to the Jewry as a whole.' (James Parkes, 1938, p. 259)

Since they had the authority to punish their own members, they were drawn closer together by shared experience of majority hostility, in joint endeavours to minimize it.

> There was one fact which contributed probably as much as any other toward the communal solidarity of the ghetto, and that was the fact that the civil authorities treated the ghetto as a community. The Jewish community as a whole was held responsible in very essential matters for the conduct of its members ... The communal life of the Jews was strictly regulated by ordinances or Tekanoth which covered every phase of life ... The punishment for violations ranged all the way from fine, imprisonment, corporal punishment, to excommunication and even the death penalty. These ordinances were usually passed by the community council, with the consent of the rabbi ... The rabbi exercised power over his congregation fairly unmolested by civil authorities, although in some instances his election had to be confirmed by them.
>
> (Louis Wirth, 1956, (ed.), p. 56)

The right of the community to dispense punishment was a vital element in its liturgical relation with the public authorities. It was essential to its general capacity to control its external relations, and was a closely guarded privilege.

> The Jewish community discouraged and even punished members who would avail themselves of the power of the civil courts or civil law against fellow-members of the ghetto. Informers, those who betrayed the Jewish community to outsiders, were severely punished.
>
> (Wirth, p. 58)

Underlying this fear (of the renegade) was the premise that the
non-Jewish world was waiting to pounce upon the Jewish community and that the tales spread by such renegades or informers
would furnish convenient pretexts for wholesale destruction ...
the morale of the closed community depended upon the conviction
that its members presented a united front to the outside world,
(and ordinances passed to this effect) are interesting examples
of internal police regulations concerned with maintaining the
equilibrium which had been achieved with the non-Jewish world.

(Howard Brotz, 1955, p. 190)

Many Jews were fearful of emancipation. They recognized that their
capacity for self-regulation and protection was dependent on formal
exclusion.

No such system could operate when Jews ceased to be a category
of non-citizens; when they were treated civilly and legally as
citizens there was no basis for a state-sanctioned and state-sup-
ported system of Jewish autonomy. Indeed, the internal opposition of part of European Jewry to Emancipation was grounded
in the knowledge that when Jews became full citizens they would
find it difficult to be full Jews.

(Freedman, 1957, p. 9)

Partly as a result of these misgivings, they were diligent from the outset
in grasping the nettle of informal community control. Established
moral ties were used to minimize the collective repercussions of the
actions of liberated individuals in the open society.

... in the opening up of the closed Jewry, all Jews have come to
thrust upon each other the responsibility of becoming 'representatives' in relation to the outside world. Living, as it were, in
a sort of glass-house, no one is exempt, let alone the rabbi, whom
the outside world would very naturally regard as a leader of the
community.

It is true, of course, that Jewish society as a whole is not a legal
corporate entity ... But though today the association is voluntary,
there does exist a considerable degree of corporate organization
in Anglo-Jewish institutions and likewise, as evidenced in such
conceptions as the 'good name of Jewry', a sense of corporate
autonomy.

(Howard Brotz, op. cit., pp. 172, 192)

Of course, not all modern societies are fully or equally open. It is often convenient for state agencies, not least the police, to allow internal colonies considerable autonomy. The immunities to regulate their own affairs, characteristic of medieval closed groups, do survive informally.

This may occur in places that we would hesitate to think of looking for them. Thus for a large part of US history, behind a façade of commitment to a *laissez-faire* 'melting pot' version of pluralist integration, immigrant communities were accorded far-reaching licence to order their own affairs. Law-enforcement agencies, especially when dealing with the more alien groups which did not expect immediate assimilation, tended to operate indirectly through contacts with effective community organizations.

The Chinese in America, for example, were a culturally very distinct group, with only a precarious foothold in the system. They needed to develop a strong internal political structure in order to carve out and protect an economic niche for themselves. For a long time the American police were content to control their behaviour through this community's own leadership. They turned a blind eye to crimes committed between its members. Instead of intervening themselves in disputes,

> ... many officials encouraged (the tongs) existence or refused to intervene so long as the wars were confined within the boundaries of Chinatown ... U.S. police agents often go to the leader of a local tong and indicate their displeasure at some activity which the association or its members have been known to commit. The leader, in turn, reprimands the parties involved and the affair simmers down. By the same token, the leader may precipitate or perpetuate a situation without the knowledge of the police.
>
> (Rose Lee, 1960, pp. 164–5)

Offences within the group were defined as private matters and not real crime at all. This police indulgence was consistent with social order and control. Not only did it make their own load lighter. It helped at the same time to create an image of efficiency by lowering the visibility of disorderly behaviour. The more private law, the less public crime. These privileges of *de facto* immunity were in the end shattered. This was not so much because members of minorities were pressing for acceptance in wider society, as because their continuation was not compatible with growing American pretensions to moral leadership of the western world. In the post-Wilsonian era of entry to world statesmanship, the political *élite* was moved to discover that the melting pot was not working. Instead of one nation they found there were still many. Since the 1920s the state, through instruments of national unification like the FBI, has strenuously swept away the fabric of ethnic immunities in a bid to establish a properly centralized social order. In the process they have created a society riven by an escalation of public crime. Penetration of erstwhile solidarity groups has both multiplied the visible offences occurring within them, and aggravated the occasions for inter-communal insult and incident.

THE DEGRADATION IN EMANCIPATION

So long as they are left alone to conduct their own internal regulation, minorities can conceal most of their disreputable behaviour from critical public eyes. The extent of such invisible delicts cannot be estimated, but must be considerable.

> A contrary factor operates to lower recorded crime rates artificially and this must be appraised as well by the investigator. Smith notes that 'outside the grosser crimes, the affairs of the Japanese seldom come before the public eye, because of the unofficial system of regulation within the group. The secretaries of the Japanese Associations have settled many difficulties between members of their own group and those of other races and thus have avoided unfavourable publicity. The Japanese are solicitous in counselling their children to commit no act which might tarnish the family name or disgrace their racial group in the eyes of the Americans.' The same situation has been reported by Robinson with regard to the ghettos of New York City. It appears then that where cohesive groups exist which are more or less in conflict with the dominant community group, some of the delinquency within such groups will be hidden, partly perhaps out of disagreement with the value attached to such delinquency by the dominant group, partly because of a belief in self-help and partly as a defence measure in order not to increase antagonism.
>
> (Sellin, 1938, pp. 73–4)

The enforcement of centralized, individualized social control blows this wide open. It would not matter, of course, if minorities were simultaneously relieved of informal collective liabilities. But since they are not, they become subject to a dual allocation of responsibility. This is the source of much of their social 'pathology'.

The problem is least burdensome for communities such as the Jews, or in post-war Britain most of the Asian groups. These possess the economic and cultural resources to maintain some influence over members. They may even be content to remain partially excluded, in violation of the commandment to integrate. But less coherent groups, or to put it another way those with no choice but to play by the rules that the open society decrees, and obliged to see themselves as free agents, are placed in grave peril by having their misdemeanours dragged out into public.

There are always some in the majority eager to fasten on minority crime as a reason for expelling or harassing or keeping vulnerable groups in their place. Anti-nationalist *élites* refuse to curtail the formal rights of minorities. So it is up to real patriots to show that minorities are unworthy of the privileges of full citizenship. Thus the vicious circles of degradation are set in motion. Anti-social activities among minorities are seized on indignantly by the popular press. This in turn spurs on police to catch and prosecute them more vigorously, and judges to sentence more recklessly.

My own study of Maltese crime showed very clearly that public interest in certain offences shot up almost overnight when Maltese immigrants were found to be associated with them. Similarly, bursts of adverse publicity carried surges of increased Maltese convictions in their wake. Exemplary sentencing against Maltese became quite routine for some magistrates. The formula 'owing to the nationality of the defendant' was actually entered in the court registers to make this clear. This application of exemplary sentencing itself constitutes a prime piece of 'extra-legal' joint liability, as the deterrent element of the individual's punishment is incurred solely by virtue of his membership of the ethnic category.

Great exposure to majority scrutiny is not the only danger from the opening up of minority communities. The revolution of hopeful expectations unleashed by the national *élite*'s confident promises of full economic and political opportunities creates many additional sources of disorder. When the third generation, or whatever cohort has been led to expect integration, finds its way blocked by the discriminating horde, then its own criminality is bound to rise. Ambitious members of this liberated generation are forced into seeking alternative avenues of advancement. Often enough, crime seems the best way of making amends and restoring one's self-respect at the same time.

For us crime has a lure which is more significant than most people think. It is a way of getting our own back on society; it is a way of gaining appreciation from other rejected colleagues whatever their colour; it is a way of proving to ourselves that we are worthy of self-esteem, able to do things and use our talents as well as our next partner in crime. Finally it is a way of surviving, protesting, and forging an identity for ourselves. Warped though this may be, in crime we are equal, we are respected.

(Chris Mullard, 1973, pp. 151–2)

Cheated youth cannot be held back by its elders from being lured into hustling and petty crime. For one thing, majority intervention in their community has deprived senior generations of their dignity and authority. Social workers and teachers hostile to traditional practices of parental control among these communities weaken the fabric of family life. They should not be surprised when these parents start to blame this interference for their children's delinquency and their own abdication to officers of the state. Punishment, as a function of leadership, becomes a prerogative of the national majority.

Once a community has become disrupted, members of a majority can, without great effort, persuade themselves that harsh measures against it are undertaken on that group's own behalf. As the Miami police chief said in hurt puzzlement to those who protested against his decision to use guns and police dogs against local criminals, predominantly negroes, 'Don't these people know that most of the crimes in the Negro districts are against Negroes? Don't they know that we are trying to protect Negroes as well as whites?' (Reported in *The Times*, 29 December 1967).

The politics of crime, and the crime of disorganization
A group opened up to the siren call of individual opportunity becomes opened up as well to frustration, disorganization and, worst of all, the competitive intervention of different interest groups in the majority. Those in favour of integration will be sympathetic towards minority bitterness, and will support interpretations of deviance which lay the blame at the feet of the majority itself. But the dilemmas they uncover are soon turned back by nationalist opinion onto the groups trapped by them.

Remember, for example, the Moynihan Report on negro family structure in the US. This showed how deviant domestic patterns were the consequence of discrimination. What it served to confirm in the majority mind, however, was the 'pathological' nature of negro culture. The question of blame got lost along the way. Consequently the report was itself strongly repudiated by Negroes like Lee Rainwater (1967) as 'whitey sociology'.

The fundamental problem is that an emancipated and disorganized group does not have any real control over its collective existence – but it does still get treated as a collectivity. There is a tension between subjectivity and objectivity. This is demeaning. It is also a provocation to resist commonsense, by asserting that the community is in reality organized, that its members are proper sovereign individuals after all.

This response has been quite strong in Britain since the 1981 riots. Up to this point, most blacks were suspicious of police figures on black criminality – seeing them mainly as the product of police prejudice and malpractices. The widespread rioting against the police during 1981 has created a new dimension to the situation. The rioters, together with the petty criminals whom the police had been clamping down on, have subsequently been portrayed, for example by Gilroy and associates (1982) as practitioners of a coherent culture of resistance. 'Social pathology' interpretations have been thrown out as part of white imperialism. Crime is now to be seen as part of a long-term anti-colonial struggle – a struggle which is also in the vanguard of class action against the oppressive, authoritarian state. Long live the black man as subject.

It is difficult to see what is achieved by this acceptance of responsibility for rebellious behaviour. The aim is clearly to impress the Left with blacks' ability to organize and resist. But only those who want to believe this are likely to be convinced. What the new presentation seems more likely to do is to fuel suspicions on the Right that minorities are indeed subversive. Politicization of crime is not going to bring down the walls of Babylon. It may well encourage young blacks into self-defeating and politically isolating gestures.

A majority community can impose all manner of contrasting demands on minorities. So it is no easy matter to remove the stigma of a degraded community. I have myself made the mistake of assuming that it is possible to construct an account which does this. In the end I think I merely confirmed existing attitudes.

My final analysis of the Maltese attempted to show how the activities of Maltese criminals in London were a direct product of the colonial experience, and that the British bore some moral responsibility for them. But when the study came out, the *Daily Telegraph* printed an article about it, under a lurid headline, which ignored completely this general argument. It contented itself with quoting snippets about the criminality. This report was circulated more widely than the book itself, and produced a very hostile reaction in Malta. In so far as I managed to influence public attitudes at all, it will have been to confirm derogatory stereotypes and prolong the Maltese baiting that feeds on them.

Following this experience, I would incline now to the view that any attention given to minority crime plays into majority hands. No explanation of crime is going to impress people whose basic feeling on the matter is that minorities are here on sufferance. If they don't want what we offer them – so the response will run – then let them go somewhere else. Scholarly studies exploring in detail the origins of criminal protest will not make them any less criminal in the mind of the general public. Nor will they strengthen the hand of community leaders. The lesson that minorities learn is that majority public opinion is only interested in results – and then only good results – not reasons. Never apologize; never explain. Before sympathy can be expected, docile behaviour is needed. No accounts of deviance coming from anti-nationalist sociologists will be good enough to excuse it.

Even where members of a majority do understand that minority problems may be ultimately, or even proximately, due to them, this will not lead to sympathy. These problems will be seen as the affairs of a different moral community. Maybe, as Enoch Powell said somewhere recently, putting his finger unerringly on the majority pulse, maybe blacks feel alienated, because they are alien.

Small wonder then that members of oppressed groups are sometimes visited by dreams of being able to recover their collective honour.

Dear Race Today

The newspapers are printing articles about black youths mugging old women ... Whether we like it or not, we have to agree that there is some truth in such articles ... Our black youths are obviously feeling the pressures of colour prejudice and are retaliating in the way they think most effective. I know of a more permanent way ... Briefly, it is to stop completely the muggings that are committed by our own people as quickly as possible, and to eventually stop all crime committed by anyone with a coloured skin. We are all aware of the fact that white people too commit crimes, but I am just not concerned with them. We must look after our own side of it. It is my dream to have Scotland Yard publish a report to say that 'Not one single crime was committed by a coloured person in Great Britain for the quarter ended . . .'. There would be no need to stand and argue forever in defence of coloureds over the causes and patterns of muggings or any other crimes.

Everard E D'Silva Haringey
(*Race Today*, November 1976)

ONTO THE TREADMILL

Proposition 101: A vulnerable minority can itself help to reduce hostility and conflict insofar as there is group control over individual members, by;
a) educating its members to an understanding of the dominant group's reaction to the minority's values and behaviour
b) careful study of the behaviours of its own members which are regarded as objectionable by other groups
c) minimizing conspicuous displays of traits of marked negative-symbol value . . .

(Robin Williams, 1948, p. 77)

An open minority lacks a clear membership with defined rights and duties towards one another. It can only hope to influence the behaviour of presumed members by conceiving a notion of group honour which it is then the moral obligation of all to uphold. Unfortunately not all members will have an equal incentive to respond to this call. So the burden will be very unevenly shared. Those actually implicated in dubious activities may need more than an appeal to a sense of collective honour to make them change their ways. For it is often the case that the activities in question are crucial to their livelihood – which may well consist of providing services for the majority which it is loth to perform for itself.

Those minority individuals who do have most to lose by a collective bad name, and who will therefore be most amenable to mobilization in the name of the group's honour, are those who are ambitious for conventional acceptance and advancement in national society, but who are finding that their own avenues remain blocked so long as the group harbours disreputable elements. The real and largely hidden value to a majority of an indirect 'collectivized' allocation of responsibility is that it places a burden on those respectable members of the community who are competing with them for honourable social positions as individuals in wider society.

My investigations among the Maltese showed that generalized blame and punishments had a tendency to attach disproportionately to the most active and prominent individuals. And it is these who pose the greatest potential challenge to the categorical supremacy of the majority. It is in the majority's interests that such people should be saddled with extra liabilities. These help prevent them from getting above their station. If the most able and successful members of the minority are morally tied to the least successful, participation in competitive areas of social life becomes for them something of a three-legged race. The main opportunities will continue to be enjoyed by members of the majority.

The general logic of this is well illustrated by lynch law in the control of negroes in the post-bellum southern United States, which is an extreme instance of the use of informal group liability in a system of domination. After Yankee victory, negroes became individually accountable to the authorities. But the legal system was backed up by customary procedures of de facto collective liability, implemented through lynching. This was itself formally illegal. But police were slow to apprehend people suspected of it, and courts reluctant to convict and punish them. So this was no more than a technicality. In fact the illegality of lynching may have heightened its effectiveness. It made its application more flexible and responsive to local white feelings. Also the negro community was not officially accorded any right to organize themselves in self-defence.

The rationale behind lynching was that the individualistic legal process would not keep negroes in their proper place. Therefore direct community action was needed periodically to teach them a lesson. After an alleged outrage by a negro, or whenever those in the neighbourhood were getting uppity, a gang of whites would capture and kill some negroes as an example to the rest. There was a random element in the choice of victims. This brought home to negroes that they were all at risk. It terrified them into earnest restraint of any rebellious colleagues as well as personal acquiescence. Randomized punishment also enabled the lynch mob to inflict pain far in excess of any original offence. This underlined emphatically the superiority of the whites.

In so far as there was any positive selection of victims, mobs usually chose members of the respectable sector of the negro community. This has led some commentators into supposing that lynch law must have been ineffective or even counterproductive. This may have been true if we are thinking only about observance of the letter of the law. But it rather misses the point of extra-legal collective liabilities.

Lynchings were not really performed for the criminal negro classes. These were legally actionable anyway. It was done to instruct respectable negroes in the fact that they had a duty to concern themselves with and control fellow members of their community. 'Responsible' negroes were in this sense more accountable to whites than the others. Writers with personal experience of the South have testified to the effectiveness of this device in mobilizing the negro community to police itself on behalf of the white majority.

The negro community was not permitted an official organizational structure and privileges. But it was informally allowed some purely internal autonomy, in the sense that local officers of the law were inclined to be indulgent of offences committed between group members. This partial autonomy was considerably less than that allowed immigrant communities in the US before 'centralization'. It was, however, enough to allow negroes to have some influence over each other's behaviour, thereby enabling the group to serve as a medium for passing on sanctions generated outside it.

The level of solidarity achieved was not antagonistic to the overall pattern of dominance. Negroes understood that attempts to improve their collective position *vis-à-vis* the white majority would be counted as provocation. So group leadership was confined to activity inside the community. Law-abiding negroes, who were the most susceptible to inter-group reprisals, learnt that the best sort of influence to exert was self-abasing restraint of troublemakers. The proper example to give was one of contentment with one's allotted station. Thus the main energy of the community was diverted inwards to spiritual and hedonistic activities. These were politically submissive and at the same time provided some recreational services for the whites.

Obviously a minority which is racially distinctive is readily subjected to long-term domination in this way. The possession of physical characteristics greatly facilitates the enforcement of joint liability. But even ethnic groupings which are not immediately distinguishable can be exploited over long periods, through encouraging, then playing on, the group's feelings of collective honour. Attaching a 'bad name' to a minority is a very effective general means of pulling back 'responsible' individuals on the brink of assimilation into a defensive and protective alignment with ethnic colleagues. This all helps keep that group as a whole in an underclass position.

Minorities seeking only sojourn are naturally less amenable to this – and are anyway less threat to a majority. For several generations most leading Polish Americans saw themselves as in temporary exile. Their main interest lay in the affairs of the homeland they expected to return to. Disorderly behaviour among community members was seen as harmful to local accommodation. But it was not an important matter, to spend valuable energy on.

Then during the 1960s a generation arose which was less moved by the idea of return. Instead they thought of climbing up out of Polonia to realize themselves as full Americans. As they did so they encountered a wave of majority hostility. This was articulated around a campaign of defamatory ethnic jokes, which persuaded many of this new wave to pull back together in mutual self-defence. Only now perhaps, as they respond to the allure of integration, are Polish Americans moving into a full minority situation.

The keener a group is to gain full admission to the national community, the more it risks being turned back in on itself into imposed and bitter solidarity. The first generation of post-war West Indian migrants to Britain were politically docile. Most of them postponed their hopes to the children who were born here. But from the mid-1960s onwards these youths, who have been frustrated by discrimination and grown tired of accommodation, have moved into a more confrontational stance. It is this which has provoked the majority to brutalize and degrade them by fastening criminal attributes on to them. In the early 1970s the crime of mugging was invented (or rather imported) to act as a focus for this public vilification, and provide a charter for police harassment.

The immediate reflex of the parental generation to this escalating cycle of discrimination, youthful rebellion and punitive victimization was to try to put pressure on their young to pull back from disreputable lives, and to grasp those chances for legitimate employment that were still available. The tone of a conference of community leaders in 1975 was that 'you cannot expect your parents and leaders in the community to continually defend you if you are determined to go about doing these wrongs'. (*Race Today*, March 1975, 'Elders Organise'.)

The implications of this were strongly contested by more militant leaders like John La Rose, who found latter-day Uncle Tomism in such a stand.

> Vigilant groups like 'Parents against Mugging' initiated by Court-ney Laws in Brixton, and now the 'Haringey Black People and Youth Action Committee' formed on the initiative of Len Dykes, Chairman of the West Indian Standing Conference in North London have now been launched. The statement which the latest group has been circulating speaks of the misbehaviour of the Black Youth ... By linking themselves to the repressive organs of the state they are being called upon to act as a sub-police ... to consolidate and defend their bourgeois class interests ... The concept of crime is a bourgeois concept of social guilt for action taken against bourgeois property ... The wageless black youth are struggling against capital's rule ... That is their challenge.
>
> (*Race Today*, October 1976)

Similar points have been made by Sivanandan (1981), who sees the oppressive state creating classes of collaborators to help police the internal colonies.

Out of these conflicting assessments and tendencies emerged groups such as the Black Parents Movement. These were responsive to majority opinion. But they did not operate just as police reservists. They tried to support youths charged by the police and to ensure that they received fair treatment from state authorities.

But however well such movements balance the contradictory demands made on them, several limitations are clear. First, they are still essentially engaged in the business of mediating with the community on terms defined by the majority. Also, they do it at the expense of fulfilling personal ambitions they once nurtured. Furthermore their influence is desperately fragile. At the same time as forcing com-munities back into themselves, the impulse to mutual control also pulls it apart by providing endless scope for mutual recrimination over the question of ultimate responsibilities.

All blacks can unite to some extent in blaming the majority – parents for preventing them from exercising traditional authority, children for continuing to exclude them even though they were born in Britain. But they also blame each other. The elders feel that their children have lost them the good reputations they arrived with. Youths argue back that their parents should not have accepted admission on the terms they did, leaving to them the job of rebelling against oppression. More recently the Rastas have rounded out the picture with their quietist variant of resistance, looking back to another land for salvation. Together they are all ensnared in the confusion of competing strategies, muddled identities and contentious efforts at organization and leadership that are the marks of an established minority.

Attempting to mediate with a hostile majority is a thankless task, as Banton noted in relation to earlier, and by comparison laughably trivial, problems of Black Britons.

> One of the most difficult problems of any organization such as the Coloured People's Society is that of deciding the attitude it is to adopt towards other coloured people in the locality who behave in a way which they cannot approve and who draw protests from the whites. To attempt to censure them when the society itself is not strong will be ineffective and will prevent the society from ever gaining their support, for it will be branded henceforth as something subservient to the whites ... (In spite of misgivings) they printed handbills addressed 'To all Coloured People in Stepney', saying that gambling in the streets got coloured people a bad name, and that if men must gamble they should not do so in public ... It is doubtful if the poster had any effect at all except to gain them the approval of a few local whites. ... Some of the coloured men in the locality complained about the publicity this occasioned; their argument was that a white man might be able to use this incident against a coloured man and say, 'There you are, you see that even your own people are against you,' and thus break the solidarity which all coloured peoples must maintain when faced with any criticism from whites.
>
> (Banton, 1955, pp. 231–2)

But even when a group does manage to mobilize itself, the energy it diverts into mutual policing will probably be spent to little avail. Deviant practices are often rooted in the very efforts of minorities to survive. Also the national majority, as the prime force behind public opinion, has the ultimate power both to determine which activities shall be counted as anti-social, and also to define and redefine the boundaries of the communities to be treated as co-responsible for their perpetration. So there is little a minority can do to counter the imputation of joint liability or to control the terms of its application. If respectable group members refuse to attempt to influence their fellows, they will be attacked themselves as accomplices. But if they do try to do so, this is open to interpretation as acceptance of collective guilt, so that those exerting the influence may become conflated in majoritarian minds with those who are its intended objects.

During the early part of this century, sections of the Italian population in the United States co-operated closely with American police, often at great personal risk, in opening up the 'Black Hand' networks that decades of police indulgence had allowed to become entrenched in the community. But this did not prevent the American press from using the designation 'Italian' to stand for a criminal, and treating respectable bodies like the White Hand Society – and more recently the National Italian-American League to Combat Defamation – as mere fronts for the mafia. What is more, most of the actual criminals were Sicilians, Sardinians or Calabrians, while it was mainland northern Italians, many of whom had previously urged the American authorities to deport criminals quickly, who have carried the main burden of community control, and whose own image and progress has been hampered by it.

It is largely an illusion for law-abiding members of an ethnic minority to suppose that they can enhance their position by looking to their collective honour. If mutual control is successful it may reduce pressure from the majority. But this is because it entails withdrawal from direct competition with the majority, and an acceptance of the role on which its pariah situation is based.

The honour system of informal collective responsibility operates overall in rather the same manner as the Hindu concept of ritual purity has done in the subjugation of lower castes in India. As a corporate property, ritual purity is contingent on the proper performance of appropriate social duties by all group members. So the desire of individuals to improve their personal status necessarily becomes channelled into a system of unremitting mutual vigilance. The code of duties includes submissive conduct towards higher castes. This effectively binds them all together in the caste position they already occupy.

Changes in group status can occur, but not simply as a result of internal discipline. They occur because of population movements or developments in the economic structure which then allow groups to foist their polluting activities onto others, and to adopt more honourable occupations. In the same way, the improvement in position of particular ethnic minorities in modern states usually takes place in conjunction with the arrival of fresh groups. As Puerto Ricans and

Cubans have moved into northern cities in the US, Italian-American criminals have been pulling out of vice, and moving into areas less offensive to American, and of course Italian, values.

The Irish in Britain currently enjoy much improved standing in society. This has taken place in spite of heightened political tension over Ulster. It is owed less to any internally managed 'purification' than to the postwar immigration of new minorities who have taken over their rougher tasks in the division of labour. Acceptance of the Irish and their growing incorporation in Britain to majority status has proceeded in spite of continuing high rates of criminality, and subversive political activity. Lambert (1970, p. 187) found that in Birmingham the Irish still contributed disproportionately to most types of crime. Since the arrival of new and more alien minorities, however, they were no longer stigmatized for this.

In my original analysis of their case I suggested that the Maltese might be a partial exception to this general process, in that they appeared to be on the point of escaping the dilemma through massive individual assimilation. Not only, as seems normal, was the doctrine of collective guilt failing to control them; but it might even fail to dominate them either. Escapist passing and assimilation were reaching very high levels. Unless further migration took place, even the disorganized rump of the community would soon be eroded into insignificance. Popular British indignation would be left with no visible Maltese to fasten on.

On reconsideration, I think I may have become carried away here. Except in the case of distinctive racial types, some considerable degree of individual wastage from a minority group may be a common feature of subjugation in any 'open' society. What matters for a majority husbanding its social resources is that some do remain identifiable and manipulable. Not all of the individuals who try to dissociate from the community will manage to do so. I noted myself at the time that the longest-established settlers were often those who expressed the strongest doubts about whether they would ever be able to change their identity. All the people that I was able to contact and interview as Maltese were clearly at risk, not least through my own actions, of being reminded of their communal obligations.

So it is, I feel, quite feasible that a massive urge to assimilate, like that of the Maltese, may not always herald the erosion of a group. It must sometimes merely represent an early phase in the formation of a minority. The original and optimistic migration motives of individuals are still powerful. Also, group members have not yet got around to developing collective responses to the imperatives of their shared problems. Only after you have been running on the wheel for some time do you begin to notice that you are not getting anywhere.

CHAPTER 8
ON THE RACK OF DEMOCRATIC POLITICS

The involvement of minorities in wider national affairs is taken by universalists as a positive measure of successful integration (Fitzgerald, 1984). Where this occurs through the absorption of different members of the same ethnic community to opposed factions and political parties, it may be cited as proof of a high degree of assimilation. Such dispersion may be seen as heralding the virtual disappearance of communities with distinctive problems of their own.

To argue in this way is surely to suspend the analysis just as the main action is getting under way. What it overlooks is the discreet collusion occurring between majority activists in different parties. This severely limits the capacity of minorities to use the political system to their own advantage.

Absorption to the national political structure does not necessarily represent an escape from oppression. It may mean a deeper entanglement in less obvious forms of it. Exposure of minorities to the conflicting demands of a variety of political interest groups gives a majority comprehensive domination over them, without the use of force. Political incorporation offers devices for magnifying and compounding the confusion and dependency of marginal groups.

Three aspects of this process are examined in turn in this chapter. To start with I look at the nationalist veto on what counts as a 'legitimate' political interest. This veto obliges minorities to pursue their concerns through parties which are basically responsive to majority interests. Ideas about pluralistic competition disperse minority communities between a multiplicity of alternative patrons. This makes their common disabilities less visible.

Next, I consider some ways in which this dispersion of minority clientship paves the way for collaboration between parties in failing to represent minority interests. In a democratic society, the explicit exclusion of minorities is redundant. The same end is served by securing their participation in games which absorb their aspirations and energy without offering them real rewards. The desire of minority representatives to change society gets channelled into contests between different factions of the majority. They become proxy warriors battling on behalf of their patrons. The main effect of democracy is to extend the exercise of political patronage more widely within the majority – well beyond the boundaries of the central national *élite*.

Following this I go on to look at how the operation of the democratic system allows parties to slide out of blame for their failure to promote minorities' interests. It is all put down to the machinations of rival patrons, and the gullibility of minorities themselves; never to lack of commitment by the party itself.

These processes are most evident in the advanced and much vaunted adversarial systems of liberal states. Here the mobility of sovereignty and diffusion of power between competing formations provides members of a national majority with the greatest opportunities for concealing the generalized relationship of dependency in which its minorities are kept. A multi-party system enjoys a great ability to extract and distribute the spoils of ethnic domination. This is surely an important factor underlying the popularity of the liberal version of democracy among stronger states in the international system.

The democratic game is risky in states unable to guarantee benefits for their citizens in the world system. In them political factionalism is potentially destabilizing and needs tight control. Minority consciousness can be problematic in these circumstances. A coercive apparatus is more likely to be required in order to contain discontent. But in those nations secure enough to tolerate internal dissent and regular transfers of power, the multi-party system can transform ethnic heterogeneity into an additional benefit for the majority. This eases the task of the political class in maintaining stability.

BONDS OF MULTIPLE FEALTY

In liberal political systems it is a 'good thing' for different interest groupings to compete in seeking power, and to take turns in defining the common good in their own favour. The contest ceases to be integrative, however, if such groups can be identified with a foreign power. Parties geared specifically to minorities are non-starters. The real or supposed attachment of ethnic communities to other states, or to alternative destinies that might be sponsored by other states, is easily construed as posing a direct challenge to the security and continuity of the host state. So minorities are unlikely ever to be accepted in a democratic society as legitimate political factions in their own right. The democratic prerogative to promote collective interests cannot extend to groups deemed inherently liable to upset the operation of the whole system. Minorities may not seek power or even a balance of power without raising such a threat.

National majorities cannot lose here. All national political parties pursue some conception of the 'national interest'. It is, however, the groups dominating the ballot box – which in democratic societies are almost by definition national majorities – which have the power to control political legitimacy. They will readily collude with parties in portraying their own communal concerns as inclusive, 'progressive' national missions. Parties implicitly favouring dominant groups are unlikely to be seen by electorates as unpatriotic; nor, for that matter, as 'nationalist' in the exclusive and unacceptable sense of the term.

Exactly the opposite applies for minorities. Their numerical power is less to start with. And even that can be diminished at the ballot box, through such contrivances as gerrymandering, qualified franchise (especially where minorities are mobile migrants) winner-takes-all style contests, federalist hierarchies, and multifarious devices for discouraging individuals from actually voting. So the effective influence they can exert on the definition of national interests is very limited. These are determined by majorities. Parties which question their definitions are liable to be deemed anti-national, sectarian and subversive.

This is an extremely pervasive principle. Parties which ignore it by giving more than a token voice to minority grievances do so at risk to their own credibility as a responsible government. The Liberal Party lost its broad appeal to electors and became eclipsed in British politics after Asquith succeeded in squeezing through Irish Home Rule. The strong Celtic origins and roots of the Labour movement that has taken the Liberal's place have always set limits to its efforts to project itself as a truly patriotic party. Even where a party stands on an impeccably universalist platform, the mere fact that it happens to appeal particularly to minority communities can feed nationalist suspicions that it is a fifth column serving alien purposes.

This is an inbuilt hurdle for oppositional movements in liberal society. By speaking for the oppressed, they are bound to attract a disproportionate number of supporters with 'external' ties. This does not apply in a colonized society. There socialist ideas usually hand in hand with nationalist consciousness, as part of a general and patriotic movement towards the achievement of independence. But in core societies socialist revolt frequently carries undertones of ethnic rebellion. Even the Chartists were plagued by their Irish connections. In the US, this century's main standard-bearer for freedom, the identification with minority or alien designs has prevented any socialist or communist party from ever attaining more than a minute proportion of the popular vote.

We should note in passing that this argument refers only to powerful and truly 'independent' states. It cannot be denied that democratic 'plural societies' exist like Belgium, Holland and Switzerland, in which political parties are more explicitly caught up in the representation of communal 'bloc' affairs. But these states are not great powers. They are generally buffer states, whose own integrity is a function of the balance of power between stronger neighbours. In them a rather different relationship obtains between internal heterogeneity and political stability.

Representing minority interests

As a general rule, then, the legitimacy of minority political activity varies inversely with the extent to which it pursues matters which are specific to minorities. The careers of our captive leaders showed that involvement is most acceptable, and gives greatest access to power, when it is clearly aligned with factions based in the national majority. Minority leaders who genuinely desire to represent the views of their 'own' communities are essentially in a no-win position. Their dilemma is that there is no representation without power. In order to exercise power it is necessary to join a party with a broad political base. This party is then liable to refuse to listen to minority grievances unless loyalty is shown to the wider programme that the party's general success depends on.

So the closer that minority representatives come to real power, the greater the pressures they will be under to demonstrate that they are not 'single-issue' activists. They may well be given a role within the party as spokesmen for their community. But to other members of the party they are merely one among several sectional interests that need to be courted. They will be expected to voice their communal constituents' sentiments. But they will be discouraged from giving too great a priority to them – as this would be electorally damaging to the party.

This is why the Labour Party in Britain is resisting the formal establishment of Black Sections aimed at increasing minority control over its policy-making. The Party would like to be able to get minority votes simply by proposing a broad democratic programme, which catered for their needs alongside others. Minority spokesmen who refuse to go along with this, and are not content to deliver passive votes, and who continue to insist on the pre-eminent significance of their own causes, are frankly a nuisance. Lobbies like this alienate the white vote. They therefore have to be kept in a lowly position in party hierarchies, in order to signal to the white voter the Party's true evaluation of the groups and the interests they stand for. It is ironic that as pressure mounts on the Labour Party to establish special sections of this sort, the Democrats are carrying out a purge of minority caucuses which, they feel, have damaged their credibility as a governing party.

The bind for minority spokesmen is complete. Dedication to minority concerns is liable to result in failure to gain admission to powerful central committees. This ensures their inability to do anything actually to promote these concerns. Conspicuous non-delivery of goods may then quickly use up their credit among their compatriots. This in turn encourages party colleagues to walk over them. The minority representative who loyally refuses to subsume his community's interests to a broader programme soon develops into that very figure – the tame and impotent intermediary, scorned as Quisling or Uncle Tom on all sides, with little constituency or audience left and only a precarious political life ahead of him – which he has striven from the beginning to avoid. This rule of inverse efficacy of representation has two major and interrelated implications. First, it means that the specific needs of minorities can often be expressed more coherently outside the main party system, by being channelled into de-politicized 'buffer' institutions. These reproduce a colonial style of administration and consultation which can protect minorities from direct confrontation with the ethnocentric masses in the political arena. The history of institutions in Britain such as the CRC and the CRE show that while not everyone in minority communities has great faith in the ability of the organizations to promote their causes, at least these causes do get an ear and a legitimate airing, which they might not otherwise receive.

The second and broader consequence is that any possible redress for minority grievances is generally carried out more effectively by persons from unimpeachable majoritarian backgrounds. One of the recurring complaints levelled at bodies like the old CARD, and NAACP in the US, and now the CRE, is that leading roles are too often occupied by paternalistic members of the dominating group. This indicates a welfare colonialism which is held to be both demeaning and self-contradictory. But some degree of paternalistic sponsorship does seem unavoidable. This does not just apply at pressure group and 'buffering' levels outside the electoral arena. It is even more true in open party struggles. The less impugnable a person's fundamental loyalty to the existing nation, the greater his chances of mobilizing universalist and patriotic arguments on behalf of marginal communities. A captive leader is the best person to convince a minority that it is expedient to cool their pressure for special treatment. Equally, majority leaders can more readily persuade the nationalist masses that minority communalism is a legitimate defence to erect, and that it will be surmountable only if the majority itself makes some concessions.

Sponsors for minority rights from within the majority have several advantages. They can convey more successfully the impression that reforms proposed are merely consolidations of, or protection for, purely individual freedoms, and do not amount to a novel set of corporate privileges giving particular groups any unfair advantage. In conveying this impression, they are helped by being in a position to admit that minorities have in the past been denied their legitimate rights, without this sounding like mere sectarian pique. By doing this they become morally fortified to lead their followers in a display of collective atonement for shared historical guilt, and in public readings of the consensualist litany that discrimination damages a majority as much as the communities subjected to it.

At the same time they may soften up their own hard line communalists. This is done by admitting privately that it should be possible to get away with a little window-dressing, or that it reflects more credit on the majority if initiatives for restitution appear to come from them.

Not all bids by penitent majoritarians are successful. Gandhi was assassinated by a Hindu fundamentalist while campaigning for toleration of the Muslim minority. His cause fell with him. Where there is no clear benefit to be gained from rolling back past injustices, then not even the most revered patriot can bring a majority to do it.

But where a nation is under severe pressure to mend its ways, then a leader with majority appeal does have greater resources for pulling it off, and for doing so with minimal disruption. This is symbolized in etiquettes of external decolonization. Attlee's Labour cabinet, short on nationalist credibility, eased its delivery of Indian independence by calling up Mountbatten to be Viceroy. De Gaulle staged a withdrawal from Algeria which Mendès-France, as an open anti-colonialist and a Jew to boot, could not engineer. And it was the Tory grandee Macmillan who sensed the post-Suez Wind of Change blowing through Africa, and declared anti-imperialism an irresistable force, to be recognized as legitimate and yielded to with dignity.

Future generations may recast Macmillan as a Yankee agent, on account of his distaff American connection and transatlantic sympathies. The Tory Party generally is potentially liable to be seen as the party of collaboration with American imperialism. However, at the time that Macmillan was operating, most British people saw the country as sharing world leadership, rather than as subject to America's. He did, therefore, enjoy the nationalist legitimacy needed to insist that there was no place for a British Empire in the modern world.

In contrast to these instances of genuine decolonization, Stalin's mission to Finland with a promise of independence was manifestly spurious from the outset. It was not carried out by an authentic Russian taking the hearts of the Russian masses with him.

Decolonization of an external empire is clear-cut and final. Securing redress for a dispersed internal minority is less complete. It keeps the minority within the same political system as the majority, while offering preferential rights that can produce greater substantive equality within the boundaries of the existing nation. The process is, however, still best carried through under a majority leader. As we saw earlier, one of the most remarkable programmes of 'redistributive' justice undertaken along these lines was Johnson's launching of the Great Society after the death of Kennedy. It was certainly no accident that it fell to a redeemed white southerner to press bold legislative measures on behalf of blacks through a Congress which hitherto had proved a democratic obstacle to such bids. All of the major legislation on behalf of minorities in the US this century was passed under Johnson, and he had to play his majority cards most insistently to achieve all this.

Now that dust has started to settle on this achievement, it is easier to discern the other side of the coin. This is that the superiority implied in majoritarian sponsorship may be more enduring than the benefits it conjures up on a client's behalf. As McAdam (1983) has recently shown, along lines sketched out by Piven and Cloward (1979), reforms on behalf of the weak may bring only very temporary respite. Unless a dependency relationship is properly broken, gains made are whittled away as sponsorship wanes or is transferred to another client. The commitment of a patron to a particular client can only be limited. Agreement on the priority of that client's needs will only be transient. Preferential rights, unlike a grant of independence to an external colony, are not for ever.

In retrospect, the lesson of Johnson's Great Society is not encouraging. It seems to be that by championing the demands rising up from suffering communities, politicians can absorb their energies and aspirations to majority-led parties. Activities which might otherwise develop in anti-nationalist directions are harnessed for domestic uses, and channelled into party contests. The consequences of Johnson's legislation are explored further in the following section.

The co-option of minority interests to national party platforms, and consequent spreading of minorities between competing groups is not the index of positive assimilation that pluralist theory would have it. It is further evidence of the successful deployment of minorities as pawns in games which they cannot engage in as principals. These games help to keep them in their secondary position in the nation.

PULLED BETWEEN RIVAL PATRONS

In their quest for a legitimate channel of representation, minorities become recruited to majority-dominated parties. This steering into mainstream national politics has the effect of spreading minority involvement across a number of parties. The result of this dispersion is to absolve each of these parties from needing to listen carefully to minority voices. It allows them to collaborate with each other in keeping minority interests marginal in all of them.

There are two types of operation here. First, all major parties produce their own minority spokesmen, who can perform like gladiators in the political arena on behalf of their patrons. Their main role will be to oppose zealously any programmes for helping minorities that are put forward by rival parties. As these attacks come from people identified with oppressed communities, they do not cast any reflection on the commitment of their parties to progressive causes.

This is a benefit that all parties share in indirectly. For since all policies that are produced are liable to this sort of attack, no policy can be seen to enjoy total support among minority groups. Consequently the majority as a whole is excused for not wholeheartedly implementing any particular programme.

The second aspect of this concerns the relation between a party and minority communities as a whole. Dispersion of minority attachments means that the same communities contain clients, simultaneously, of several parties. Majority patrons in any party can use this as an excuse for holding back from total commitment to their own protégés. If minority activists in other parties believe that another policy is needed, then maybe it is worth considering. Conversely, if spokesmen already inside the party do not like the proposals for reform that are being prepared, it will not be too difficult to recruit some new ones who do. There is no need to be bullied; no reason to let the tail wag the dog.

The aftermath of the Civil Rights legislation in the US in the 1960s is instructive here. It shows the homeostatic quality of the party system. Support among some minorities for reforms put forward by one party can be balanced out against minority opposition from other quarters. The overlapping lines of clientship created by parties competing, or appearing to compete, for the ethnic vote give each party leverage for extracting even greater displays of loyalty from would-be representatives.

The Democratic Party which committed itself in the 1960 campaign to Civil Rights already enjoyed a large share of the white minority vote. In adopting this new commitment it was pursuing two aims. On one hand it was vying with the Republicans to be the party to improve the nation's image abroad. On the other it was bidding for a larger portion of the black vote.

The key 1964 Act did not spell out in detail how it was proposed to roll back generations of discrimination. But as executive orders appeared under it, over the next few years, it became clear that the democratic administration was focusing its concern sharply on the most underprivileged groups. Certain communities – blacks, orientals, American Indians and Spanish Americans – were identified as having the most fundamental need for enhanced opportunities. It was, accordingly, these groups and only these, who had target quotas set for them.

The effect of this unfolding programme of compensatory rights for scheduled communities was divisive. Critics of the idea of affirmative action had all along pointed out that it would operate to create new grievances. This now came about. Among those who were now placed at a competitive disadvantage by the new policy, anxiety and resentment were provoked (Roucek and Eisenberg, 1982).

Significantly, this did not occur so much among poor whites. These were still numbed and immobilized by collective guilt. Where it mainly took place was among the middle-placed ethnic groups in the American national hierarchy – that is, the groups whose vote the Democrats took for granted.

During the formative years of the civil rights movement, idealistic members of relatively well placed minorities had found themselves playing an intermediary role between the WASP *élite* and the truly dispossessed. These groups felt secure in their own rising station. Remembering the problems faced by their forebears, they put themselves forward as allies for those most in need of support. This was perhaps partly undertaken in the hope of minor benefits for themselves, such as removal of remaining barriers holding them back from acquiring full *élite* status. But the principal motive, befitting aspirants to a leading position in the nation, was undoubtedly to offer advice and help to the real underdogs.

The successive affirmative action orders implemented by Johnson soon undermined this category of civil righters. Granting of preferential rights and accelerated social mobility to only the most deprived communities did nothing to help the less well off members of groups just above them in the pecking order. These had an unfair fight on two fronts. Groups below them were now officially cosseted. The incumbent majority above them, however, retained their traditional advantage, as limitation of special provisions to the lowest groups meant that competition for *élite* positions could still be rigged by the WASPs against unwelcome outsiders.

Affirmative action soon galvanized members of these intermediate groups – Italians, Irish, Jews and so on – into new lobbies. These were resentful of the limited reference of government action, and hoped to use the participation of some of their number in the Civil Rights movement as a lever to extend its benefits to their own groups. The late 1960s witnessed the spawning of a plethora of minority pressure groups. All set about rediscovering their ethnic identities and problems in competitive bids for inclusion in the excursion to substantive equality.

However, the lines failed to be redrawn. Also, the realization gradually spread that nearly everyone could define himself as subject to some collective disability. If each was given special help, they would all be back where they started. So the spate of me-tooism yielded to a harder mood. Groups excluded from its benefits re-examined the idea of positive discrimination itself. They soon found it to be un-American.

The swinging pendulum

The result of all this was to send several minority communities looking for new patrons, bringing party politics back into prominence. The concentration of Democratic attention on the problems of blacks and other underdogs caused them to lose many of their traditional voters in the middle of the American ethnic hierarchy. White minorities were goaded into becoming champions of the Republican cause.

White ethnic identities had been reawakened in the early 1960s by semi-altruistic participation in civil rights. They had then been teased into urgent mobilization by the programme of positive discrimination. Finally they matured during the 1970s into reassertive celebrations of the American Dream. Polish, Irish, Italian and above all Jewish Americans rediscovered their own histories of settlement. And they saw them as success stories revolving around and confirming the original American values of freedom and enterprise. Ethnic legends were rewritten to show how their struggles to break into American society had not only made them. They had made America too.

Figures like Moynihan and Glazer had helped to pave the way for Civil Rights by their analyses of continuing obstacles to integration. Now they sidled over to the Right to attack statist sponsorship as unconstitutional and bad for everyone. They declared that non-meritocratic appointments could only lower the calibre of personnel. Incentives would be reduced, and national efficiency drained. Such appointments would also, as 'tokenist' measures, devalue the efforts of all members of groups eligible for them, undermining their self-respect. No one would be able to feel, and to convince others, that he really deserved and could handle his job. In the longer run the soft road of positive discrimination would enfeeble the challenge of listed communities. It would be held against them, as it had been after the first Reconstruction, as evidence of their innate inability. Only a return to personal endeavour and enterprise could save the nation.

These were good years for the Republicans. Nixon was able to draw on the growing resentment of 'white ethnics' in his 1972 campaign. This saw a desertion from the Democrats of many traditional supporters of that party. Bussing and preferential educational and work opportunities for negroes removed Irish and Jewish support for civil rights. It split the movement down the middle, leaving negroes directly dependent on WASP patronage of the likes of Mayor Lindsay.

The New Right which emerged during Nixon's Presidency, as mouthpiece of the silent majority, was in large part a movement of middle ethnics caught out by affirmative action. Many of Nixon's henchmen were super-patriotic middle Europeans. These proceeded to attack civil rights as an élitist conspiracy designed to maintain support for a WASP establishment. They dedicated themselves to replacing the Democratic world with one in which minority enterprise could flourish, and genuine talent would be rewarded. Under their inspiration, the Office of Minority Business Enterprise was set up to show blacks that there was a surer way to find salvation.

A high tide of reaction and middle-American fundamentalism was reached with the Bakke case. It was this which finally confirmed the anti-statist view that positive discrimination threatened the constitutional rights of the individual. Bakke was a white student refused admission to medical school. After finding that black applicants with inferior qualifications had been allowed in through benign quotas operating in their favour, he sought legal redress for encroachment on his individual rights. He submitted that affirmative action guidelines discriminated unfairly against individuals in non-listed communities. This was echoed sympathetically across middle America, at a time when conflict between blacks and other minority communities was greater than it had been for decades.

A Supreme Court ruling in 1978 upheld his position. The Civil Rights Act itself was not declared unconstitutional. Nevertheless the ruling undermined what little confidence there was left in the Great Society. Blacks felt that once again they were being asked to see their goals as conflicting with national integrity and values. Any procedure for giving certain minorities preferential rights as groups was bound to be at the expense of individuals in other communities. Many blacks felt this should be openly recognized and accepted. But it was not.

The swing that had taken place in the party pendulum had done no harm to the WASP majority. It wiped out gains that negroes thought that they were making under the affirmative action programme. Mobilization of the black community pulled most of those who thought that they had made it back into membership of an excluded and underprivileged group once more (Van den Berghe, 1975, p. 275). After a promising start in its own terms, and fulfilment of all cosmetic requirements, the schedule for positive discrimination faltered before it had made any noticeable inroads into traditional WASP supremacy.

New gladiators in the arena

Several critics of affirmative action had predicted that it would let blacks down. What few had foreseen was that the dirty work of blocking negro advances would be performed on behalf of WASPs by minorities occupying intermediate stations. White ethnic groups have thereby increased their own visibility, and now take the blame for the backlash.

Having used their rediscovered ethnicity to revive the American Dream of their patrons, many are now finding this identity a burden again, that would have been better left forgotten. It is no longer any help in cementing an older brother bond with negroes. That relation appears to be irretrievable for the moment. And it is certainly a barrier to full membership of the national *élite*.

Hyphenates have been extraordinarily prominent in the New Right. Jews dominate journals like Commentary, Midstream, Public Interest, and the New Republic. Intellectually they are leaders. But their essential role is still that of eager client – exemplified in Norman Podhoretz's protestations that what is good for the US is good for Jewry and Israel. But for a minority community, with its own unique constellation of ties, consensualist patriotism is a hard road. Bitter debates rage all the time among American Jews over the need to protect special interests. Henry Kissinger is still fiercely condemned for his alleged betrayal of Israel to American designs. And the reactionary policies of Begin have complicated the matter further (Hertzberg, 1982).

Moreover, and as a result of their leadership in reaction, these intermediate groups have had their own challenge to the majority pushed back. They are prime victims of the very fundamentalism they were instrumental in unleashing. In the early 1970s they took a stance as super-patriotic red-necks. By doing so they set themselves up as targets – not just for the liberals and the Left, but also in turn for the more discreet but still highly effective WASP nationalism for which many like Schrag (1972) had written premature obituaries.

The nimbleness of hyphenates in changing horses when it suited them could be held to display an underlying opportunism that was distinctly un-American. Shifting so fast from the Democratic to Republican camps somehow highlighted their continuing true marginality. The rapid sequence of transformation, from quiet assimilation, through strident self-interested collectivism, back round to a transparently partisan endorsement of bedrock constitutionalism, could not help but compound majority suspicions about the superficial and tactical nature of any ideological posturing by client groups. It has thereby weakened their collective claims to a more responsible standing in the national body.

This identification of the middle ethnics as the chief reactionary component in the nation has assisted the revival of a purged WASP majority as the natural guardian of American morality. Renewed hostility between blacks and other minorities has confirmed WASPs as the only group able to hold the show together. The New Right reasserted the sanctity of individual rights, the priority of national unity, and a formal rather than substantive notion of equality. All of this now reads as a restatement of the central position of the descendants of the Founding Fathers. After a decade or more occupied in denouncing WASP domination, American society has reunited around them again.

It has perhaps done so even more strongly than before. The exposure of prejudices within minorities has assisted in the moral elevation of the long maligned poor white. We now see the phenomenon of a progressive WASP identity throughout the whole union. This was epitomized by the election of Carter. In the Nixon years ethnic lobbies revealed their narrow hearts, and middle-European fixers helped to bring the political system into disrepute. In reaction to this the nation, including black voters, turned to a re-born southern white for president. This decisively endorsed the WASP majority as the repository of the nation's conscience and abiding virtues.

Here is the basis for the remarkable surge of WASP self-confidence that has taken place under Reagan. Protestant individualism is rife. Everyone knows his place again. Blacks aspire to be minstrels and sprinters. Catholics and Jews learn to be grateful for toleration of their rites. The Democratic Party once more speaks for the down trodden hyphenates. The cycle is complete. Homeostasis is manifest.

TAKING THE STRAIN

Such a degree of stability in ethnic stratification could well become politically embarrassing. The failure of majority patrons to secure lasting benefits for client groups in the political arena cannot be concealed or denied. It can, however, always be blamed back onto the democratic system itself. The dynamics of transfer of power are critical here. They leave a majority free to renege on promises at almost any time, leaving minorities to take the strain.

Nothing is more reliable in a smooth running democracy than the periodic shift of power between competing groups. With the need for regular and frequent re-mandating of the executive by the people, no policies can be regarded as sacred. On the contrary, they can be rescinded as the result of a mere handful of voters actually changing their minds.

This mobility of sovereignty and the inevitability of flux gives patrons a great deal of room in which to escape from commitments. The frailty of office, the constant need to outmanœuvre opponents, and the inability of minority clients to commit themselves whole-heartedly to the fortunes of a particular party, all provide abundant justifications for abdication from inconvenient undertakings, and redrafting of promises for the future.

Knowledge of the possible or impending transfer of power offers an evergreen charter for postponing action to riper times, or for legit-imately refusing to make any firm promises. A patron is no use out of power. So the general task of acquiring or keeping office must always outweigh considerations of specific policies. Everyone knows, when talking privately in committee rooms, that there is a great sea of ethnocentrism lying not far below the fog of public debate. To attempt too much for minorities too quickly is a sure way of losing the popular support on which the power to do anything at all is based. Extreme caution is always to be recommended. No patron can help a client who demands too much.

It may even be expedient from time to time to make a tactical display of hostility to minorities. Your clients must of course not take this as a true measure of intent, but recognize it for what it is – an ability to cope with the political realities, by giving the masses a little evidence of majoritarian machismo.

A tightening of immigration controls is usually sold in this way to minorities in Britain, as a precondition for good community relations – that is, majority tolerance. Readers of the Crossman diaries are familiar with the argument that it may be necessary to do some unpleasant things in order to prevent opponents from doing worse. Rival parties are prepared to go much further in plumbing the depths of populist sentiment in their quest for votes. A small tactical retreat is preferable to a major defeat. Both Labour and Conservative governments in post-war Britain have used the threat of growing support for movements like the National Front, as justifications for adopting harsh measures themselves.

When several parties try to shunt blame for treacherous policies onto each other the underlying collusion may show through a bit. Each of the major pieces of legislation introducing controls on immigration to Britain – the 1905 Aliens Act and 1962 Commonwealth Immigrants Act – has been brought into being with some misgivings and against strong, principled opposition. But soon after passage each has been administered by a different party which had fiercely resisted it as a bill. All of the parties involved have subsequently been able to offer a range of explanations for their conduct, depending on whom they were trying to impress.

Thus parties initiating restrictive legislation have argued to the masses that they were the ones with the courage to do what was needed. To minorities and international critics they have claimed that it would have been done anyway. Those inheriting the laws have sought nationalist accountability with the argument that they did accept the legislation – and that it was always their intention to do so. They have mollified the universalists with the plea, justifiable for Liberals after 1906, that they were able to make some relaxations in the execution of the law when they took over office.

On both occasions, it was the party system itself which enabled patronage to survive a decidedly awkward test. It did this not just by diverting the blame for action taken when in office, but also by making it feasible to take an idealistic line while in opposition. The frailty of tenure in the democratic circus means that a party can automatically unload onto its opponents a good deal of moral responsibility for what it does. Awareness that policies are easily defeated, or can readily be changed, amended or subverted at a later date even if they are passed, makes it much easier to pose as a genuine patron in the first place.

Ian MacLeod impressed many Africans as colonial secretary at the Kenya constitutional conference. One line that went down well was his frank confession about the difficulty of getting his harder line colleagues to yield on certain points. He was, as a result, able to protect the image of Britain as a caring power, without actually giving much away in the independence settlement: a very polished double act. When it comes to patronage inside a state, where few concessions are likely to survive long anyway, it is even safer to make speculative proclamations. Oppressed groups can be forgiven for finding some hope in them. There is always just a chance that promises are genuine. There is always a market for new beginnings.

Democracy enjoys a great advantage here compared with monarchy. A consequence of the extension of sovereignty to the people, is that the sovereign no longer speaks with one voice. It can, therefore, fail to honour pledges made by one set of its representatives without seeming to be dishonest as a whole. Monarchs have difficulty in breaking agreements (Carr, 1968, pp. 29–30). But democracies can keep their commitments ambiguous. Public opinion is neither homogenous nor consistent. So a party – especially a populist party of the sort advocated by full-blooded democrats like Tony Benn – can pursue contradictory objectives simultaneously with a reasonably clear conscience.

Parties can avoid making absolute pledges themselves. They can, however, demand absolute loyalty from their minority members. More double standards apply here. Thus a major political party would not in practice want all minorities, or all members of particular minority groups, to support them. It would endanger the party's own nationalist credibility. This is not a consideration that needs to be – or even could be – aired publicly. Because of this, a party is not prevented from pretending to seek total support of this kind. This is a valuable tactic. For it enables them to hold the fact that they haven't got unqualified minority support against those minority individuals who are actually in their camp. Groups that can't commit themselves wholeheartedly to a single patron – so the argument runs – are obviously too confused, volatile or unreliable to be worth struggling too hard on behalf of.

Thus majority patrons first of all use the party system to divide ethnic communities. Then they collude in exploiting this dispersion to put a squeeze on the loyalty of their own clients. Using their majoritarian prerogative to define minority individuals unilaterally as members of 'groups', they can issue abdicatory ultimata to them. Any alliance with their rivals by any group members will be taken as a betrayal of their trust. The Democrats, for example, insisted in their 1948 campaign that unless enough blacks voted for them, then they would drop their pledge to fight for Civil Rights.

The reasoning behind this is brutally simple. Either minority groups do have strong common interests and should stick together in seeking out the most appropriate patronage. Or group members have mainly divergent interests, in which case those in one's own party should drop their tiresome demands for special treatment and knuckle under as loyal party hacks. If they can't agree internally what their priorities are, then maybe they don't really have any common interests that need pursuing.

The alternative to party loyalty is political impotence. So most minority politicians are forced to moderate their stance. This is the sort of pressure which tamed the post-reconstruction generation of leaders into good party men, and steered Roosevelt's Black Cabineteers into opposing the creation of a special Negro Bureau. Client groups are rarely able to achieve unanimity on anything under the circumstances. Parties therefore have *carte blanche* for ignoring their own minority spokesmen. Who do they speak for anyway? If Mr Balfour had given ear to Edwin Montagu, let alone Israel Zangwill, what would be the status of Palestine today?

Knowledge of how loyalty is extracted from minority clients is also useful in dislodging or discrediting those in rival parties. These are taunted as stooges and ballot-fodder. They are told that they would not be subject to such disgraceful pressures in the tormentor's own outfit.

Sometimes a minority spokesman is persuaded to cross the floor. Ambrozine Neil helped to bring down the Labour council in Brent recently by responding to Conservative suggestions that Labour was taking the black vote for granted. The move certainly shook Labour complacency. The development of Black Sections there is now far in advance of most constituencies. But the black caucus is operating in a situation of reduced trust. The Labour Party can now resist their demands by accusing them of merely trying to use the party, and of not really being socialists at all.

Sometimes the taunting of rival clients backfires, and fails to give the impression that they would indeed fare better elsewhere. It is especially liable to this when the taunter is himself a captive. This was the case a few years ago when Keith Joseph was drafted in to canvass in the Newham by-election. His mission was to attack the Labour Party's assumption of an automatic right to the Jewish vote. Unfortunately the fulsome praise for his efforts which appeared in the *Daily Telegraph* and elsewhere inadvertently made poor Sir Keith appear something of an Uncle Tom himself in the Tory ranks.

Not that this mattered much to his Tory patrons. He probably won them some votes. And it all helps to maintain divisions and mobility in minority support, while reinforcing the notion of collective identity and solidarity of the groups in question. In the ensuing eagerness to demonstrate resistance to cross-party courting, minority gladiators are goaded into even more zealous proxy battling on behalf of their masters.

The outcome of this competition to provide patronage and acquire clients is a bewildering tangle of claims and counter-claims on loyalty, set in a constantly changing scenery of policy initiatives. Changes proposed are usually justifiable, in that existing provisions are not adequate. But it is doubtful how far they are actually expected to work. MacDonald has observed (1977) that they exist largely as bids for minority votes. Through counter-bidding, parties can end up passing clients between themselves rather than actually finding solutions. No solutions need even be put forward, only a kaleidoscope of partial solutions. Frequent changes of direction and emphasis are useful in concealing the lack of genuine commitment to minority causes.

In the end what is achieved is continued dependence. The iron law of residues applies. If we take away the ephemeral content of concrete proposals, the historical dross, what we are left with is enduring relationships of patronage and clientship. In this the role of minority groups is to furnish yes-men and cheerleaders for whoever can use them.

Dislocation and immobilization

The durability of this relationship is currently obscured rather than illuminated by use of the concept of internal colonialism. In an age that has seen massive decolonization on the world scene, this concept tends to imply that domesticated minorities have similar prospects for liberation. This is not the case. Internal minorities have limited chances to unite and mobilize. They are far more mixed in with a majority population, and are usually greatly outnumbered.

Participation in the dominant community's political system sets the seal on this weakness. Complex involvement in the domestic struggles between different sectors of the dominant community make it virtually impossible to organize in working out a coherent strategy of their own. As long as some gains seem to be achievable through the national party system, then the appeal of purely inward-looking or separatist movements is bound to remain limited. Yet while such gains remain incomplete, then the desire for greater independence will not lie down either. The community hangs awkwardly between alternative aims and consciousness.

In the day-to-day struggle for survival and progress, however, and in the context of changes in public opinion, governmental policies, legal and judicial precedents, it becomes increasingly difficult to maintain a social movement dedicated to one goal alone or to live one's life totally according to one ideal or the other. The difficulty with the integrationist mode is that, as racism beats him back, the black man is drawn toward separatism as an alternative mode of adaptation and action. With separatism, as blacks gain more opportunity, solidarity declines. The two themes – integration and separatism – are therefore in constant interaction, each vying at different times or stages of history for the all-consuming interest of black people.

(Blair, 1977, p. 27)

A group that is united stands some chance of minimizing the offence it gives a majority; but one deeply divided on itself faces trouble in all directions. Every strategy drawn up by a faction or sub-faction is liable to dismay some portion of the patron community. Division into factions strengthens a majority which controls them all. But it is weakness for their clients. Since emancipation Jews have been open to attack variously as revolutionaries, finance capitalists, anti-patriots and free-thinkers – to mention but a few. Each time reprisals are exacted against any one of these visions of them, everyone in the community is at some risk, regardless of their factional location within it (Carlebach, 1978, p. 16).

Unity is just what an internal minority cannot achieve. Attempts to mobilize usually just multiply internal dissentions and fuel group factionalism. Charges of collaboration are aggravated. Even further demoralization is produced. The most common response to impotence in the political arena is a withdrawal of interest altogether. It is not rational to dissipate energy for ever in pursuit of such elusive goals. So as each generation discovers the scale of handicap facing it, there is a tendency to retreat and seek satisfactions in areas where the majority cannot or would not want to compete.

Symbolic participation continues, in order to placate integrationist patrons. But the main response among minorities to rebuffs is withdrawal into private life. Big prizes that can be won from the democratic rotation of power are left to be monopolized by their majoritarian patrons, from whom they may hope to receive the occasional perk if they play their cards right. At the political level the situation is not very different in its basic features from that described by Myrdal as obtaining under segregation, and where the best response to an ambiguous political system lay in having an ambivalent attitude.

Compromise leadership in Southern Cities:

In the rural South only accommodating Negro leadership is as yet possible. In Southern cities – except in the smaller ones – single individuals and small groups of followers around them use the protection of the greater anonymity of the segregated urban Negro community to raise cautiously the banner of Negro protest. For instance, they try to get the Negroes to attempt to register as voters; and they support local branches of the N.A.A.C.P., a national protest organization. The protest has little or no effect locally, but it has the symbolic function of keeping the flame of protest burning in the community. The president of the N.A.A.C.P. branch in one of the smaller capitals of the Deep South, a distinguished, elderly gentleman, a postal clerk who for many decades because of his economic independence as a federal employee had led a cautious fight for Negro interests in his community, during a conversation as to whether there were any other similar organizations in the city, said:

'Yes, there is the League for Civil Improvement.'

'Why do you bother to have two organizations with the same purpose of trying to improve the position of Negroes?'

'Sir, that is easily explainable. The N.A.A.C.P. stands firm on its principles and demands our rights as American citizens. But it accomplishes little or nothing in this town, and it arouses a good deal of anger in the whites. On the other hand, the League for Civic Improvement is humble and 'pussyfooting'. It begs for favors from the whites, and succeeds quite often. The N.A.A.C.P. cannot be compromised in all the tricks that Negroes have to perform down here. But we pay our dues to it to keep it up as an organization. The League for Civic Improvement does all the dirty work.'

'Would you please tell me who is president of the League for Civic Improvement? I should like to meet him.'

'I am. We are all the same people in both organizations.'

(Rose, 1964 (ed.), p. 254)

CHAPTER 9
TRIALS OF COMMITMENT

Ordinary members of minority groups can avoid most of the distress created on the political stage, by leaving it clear for those who can be sure of getting something out of it. But there are still plenty of other difficulties that they are subject to, and which people in the majority can play on to assure themselves of dominance. Minority individuals, suspended in limbo between the promise of full integration and the fear of continued exclusion, are faced all the time with impossible questions about their identity. They must try to resolve them, in order to make sense and take control of their existence. But ultimately these are matters which only the majority can determine; and the majority has nothing to gain by sorting them out.

The basic level of uncertainty for minority individuals concerns whether it is realistic to see themselves as free agents in society, or whether it is not better to let official ideology be damned and to congregate with other people sharing the same experiences of rejection. This problem of the relative emphasis to give to personal rather than to collective action is commonplace enough. It is felt in some degree by all members of society. But it is made distinctive and more unsettling for minority individuals by the way in which it ties in for them with a second dimension of choice.

Their difficulty is that the groupings they are most likely to be pushed into forming are ethnic communities. These, by definition, have a problematic relation with the state. They are subject to majority suspicions about their loyalty to and place in the nation. In these circumstances, no decision about identity can be the right one, or even the final one.

If minority individuals do opt for a collective approach to their problems, does this entail, or will it be construed as indicating, a lesser commitment on their part to the nation as a whole? If, on the other hand, they renounce ethnicity and decide to plunge wholeheartedly into the rat race, without group protection, what will be gained? Will they be allowed by the majority to forget their communal identity? Will less courageous or fortunate compatriots refrain from looking to them for help, or rushing along after them in the trails they have blazed? Will competitors in the majority disdain from suggesting that their needy compatriots might have some fraternal claim on their compassion and charity? There is a multitude of tests here which compromise the patriotism of the new recruit.

THE OBJECTIVE TEST OF CULTURE

Many traps are concealed in that vast and vague dimension of life we call culture. On the face of it this is so much freer from agonizing decisions than the hurly-burly of politics. One thing, however, that we cannot do in culture is to avoid making choices. The need to make cultural decisions does, in fact, pervade everyday life. We all have to speak in a language or languages, exercise culinary and sartorial tastes and so on, and to do so with unremitting frequency. Even if single acts do not appear to have great significance, they are part of an accumulation of habit which may be formed before its full implications become obvious to us. We participate in culture so unconsciously that we may never think of it as a decision-making area at all. But it is. And this is just where it derives its value for majoritarian tests.

The duality of modern society is readily detectable here. Cultural practices are given highly divergent evaluations by different sectors of majority opinion. Enlightened classes are usually wedded to a voluntarist outlook, treating them as matters of open individual choice and discretion. 'Culture' is seen primarily as a vehicle of self-expression and discovery. Diversity of cultural traditions is accordingly valued as an asset and enrichment. It enlarges humanity's choice, by multiplying the satisfactions available to individual producers and consumers.

This humanistic view of the cultural market place has been given theoretical backing by the labours of people like Franz Boas and the cultural anthropology emanating from under him at Columbia University. The line taken by Boas was a reaction against the exclusivist and racialist theories of culture associated with Germanic nationalism and social Darwinism. He insisted that cultural activities are responses to local environments and stimuli. They are transferable between groups and individuals as new settings are created and adapted to. All cultures are equally bound by their contexts. So they are all intrinsically equal. Moreover, since the communities in which it evolves are fluid and overlapping, the whole of human culture is ultimately a seamless web, permitting the intermingling and co-operation of all in an unfolding future.

In Boasian terms, which brought up to date a venerable liberal tradition of regarding culture as something to be adopted voluntarily, and not imposed, minority culture is not problematic. Members of national minorities have every right to see themselves as acculturating to the way of life of a national majority. They may, equally, look for pluralistic diversity, or cultural autonomy in the Austro-Marxist sense, or contribute to the evolution of a new hybrid culture, or pursue any conceivable combination of these alternatives. What is important, and the only thing that is important, is that they do not have something thrust on them against their wills. This would inhibit the capacity of diverse traditions to merge freely and cross-fertilize in the generation of new cultural responses to emerging challenges. Individuals with different backgrounds should be genuinely free to adopt and adapt whatever elements of whichever heritages they find pertinent to their own lives. Where they are, they participate in creating a forward-looking and vigorous way of life.

Attractive as this vision may be, it has its limitations and blind spots. What it refuses in particular to countenance is that most people are not normally operating in situations where cultural choices can be free. Cultures are fluid and open to individual modification all right. They do change, overlap, meet in a seamless web and so on. But at the same time they are strongly rooted in group ways of living. They are to an important extent collective enterprises. So they lend themselves to the indirect expression of communalist designs and sentiments.

To a communalist, culture signifies group membership. It is an emblem of group solidarity, providing definitions and symbols for maintaining the coherence and self-respect of a group *vis-à-vis* other groups. In these terms a common culture is the means whereby members of a community can construct a favourable account of themselves in relation to the rest of the world. Language is the medium of group consciousness, and literature the repository of communicable and partisan collective memories.

Culture tends all the time, therefore, towards invidious judgments. It is the medium whereby dominant groups try to justify their treatment of weaker, and weaker to articulate their resistance to more powerful (Adam, 1971, p. 22). Even 'liberal' nations like the British, who like to claim that their shared culture is the result of, not a reason for, common statehood, have used mobilization around cultural emblems to help establish their national identity. I am not just referring to the apprentice boys of 'Derry. It was, after all, through reformation marking the rejection of Catholic control that the British Union achieved, and still maintains, its political integrity.

It is very difficult to resist this communalist logic of treating culture as an index of political loyalty. Even liberals find themselves carried along by it in practice. Don't forget Versailles. When the crunch came and western powers needed to operationalize the principle of self-determination, they slipped easily enough from a voluntarist position into using culture as an objective indicator of group commitment. Minorities to be invested with collective rights were identified from above, according to linguistic criteria. Their destiny was defined in terms of history, rather than surrendered to the market. Choices supposedly belonging to individuals were in the event made by powerful groups on behalf of the lesser.

Part of the routine power exercised constantly by a national majority lies precisely in just such an ability, recognized in Guy Héruad's 'ethnopolitics', and by Hechter's application of internal colonialism, to use culture as a marker for sealing off colonized groups. The dominant community in a nation does not evaluate minority cultural performances as contributions to humanity's choices. It looks at them in terms of their capacity to mediate subordination. Maintenance of separate traditions is acceptable if it implies submission in secondary status, but not where it embodies a demand for parity of esteem and rejection of majority control. National education typically operates as a system for grading or devaluing cultures other than that of the controlling community.

By the same token, cultural assimilation is looked on kindly by a majority in so far as it conveys a desire by minorities to conform to majority mores. For this expresses an appreciation of their superiority. But many in the majority will draw the line at minority individuals acculturating in order to pass as members of the majority and escape from subordinate status. The young Hitler, arriving in Vienna from the provinces, was horrified by the prevalence there of assimilated Jews. He immediately sensed a communal plot to infiltrate and control national life.

In the later decades of the nineteenth century very many Jews throughout Germany had, for a variety of reasons, enthusiastically set about recasting themselves as Germans. Bermant notes, however, that 'all remained Jews in the eyes of Gentiles, who found their sudden rush for the forefront of European life startling', (1978, p. 44). As in fifteenth-century Spain, seventeenth-century Poland, and perhaps present day America, hostility to Jews is greater, the closer they feel themselves to acculturation.

The minority individual attempting to adopt the majority's ways is regarded as fair game by most nationalists. The recently Anglicized, Russified or Magyarized person is often visible on account of his over-punctilious manners and rigidity of performance. These make him an easy object of ridicule. Whatever he does can be questioned from some quarter for its authenticity. Novak points out in his illuminating study (1971) that majorities can use the dominance of their culture to make behavioural demands on a minority individual which they could not hope to meet themselves.

Any deviation from orthodox practices opens him to the charge of being inadequately schooled, and contaminating a culture by his vain pretence at its command. If, on the other hand, he sticks too closely to prevailing modes he will be accused of being nothing more than a mere imitator, who is incapable of constructive innovation, and hence is purely parasitic on the traditions onto which he has latched himself.

Successful mastering of a culture is redefinable by critics as a form of failure, of using it while giving nothing back in return. Wagner was most scathing about the achievements of Meyerbeer, one of the foremost composers of his day.

> As a Jew, he owned no mother tongue, no speech inextricably entwined among the sinews of his innermost being; he spoke with precisely the same interest in any modern language you chose, and set it to music with no more concern for the idiosyncracies than the mere question of how far it was ready to be a pliant servitor to Absolute Music.
>
> (Quoted by Bermant, 1978, p. 189)

This sort of judgment rests on the communalist idea that there is no honourable place in a nation for groups that have not made their own distinctive contribution to its way of life, making it their heritage too. It is this which then drives many formerly acculturating individuals back into renewed interest in their own traditions. Their hope is that they will find there an appropriate cultural dowry that will buy them some respect and an acknowledged stake in national life.

WEIGHING UP THE EVIDENCE OF ROOTS

> Every colonized people ... finds itself face to face with the language of the civilizing nation; that is, with the culture of the mother country. The colonized is elevated above his jungle status in proportion to his adoption of the mother country's cultural standards.
>
> (Fanon, 1967, p. 107)

Communities which do not have the power to impose their own values on a society are often taunted for their 'warped and inadequate' attempts to adopt the dominant culture. They may as a result be tempted into gambling the accommodation which they have already achieved. Hazardous journeys are undertaken into distant and ancient places in the search for something of value to contribute to national life. These are journeys from which they will be very lucky to return in better shape than they set out.

One obvious snag of such bids for pride through rediscovery of roots is that it will carry individualists into communalist territory. Members of a majority have the nationalist legitimacy to make innovations to national culture, without being denigrated as deviants or conspirators. Minorities, however, are made to feel that they have no right to interfere with a culture unless it is one their own community has helped to shape. Consequently it is often the most individualistic people, with the greatest creative urge, and who are most likely to feel any disparagement of their personal efforts, who become subject to the strongest pressure to undertake a retrieval of communal assets and pride.

What is worse, the communal sentiments that are activated relate to a group which, almost by definition, has little legitimacy in the host state. The distinctive focus of minority identity is always external to their host state. The process of being herded back into it, and having one's consciousness of membership heightened, necessarily entails a spiritual repatriation. At the moment of reawakening of satisfaction in its ancestral endeavours and achievements, a minority becomes metamorphosed from its previous, merely subordinate or dependent status, into an alien and potentially hostile presence.

During the hopeful years of affirmative action in America, blacks like Haley retraced lines of descent back to their African origins, in order to start assembling a patrimony which they could bring with them as they were admitted to full membership of American society.

But it did not work out like that. The surge of collective sentiment which was elicited had the effect of turning blacks into an 'ethnic' group, with all that entails in American political life of conspiratorial tendencies against the Union, instead of the Black Americans which they had essentially been since the fading of Garveyism. Irving Howe's 'Land of my Fathers', responding partly to the rise of Jewish self-esteem after the six-day war, and partly to the mood of me-tooism in the wake of Civil Rights, had a similar outcome.

This is not all. The external identity which is summoned up may not in the event be able to produce a dowry. The roots of minorities reach into archaic states, and weaker contemporary nations. Explorations in such places are unlikely to uncover anything which will impress a host majority as offering a valuable addition to its national life. Those items most likely to be of interest to hosts are usually trivial bits and pieces that tie in with minority servicing roles. Studies attempting to document the 'cultural contribution' of minorities end up (like Borrie, 1959) as embarrassingly thin inventories of colourful folk-lore, quaint musical genres or modes of dress, and exotic culinary concoctions.

The tracing of roots back to a peasant existence, let alone into the bush or jungle, is not going to cut much ice in an advanced metropolitan society. What generally strikes observers in the majority is the barbaric quality of the artefacts that their clients dig up. Many caring members of the host *élite* find they are caught here in what might be called Gladstone's dilemma. Their initial enthusiasm for the principle for cultural diversity is neutralized by the unpalatable content of what is being patronized. The Protestant Yeats was very keen on the idea of reviving Irish peasant culture until he discovered the nature of unchained Catholicism. Some in the race relations industry today contrive to believe in the need for an appreciation of minority cultures while holding serious reservations about the practices these embody.

Many in modern metropolitan societies believe, either from passion or patriotism, in the virtues of tolerance, democracy and egalitarianism and so abhor élitism, tribalism, arranged marriages, wife-beating, Purdah, Halal slaughter, cruelty to animals and so on. They find it hard to stomach the cultural claims of groups from backgrounds where these brutalities are found. This applies even if the communities in question were brought into servitude through force and fraud.

Equally, minorities venturing back out in search of lost treasures that their ancestors have been guarding over for them are all too likely to apply their hosts' criteria when deciding what to look for, and evaluating what they find. For the Salman Rushdies of this world, examination of roots does not bring pride, but moral confusion. Minority critiques of host majority practices are usually phrased in terms of majority values. There is a measure of ambivalence inherent in the critical process.

Another factor which does not help is that where recognizable 'homelands' do currently exist, these are probably cultural colonies of the host nation. Spiritual pilgrims to ancestral dwelling places may be shocked to find that their cousins who have remained at home have succumbed to what Bulhan (1979) calls auto-colonialism. They have espoused the very values their visiting relatives are in flight from.

Independence in Africa brought a rich harvest of irony in this respect. It has inspired black minorities in the West to look to Africa for inspiration and self-respect. But in Africa itself, the acquisition of political power removed inhibitions about adopting the values and life-styles of the former masters. Klineberg (1961) recounts the case of an African speaker who was criticized in 1950 by American Negro groups for turning up in African robes, and then in 1960 for appearing in a western suit. Exile communities and homelands march on hand in hand, but remain out of step.

The cult of negritude is stronger in the metropolitan centres of Europe and North America than amongst the masses in Africa.

> Those most involved in the nationalist movement in its political and social aspects have faced a number of difficulties, not least of which is that 'negritude' as a concept is operating with diminished force in Africa as African nations strive to modernize ... In short, their underlying values seem largely white 'middle class'.
>
> (Rothman, 1974, p. 420)

Even fathers of black consciousness have recanted just when the diaspora community needed them most. Sekou Touré told the sixth Pan-African Congress:

> ... the reclamation of Pan-Africanist identity requires a fight against racist, segregationist and Zionist movements and any attempts to encapsulate the movement in a particularistic identity, for these are retrograde tendencies which place Pan-Africanism in a geological garden of stagnation.
>
> (Speaking at Dar-es-Salaam, Autumn 1974)

The journey to trace roots may just bring disillusionment and renewed resignation. Rastas have learned that Africa does not offer them a useful contemporary model, let alone a feasible alternative home. Africa today is still part of Babylon – perhaps more a part of it than ever. Their contemplation of dim horizons has all the appearance of a new wave of quietist retreat – resistance lodged at a noble level where it offers no threat at all to continuing White supremacy.

The roots of suffering to minorities are often the foundations of supremacy to their colonizers. These often seem to find the unravelling of their own unsavoury past, which is dug up at the same time, quite stimulating. For every liberal whose conscience is moved by tales of treachery and force in subduing distant territories, or the horrors of the middle passage, and the continuing injustice in communal exclusion, there may be several communalists who find in them evidence of their own past and present glory. History confirms the power of their collective will. What parity of esteem is there in the rediscovery of conquest and despoliation?

All of which means that the idea that minorities can hope to improve their place by proudly standing by their own cultural heritage is a snare. As Bierstedt (1948) pointed out, following de Tocqueville and Simmel, what counts is demography. A physical majority, especially when bolstered by democratic concepts of the divine right of the masses, can determine which practices are adopted as the central tradition and way of life of a people. The ability to contribute to the culture of a nation is mainly a matter of relative power. So the dominant group is bound to be the arbiter of what is done, and of what values are attached to different ways of doing things.

The 'pluralism' of American society, for example, is ordered according to WASP preferences. Even within ostensibly separate religious traditions, Protestant values intrude and impose.

> Religious faith and practice in America have been influenced in important ways by the Protestant etiquette ... Perhaps the most striking adaptation has been the tendency of American Jewish theologians and rabbis to play down the teaching that the Jews are God's own chosen people.
>
> Similarly the Catholics in the United States have de-emphasized the belief that the Church of Rome is the one true church ... The hierarchy has actively discouraged its priests from teaching the

ancient doctrine of 'extra ecclesiam nulla salus – There is no salvation outside the Church' ...

Thus the Catholics, like the Jews, have come to terms with America's religious pluralism. But in minimizing the differences that separate them from the Protestant denomination and more importantly by renouncing the claims of superiority made by their own traditions, both groups have given up distinctive, perhaps vital elements of their religions. They have adopted what the Jewish theologian, Arthur Hertberg, called 'split personalities'. That is, he said, 'each sect is to remain the one true and revealed faith in private, but each must behave in the public arena as if its truth were as tentative as an esthetic opinion or a scientific theory.'

... by demanding of Jews and Catholics that they act in public as though they are merely available options for consumers of religion, American society has, in effect, demanded that they act as though they are Protestants.

(McGrath, 1979)

A dominant community can patronize and trivialize minority practices as long as it wishes to. As the arbiter it can call on libertarian conceptions of the sovereignty of individual choice to justify a gourmet's approach to diversity. Minorities are thereby permitted to serve up exotic confections, to amuse jaded metropolitan palates with their freshness and presumption.

The majority, meanwhile, gets on with the serious job of providing 'core' values and the key institutions of law and political constitution. Proclamation of a pluralist intent makes little difference. It was when Stalin signalled a move to official endorsement of cultural autonomy for minorities that Russian culture was brought back into its central and unifying place. Someone has to hold things together. Within prescriptions for tolerance or multi-culturalism there usually linger some flag-waving references to the dominant group's superior capacity to integrate all the other communities into a single happy family.

A society which has provided the modes for other societies by evolving democratic forms that respect the individual, and which has known how to combine tolerance with dissent, now has the chance to set a further example by proving that men of many races can live together in justice and harmony.

(E. J. B. Rose *et al.*, 1969, p. 756)

The idea of majority arbitration need not conflict with the Boasian principle that all cultures are equal as adaptations. It is all a matter of what is being adapted to. Boas' relativism rests on a notion of culture as adaptation to environment. So it is reasonable for an autochthonous majority to argue that it is, by virtue of long evolutionary adjustment, the best judge of what mix of cultural items is appropriate to local circumstances.

But where the dominant group are not natives, they can call on the same ideas to overrule local claims. All they need to do is to present their own life-style as a superior overall adjustment to a wider environment. Aboriginal Australians argue, justly, that their provident culture is a perfected response to their harsh and unpredictable habitat. But European settlers can reply, equally, that their way of life is capable of locking Australians into a broader and more productive interchange of goods and services from which they all can benefit.

ARRESTED IN THE LOBBY

It is as if a man who has built himself a pleasant house and is leading a comfortable existence suddenly finds a horde of impecunious relatives descending upon him.

(Nathan Glazer, 1957)

The revival of consciousness of a cultural community does not only arise out of a desire to rediscover roots. The past can also turn up uninvited on the doorstep, in the shape of new waves of immigrants who are lumped together with existing communities through majoritarian treatment and definitions.

People of the Jewish faith are old hands at dealing with this. They know the cross-pressures it sets up within their communities. There is initially a strong impetus within local Jewish groups towards the exclusion of new arrivals. This is prompted both by possessiveness in relation to the stock they have already acquired in the national system, and the desire to appear loyal patriots. Sam Gompers for example, the Jew of Dutch extraction who presided over the American Federation of Labor, combined service to class, nation and established Jewish interests when he supported the restrictive Immigration Act of 1924.

Garrard notes, too, that it was Jews who were the first to resist the waves of exiles from persecution in Eastern Europe, near the end of the nineteenth century.

In fact, over the first decade and a half, it was the Anglo-Jews who noticed and worried over the arrival of the immigrants; it was they who were concerned to keep them out rather than Parliament, which contented itself with expressing its sense of outrage at the pogroms that produced the exodus.

(1971, pp. 23–4)

A letter appeared in the *Jewish Chronicle* from a member of the Jewish Board of Guardians, advocating restriction, several years before attacks on the immigration started in the English press.

However, and as this English case showed, the pressures that are put on a local minority community to receive needy colleagues as their own people are extremely difficult to resist. Anglo-Jewry was comparatively well placed to hold off new additions, and managed to do so for some time.

England's geographic position permitted the Jewish community to send immigrants either forward to America or back to their native places. From the eighteenth century, the community encouraged emigration to America and the Colonies to reduce the number of its poor and the burden which they laid upon more affluent Jews.

(Gartner, 1960, p. 49)

One of the main fears was that poor Jews would become a drain on communal resources. The richest Jewish families tended to take the line that while newcomers should of course be regarded as having the right to seek asylum in Britain, they should not be seen as having a call on Jewish charity. But, according to Talmudic instruction, all of Israel is responsible for one another. Under the initiative of more recent migrants, with less to lose, the community gradually mobilized its wealthier elements into providing support for impecunious new arrivals.

The poorest Jews who were the direct economic competitors with the impending immigrant hordes remained the most hostile. Over a period, however, the community was pulled together by the issue into a more coherent and welcoming body. By the late 1890s it had created a lobby generally supportive of the rights of immigrants. This was effective in securing some safeguards for religious refugees from the legislature during the committee stage of the second Aliens Bill.

Some Jews, notably Primrose Leaguers following in the steps of Disraeli, aligned openly with the anti-alien movement.

The conservative M.P. for Islington, Benjamin L. Cohen, informed the anti-alien lobby in Parliament that he and certain other Jewish M.P.s were 'disposed to assist in the establishment of such regulations as would discourage the immigration of undesirable persons', ... (and told fellow Jews they should) 'make it clear not to endeavour to oppose any action which the responsible advisors of the Crown may deem necessary for the national interests which we are as desirous to protect as our fellow-citizens ...' Cohen voted for the Aliens Act in 1905, and received a baronetcy soon after.

(Gartner, op. cit., p. 55)

The overall outcome of the affair was to weld the Jewish community, including the new arrivals, into a self-reliant and redistributive corporation. This saved the majority community, in the form of the Poor Law Commissioners who were reluctant to spend public money on members of the Jewish faith, considerable embarrassment and expense.

Underlying this drawing together was the calculation by Jews that once the issue had arisen and taken hold, there was no way in which they could avoid collective liability in some form. One way or another the majority could press them into aligning with the newcomers. If they stood up for the right of Jewish refugees to immigrate, then the only way to fend off the charge that they were saddling the state with a heavy burden of provision for the destitute was to welcome them into their own house. If, on the other hand, they opposed immigration, might they not be admitting grounds for their own expulsion on some future occasion? As a speaker at a meeting of the Board of Guardians suggested, 'The letters which spell exclusion are not very different from those which compose expulsion.' (Gartner, op. cit., p. 55)

The Jewish response was determined ultimately by British ascriptions of fraternal solidarity to them, on the basis of objective cultural criteria. These did not just come from people hostile to Jews. This is true also of equivalent pressures on minorities today. Present day internationalist championing of the rights of immigrants is no less communalist in its working assumptions about the common interests uniting newcomers and existing settlers. It may not be consciously thought through. There does, however, seem to be some particle of nationalist collusion in the behaviour of those libertarians who orchestrate pro-immigration lobbies in metropolitan nations, when they presume to speak for minority communities as a whole.

Where these lobbyists are class warriors fighting to change society, they may well conceptualize minorities as spearheads for an international revolution. In their own terms they are giving priority to class, and merely playing on communal sentiments to that end. The same could be said of the Left at the end of the nineteenth century, who rejoiced at the arrival of poor Jews because it sapped the wealth already accumulated by their richer compatriots.

Those engaged in such stratagems should, however, take care to ensure that they do not have mixed motives here. They are using minorities as pawns and lobby fodder in ways which they might hesitate to apply to others. Activists may hasten their revolutionary goals through imposing communal liabilities onto members of minority groups. More likely they will not. What they will succeed in doing anyway is to increase these minorities' appearance of solidarity and of prior loyalty to anti-national causes.

Members of minority groups who do not want to be co-opted in this way to majoritarian programmes resent being herded into lobbies.

> The Labour Party has for many years now considered the black vote to be its sole property and in furtherance of the protection of this vote have evolved a particularly sordid brand of racialism. Socialist politicians have systematically instilled in the coloured population a dread fear that under any other government their stay in this country could only be temporary. This has greatly stressed good race relations whilst deliberately increasing the divide between black and white. ... It is strange that a great number of assumptions on the discussion of immigration are prevalent. The strangest of all in my experience is that settled immigrants do not want immigration controls, and yet we have specific evidence from Leicester sources which indicates that many Asians would welcome a move towards further controls. They argue with some force that we should be more concerned with the effect of further immigration upon the integration of those already here and how this might be hampered.
>
> (Javed Khan, Letter to *The Times*, 8 February 1978)

These are the writings of a gladiator. But they have a point. It is members of existing minorities who stand to suffer any fall-out from pro-immigration campaigns. Internationalists in the majority fail to give enough consideration to this. They can themselves make a case on behalf of immigration without losing political legitimacy. This is not true of those who are recent immigrants or liable to be communally identified with them.

Majority idealists, activated by humanitarian conscience and charity, have no obvious sectarian interest in immigration. They can present a universalist case for the admission of newcomers – considered as refugees, deserving poor, or subjects of a former Empire who should not be abandoned etc – which cannot be attacked *ad hominem* by nationalists. It may even convince some that measures of this sort are needed to protect the good name of the nation.

This position is not available to minority individuals in the lobby, or that the lobby likes to think it embraces. When such people plead for an open door policy this is almost invariably seen by nationalist opinion as pursuance of their own sectional goals, even perhaps as entertaining subversive designs with alien compatriots. Pro-immigrant activists would do these individuals a favour, and maybe the cause too, by being more cautious before citing them as solid grassroots supporters.

Minority individuals can, of course, communicate universalist aspirations very effectively. I suggested in chapter 2 that progressive ideologies depend a great deal on the energy and inspiration of oracles reared in such backgrounds. But they will lose credibility if they appear to focus on issues which principally benefit groups they belong to, or could be construed as belonging to, themselves. In the eyes of solid citizens like David Owen this will appear bogus and partisan.

> It is of course entirely right and understandable that, in fighting for human rights, Jewish groups should concern themselves mainly with Jews ... But the fact that this concern is displayed so conspicuously and at times almost exclusively in the cause of Soviet Jewry does in my view tend to limit the effectiveness of the groups concerned and may even cause some resentment among those who are competing for public sympathy and support on behalf of equally deserving cases which do not involve Jews. The force of Jewish lobbying in this area would be greatly strengthened if it were quite consciously and visibly extended to cover other ethnic and religious groups, not only within the Soviet Union, but also elsewhere.
>
> (David Owen, 1978, p. 45)

As usual national majorities stand to win all ways. They can mobilize established minority communities to effect a privatized care and financing of destitute refugees. Then they can expose those who carry this burden for them as being alien themselves. This transformation of settled migrants into co-exiles with the newcomers also brings people who may be forgetting their place down a peg or two. Those available for drawing against their will or better judgment into pro-immigration movements are themselves kept a little longer in that other lobby, of incomplete admission to the national body.

Thus the term 'kike', first coined by German Jews as a derogatory stereotype applying to the new Russian immigrants, was now used by gentiles when referring to Jews in general, the cultivated and Americanized German as well as the impoverished and alien garment workers on the Lower East Side. This was, of course, a terrible shock to the established Jews, especially the cultivated elite, some of whom became anti-semitic themselves ...

This new situation might well have precipitated a caste division within the American-Jewish community. For, after all, the difference in 'race and habits' as between the newer 'Russian' and the older 'German' Jews were far greater than the cultural gulf dividing the Americanized German Jews from their gentile neighbours.

(But, and instead) increased anti-Semitism among gentiles created a new and rigid caste barrier which now excluded all Jews, as well as convinced Christians of Jewish origins, from communal or associational participation in the larger gentile society, especially at the elite level.

(Baltzell, 1970, p. 329)

Ordeals of marginal men

Thus the Jew has been alternately encouraged and restrained by forces outside as well as inside the Jewish community to assume a half-way position relative to the Gentile's world, neither completely in nor completely out. It is this peculiar position between the two peoples which we shall designate as 'marginal' ... The marginal man is the individual who lives in, or has ties of kinship with, two or more interacting societies between which there exists sufficient incompatibility to render his own adjustment to them difficult or impossible. He does not quite 'belong' or feel at home in either group.

(Stonequist, 1942, p. 297)

For minorities there are no safe houses. Communal politics penetrates within private lives. It disturbs the growth of local roots and clarification of identities. If no choices are allowed by the majority to be complete or final, then the only way to keep going at all must lie in being unable to make any decisive commitment.

At times individual members of minorities, even whole generations, may begin to feel that they are approaching a workable resolution of existing demands on them. But so long as it suits a majority to keep up conflicting demands and pressures on them, their accommodation will be inadequate. Others in the community will discover this. The children of those who have tried to integrate are better than their parents at seeing how they are still treated as outsiders. They (Peter Rose, 1977) are the ones to return to ghetto life. What the son forgets, the grandson is made to remember.

On the British scene, a submissive generation of Caribbean immigrants has been succeeded by rebellious and negative children. Conversely, a collection of introspective, incapsulated Asian communities looks like producing a new breed of avid assimilators. Where no solution is adequate, then a mixed or alternating response is elicited.

The marginality of identities resulting from this keeps minorities available as a reserve, semi-domesticated stock of energy. Many occupying the reserves will have fantasies about moving on after a brief sojourn to greener pastures. Some will do it. But for most of them there is nowhere to go on, or back, to which offers better living. The servitude they undergo therefore requires no tangible walls or restraints. Their own irresolution is sufficient to keep them where they are. Until they can decide who they are, then they cannot be whole people at all. In the words of Du Bois:

One ever feels his two-ness – an American, a Negro; two souls, two thoughts, two unreconciled strivings; two warring ideals in one dark body, whose dogged strength alone keeps it from being torn asunder. The history of the American Negro is the history of this strife – this longing to attain self-conscious manhood to merge his double self into a better and truer self. In this merging he wishes neither of the older selves to be lost. He does not wish to Africanize America, for America has too much to teach the world and Africa. He does not wish to bleach his Negro blood in a flood of White Americanism for he believes . . . that Negro blood has yet a message for the world. He simply wishes to make it possible for a man to be both a Negro and an American without being cursed and spit upon.

(Du Bois, (1903) 1968 ed., p. 16)

PART IV:

THE FRAMEWORK OF CONTAINMENT

CHAPTER 10
THE POWER OF COMMUNALISM

The nature of progressive nationalism
The orthodox view in responsible political and academic circles is that
the exclusion of minorities, and idealistic attempts to integrate them,
are separate and opposed forces. They may inhabit the same people
at the same time. But they are irreconcilable adversaries. Moreover, it
is idealism which will triumph in the end.

> The popular explanation of the conflict in America between ideals
> and actual behaviour is that Americans do not have the slightest
> intention of living up to their ideals. This explanation is too
> superficial. To begin with, the true hypocrite sins in secret. The
> American, on the contrary, is strongly and sincerely 'against sin',
> even and not least, against his own sins. ... America's handling
> of the Negro problem has been criticized by white Americans
> since long before the Revolution and the criticism has steadily
> gone on and will not stop until America has completely reformed
> itself.
> In a great nation there is, of course, division of labour. Some
> Americans do most of the sinning, but most do some of it. Some
> specialize in muckraking, preaching, and lamentations; but there
> is a little of the muckraker and preacher in all Americans ...
> superficially viewed, Americans often appear cynical. As a matter
> of fact, this young nation is the least cynical of all nations. It
> labors persistently with its moral problems. It is taking its Creed
> very seriously indeed. The cultural unity of the nation is this
> sharing in both consciousness of sins and devotion to high ideals.
>
> (Arnold Rose, 1964, p. 8)

It is this sort of position which is actually the superficial one. It refuses
to see that exclusion can itself call on supportive moral precepts of its
own – a point I shall take up shortly. But where it is most flagrantly
blinkered is in failing to consider the communalist calculations which

lie not far below the surface of conventional idealism. We are all against sin. Most anti-segregationists however surely do not disapprove of exclusive practices *per se*. What makes them offensive is the damaging effect that they may have on the nation's image and standing in the world.

We must not forget that Myrdal's study, from which the above quotation is a summary, was commissioned by 'idealistic' American patriots. They were anxious to tackle a problem that was impeding US accession to world leadership. This sort of breast-beating is more cynical than the common sense scepticism with which it takes issue.

Where libertarian sentiments are underpinned by such considerations, then they are unlikely to prompt behaviour against group interests. So if humanism and majority communalism find common cause, it is the latter which will hold the whip hand. A good deal of liberal philosophy seems to consist of attempts to deny or obscure this. And these labours all assist patriotic ends – whether this is intended or not. For, in so far as efforts to show the power of humanist impulses do carry conviction, they contribute further to a successful concealment of the true force of communalism.

Communalism works best in the dark. That power which it does enjoy in modern society is contingent on a large measure of public oversight and denial. The modern world system, which communalism is obliged to operate through, would not hold together at all unless most people, including most of those who are inclined towards communalist values and purposes, formally conducted their lives according to the ruling fiction that humanism is in control.

All this surely encourages dissimulation. Some of the people engaged in promoting communal causes must sometimes or in some contexts deliberately cloak them in universalist attire, in order to confuse their opponents.

This is not likely to be true of national governments or majority groups considered as corporate entities. Duplicity at this level is unconscious and indirect. It is a line of least resistance, arising out of the need to meet and balance contrary pressures. Nevertheless, they cannot deny all responsibility for it. They are guilty at least of oversight in the way they articulate their various aims and policies.

For it is not inherently difficult to appreciate either that 'progressive nationalist' formulae permit deception, or that the cover for majority communalism thereby provided has been an important factor easing the official adoption of progressive codes. If powerful groups do not recognize this, it must be because they do not want to know. Their collective hypocrisy lies in toleration of double standards which hurt others but not themselves.

To avoid being drawn into this humbug, we need to unravel and clarify the relationship between liberal creeds and majority communalism. The first step lies in recognizing that there are very real differences between the two major moral systems involved. Consensualist theorists have a knack of using concepts like 'community' and 'class' in a loose, overlapping way. This has the effect of running the two moralities together and blurring the lines between them. We must resist this, and clearly establish the distinctive properties of the opposed ideologies.

Having done this, we can then move on to a fuller appreciation of the ambiguity of the progressive nationalist formula. The idea of the enlightened nation does not produce a complete merger of the opposed principles it embodies. This would be impossible. What it does do is to fix a concept and level of group identification which is open to diverse evaluations.

The modern nation has a very different significance for its various elements. Liberals experience it as an artificial curb on their natural freedoms. They will only tolerate it, if it is seen as a step towards an open society of all humanity. To communalists, on the other hand, it generally represents a stretching out of fraternal solidarity to its effective limit. For them, it is only worth belonging to if it opens up access to benefits controlled by that nation's state machine.

The idea of the progressive nation is thus open to alternative interpretations. Its formulae allow for highly divergent legitimations of state actions and institutions. Different sectors of a national society can agree to support them, even though their reasons for doing so may be quite contrary. It is this flexibility which is the key to its general acceptability.

The political success of humanist creeds, as marked by their formal enshrinement in state institutions and international conventions, has to be seen in the light of this constructive ambiguity. Later sections of the chapter expand this point further. Before this can be tackled, the specific character of communalist morality needs to be looked at in more detail.

THE FRATERNAL IMPERATIVE

Most commentators, like Myrdal, do not regard communalism as informed by ethical considerations. Morality is implicitly equated with humanism. Anything not conforming to this is treated as merely 'selfish behaviour', to be contrasted with 'idealistic values'. No wonder that such commentaries are constantly being surprised by the tenacity of communalist ways.

Communalism cannot be dismissed as a moral failure or vacuum. It is grounded in ancient and well-tried principles for relating individual to group interests. What distinguishes them in practice from humanism is that they are particularly relevant to humble folk – the 'losers' in the open society. Communalism is a philosophy for the weak. Its development in nationalist form in the modern world is best understood as a reaction to the self-serving transformation of utopian humanism by liberal *élites* into a philosophy for winners.

This usage of humanist ideals is not inherent in them. Their basic moral conviction is that social groups are subordinate to the individuals comprising them. The natural rights of individuals are ultimately more important than any requirements of social organization – in principle even than those which may be instrumentally necessary to implement and defend human rights themselves. In the full-blown libertarian version of this doctrine, social arrangements are to be regarded as valid only in so far as they are freely consented to by the individuals they impinge on. Even this validity is itself conditional. No social commitment is legitimate which takes away the natural freedom to enter into alternative relationships or contracts in the future.

Taken at face value, this creed does have a unifying and liberating appeal. In its original form as a critique of closed feudal society, it held out a prospect of democracy and social justice in which all could hope to share. During most of the seventeenth and eighteenth centuries, ideas about natural human rights did carry genuine revolutionary implications. They conjured up a dream around which a variety of elements hostile to feudalism and its ideology of Divine Right were able to congregate.

The consensual spirit of the enlightenment declared that removal of the medieval fetters of hereditary obligations and suffocating hierarchies would free everyone to discover their true selves and special talents. They could then enter voluntarily into productive agreements for the exchange of services. This would enlarge their contribution to the common good, while ensuring that the social rewards they received were commensurate with it. In this way a rational division of labour would evolve, grounded in consent and awareness of the needs of individuals to express and develop themselves. It would overcome once and for all the ancient conflict of interest between individuals and society – the secular foundations of original sin – and herald in an eternity of harmony and prosperity for all. It was a vision at once morally inclusive, and insistent on the importance and beneficent power of rational human choice.

Its eventual usage in formal state constitutions, however, owed less to its capacity to inspire consensual revolutions than to its opposite and less immediately apparent facility – that is, in legitimizing a new type of authority for those establishments arising out of them. Ideas hostile to privilege under one type of régime take on an exclusive character when admitted to the defensive armoury of another. As anti-feudal elements joined ruling establishments they found that libertarian values were easily forged into an expression of their new-found conservatism.

Humanists admitted to a share in power lost no time in closing the gates behind them by reformulating their creed as an attack on only certain types of oppression and inequality. By concentrating attention on more formal aspects of natural rights, and arguing that their own *élite* status is due to useful and arduous effort, hard-nosed individualists can easily turn the vision of the open society into a justification of their own supremacy. The libertarian idea that merit, and only merit, must be rewarded is readily reworked into a self-congratulatory charter with which the powerful and successful can authorize generous benefits to themselves from social resources. The society open to all talents soon becomes for practical purposes one in which failure to display special ability is treated as sufficient grounds for consignment to a life of submission.

There is little in this for ordinary people. A liberal ruling mandate has diplomatic value for a nation in its external affairs. But it is harmful to domestic relations between classes. Slogans extolling individual freedom and opportunity, on the grounds that talent is scarce in the world and needs encouraging, implicitly devalue the social contributions of all but that fortunate few who monopolize the more prestigious activities. They make a mockery of the lives of the toiling masses. In no way do they provide a satisfactory basis for securing their allegiance to the state.

It is not talent which is scarce. What in reality is severely limited is the chance to develop and use it and have it appreciated. A complex division of labour creates a preponderance of menial and highly regulated jobs. Meritocratic cults of self-achievement and fulfilment make it that much harder to motivate people to perform these humdrum tasks. Insisting on the need for competition to fill higher positions in society, or defining tenure of lowly occupations as personal failure, inevitably devalue the social contribution of the masses. This aggravates the tensions latent in the social division of labour.

Ordinary people can usually tolerate liberal individualism as an official ideology, so long as it serves foreign policy ends. But they cannot be expected to take its ideas seriously. It does not correspond to their actual daily experience, in which an incumbent *élite* can be seen to preserve for its own members and their offspring a better than equal opportunity. Nor does it provide a desirable or credible conception of how things might be. It is surely not rational to commit oneself heavily in a game with so few winners and many losers, unless you have reason to believe that the dice are loaded in your favour.

Michael Young's satire on Meritocracy (1958) gives us ample reason to suppose that there is no way in which genuinely free members of a society will acquiesce in a competitive process which persistently defines them as failures. They are bound to feel that the contest has been rigged against them. If they are allowed to challenge the system and replace it with a friendlier one, they will try to do so. Members of a privileged and protected upper class can play at competitive opportunism without much risk of disappointment. But most participants in a social system are better advised to embrace a different kind of philosophy, more respectful of the real odds.

The sort of moral system that the majority of people can in fact respond to is one which puts a fraternal obligation on communities to share benefits among their members, regardless of how talented or important they are. Calling such values collectivist does not mean that people responding to them are any more or less selfish than those subscribing to individualism. This is where, I think, primordialism goes wrong. It is more to the point to regard these different value systems as offering alternative moral strategies for reconciling individual and group needs. Each caters for individual interests in different ways.

Individualism insists on linking valued social benefits to personal merit and contribution. This is an appropriate vehicle for the self-seeking of those persons able to make a significant input to society. People occupying important positions, or possessing specially valued skills, can usually make a good case for recognition of their own claims on such a basis. The less privileged have little to gain by this strategy. They stand a greater chance of winning valuable rights or benefits if they act together in solidary combinations, and press claims by virtue of group membership.

Fraternal groupings provide their members with intrinsic satisfactions, such as conviviality and the assurance of mutual personal respect. However, they also need to be seen as mechanisms whereby their members can pursue joint material interests. The potential pay-offs for collective action are smaller than those for freely acting individuals. This is because the pooling of claims entails a corresponding division of the spoils. The limitation on possible gains is offset by greater security. For a loyal member can automatically expect shares in utilities controlled by the group.

Fraternalist principles are not made use of in present day constitutions. However, if we look at the norms by which most people in modern societies actually regulate their everyday lives – in domestic relations, at work, and within local communities – frequent recourse is, in fact, made to values which put satisfactions available through group membership and service, before individual freedom and aspiration.

It is in terms like these that popular political legitimacy can be achieved. As liberals have prised the masses out of traditional feudal domains and imposed harsh liberties upon them, they have been obliged to accommodate themselves with alternative principles of this sort, in order to give the people a genuine stake in the system, and acquire their support for the new régimes.

Distinctive properties of fraternalism

This accommodation has not been open and direct. Elites in secure, established nations usually prefer to conceptualize popular fraternalism in class terms. This transforms it into something more compatible with humanist precepts and tastes. If communal sentiments are dressed up as contractual and voluntary bonds, they can be admitted without undue bother to a progressive and consensualist analysis of modern trends.

These presentations do have some plausibility. The most forceful and visible demonstrations of instrumental collectivism occur within the trade union movement. Union leaders are happy to allow their members' actions to be described in terms of class action. This enhances their legitimacy and effectiveness. But in truth conventional notions of class have limited power to explain even these categories of behaviour. Fraternal actions necessarily follow the logic of group-oriented morality. And this, unlike textbook 'class', runs counter to virtually everything that the humanist enlightenment specifically stood for.

To start with, fraternalist values are inescapably hostile to voluntarism and individual freedom. They have no valid conception of natural and universal man. Only those groups from which the strong cannot readily opt out are capable of supporting their weak. The only human rights which can be admitted are those logically attendant on duties to the collectivities providing them.

To allow members a contractual view of their commitment runs the risk of slipping into mere associations of convenience, incapable of extending mutualist services. To a convinced fraternalist the source of meaning in life, and the way of getting access to valuable assets, are both seen to lie in participation in the affairs of a particular group. There are only two meaningful dimensions of choice. One concerns how far to actually be a morally responsive member of the community in question. The other has to do with at which level of group identification to lodge one's major commitment.

The second of these considerations indicates an even more distinctive aspect of fraternalism, placing it further outside the humanist tradition. This is its inherent relativism. True liberals believe that it is possible for people to serve and align with all humankind. They are citizens of one world, scornful of lesser allegiances. In seeking to promote absolute goods from which everyone can benefit, they are disposed to pay most attention to utilities which can be expanded indefinitely.

Collectivists on the other hand are bound to take a more sectional view. They are aware that securing benefits for members of one's own immediate fraternity usually entails withholding or even removing them from others. So they tend to become fascinated by zero-sum, mercantilist accounting. Fraternalism leans towards particularistic moral evaluations, which are deeply relativistic in at least two important senses.

First, all such moral judgments are relative to group membership. Behaviour cannot be reviewed except in terms of its effects on the fortunes of a particular community. For example, in a tribal society, where such values play a dominant and explicit role, the moral value of an act of homicide depends on the closeness of relationship between killer and victim. Killing a person from a distant tribe may get minimal condemnation. Sometimes it even elicits approval. On the other hand, the murder of someone from a neighbouring group will be regarded as a serious offence, inviting reprisals and requiring damages or punishment. While the deliberate killing of a member of one's own immediate community is such an enormous and self-wounding transgression that it may remain unpunishable, and beyond atonement.

Second, the actual definition of membership of the moral community is itself situational. It may well fluctuate between one moral assessment and the next. All dimensions of communal identity – kinship, tribe, race, territorial group and so on – lend themselves towards some measure of structuring into 'pyramidal-segmentary' systems (Levine and Campbell, 1972). Members of any specified collectivity may themselves as owing prior loyalty in some contexts to constituent sub-groups, and in others to higher-level, more inclusive groupings. Moreover, group identity at any level is defined largely through opposition to those other groups with which, at the next higher level in the pyramid, unity is achievable.

Such fluidity of identification shows up readily in an area where no vital interests are involved, like support for a local football team. Soccer fans in North London divide fiercely between Arsenal and Tottenham. But these unite against non-London teams, especially a distant team like Liverpool – a major common enemy in the English League. This, in turn, would not prevent them from taking pleasure in the contribution of individual Liverpool players to the success of the national team. Many might even find it in themselves to support Liverpool itself, when it is appearing as quasi-national representative in the European Cup.

This relativity of loyalty and identity mitigates the involuntary aspect of fraternal duties. It allows some room to manipulate allegiance, without breaching the general rule of unconditional dedication to the group. You may not be able to change your location in the structure of inter-group relations. But it is feasible to expand or contract the boundaries of the community to which you profess greatest loyalty, according to whether you are seeking access to a desirable identity, or moving to exclude fraternalist claims by others. Thus the most confident expressions of Scottish nationalism this century, resisting English big brother 'British' solidarity, took place when the estimated value and life-span of North Sea Oil was at its peak. The potential benefits to be derived from exclusiveness were very great.

The intrinsic relativity of group identities is not the only factor which complicates the exercise of fraternal obligations. In practice there are usually several different dimensions of group identity available. These compete as axes of mobilization. In the sub-continent, for example, caste, religion and colour interact to generate a mosaic of communities. Tamil-speaking Hindus and Moslems may unite in one context against 'Aryan' domination, while fracturing in others (Béteille, 1971).

There may, also, often be uncertainty over how groups do fit together in larger aggregations – allowing for further collective manipulation. Macedonians have shifted between seeing themselves as Serbs, and as Bulgarians; Silesians similarly have alternated between Polish and German identity, in attempts to align with the entity which is currently dominant at the higher level. The vagaries of history – as when sudden political splits impose arbitrary divisions, like in Korea or postwar Germany – prevent clear and unambiguous pyramids of identity developing along any particular dimension.

There are many complications. But the basic problem is that all dimensions of group membership are subject to the logic of relativity. This inherent fluidity is a potent source of difficulty in implementing communalist values. In the last analysis, these values are able to define as moral any individual who is judged by others, at any level of collective mobilization, to be responsive to their claims, and to be seeking his own satisfactions through participation in their joint endeavours. But these values are in themselves impotent to determine at which level they should operate. So they contain an awkward tendency to undermine the very groupings in which they are applied.

Within any framework of communal loyalties, it is always the smaller and more intimate groups in which the most compelling mutualist claims can be made. The moral universe of a collectivist consists, in the final analysis, of concentric circles of ever-widening, ever-weakening commitments. The only irreducible loyalty is to oneself. Communal identities form an extension of egoism. This works outwards through social bonds which, by acknowledgment of multiple interdependence and indebtedness, mediate between oneself and an increasingly hostile outer world.

A fraternalist claim to inclusion or redistribution within a particular group can always be denied by retreat to a lower level, more exclusive identity. At whatever level we call ourselves brothers, some of us are inescapably closer, and share more interests, than others. There is no way of resisting the logic of this. You cannot help everyone equally. You have to start, and stop, somewhere (Worsley, 1967, pp. 78–82).

Certain levels of group consciousness need to be invested with special significance from a source *outside* the communalist dimension of morality. Otherwise any exercise of fraternal claims is liable to cause communities to fracture into ever smaller and more exclusive units. Ultimately the delicate fabric of mutuality is stripped away altogether, to expose the vulnerable egoisms at its heart. Charity begins and ends at home.

This fractious aspect of communalism renders it inappropriate as a governing ideology in a complex society. It possesses little power to bind groups together. Paradoxically the self-seeking encouraged by individualism is in some ways less disruptive of group organization. Individualism shows people they can avoid particular moral claims on themselves by confessing a stronger attachment to the higher and more inclusive community of all humanity. By doing so, it gives their selfishness a potentially unifying and constructive form. The avoidance of unwelcome claims is turned into a virtue. In contrast the only escape-routes to such claims that fraternalism itself can offer are exclusive and inward-looking. They lead towards the erosion and denial of all group ties.

So communalism can never operate entirely by itself. In very simple societies with rudimentary political articulation, segmentary loyalties turning on relativistic moralities play a more prominent part in organizing public affairs. Even here, though, other principles, such as rules of exogamy encouraging intermarriage between communities which are structurally distant and potentially hostile, are always to some extent present as countervailing forces. These help to set a wider conception of an over-arching common good, and to stabilize the major effective focus of group feeling at an appropriate level of identity.

As societies become more complex, and state-systems develop, frequency of contact ceases to be so related to closeness of relationship. Strangers have to be dealt with all the time. Inter-group relations cannot therefore be governed by relativistic morality.

Public values have accordingly become increasingly reoriented around universalist notions of an impartial rule of law. The transition from feudal to modern régimes marks an important watershed in this process. It has seen particularistic behaviours largely outlawed in the public domain. In so far as liberal *élites* have been obliged to allow fraternalist claims from the masses, this has necessarily taken place in a roundabout and discreet manner.

The licensing of nationalism

Liberals cannot stomach fraternalist propositions in a pure form. What they may be prepared to do, however, is swallow a sugared pill, by allowing a role to nations in the building of the new humanist social order.

The first humanists to form governments soon appreciated that a society of all mankind could not be created at a stroke. Many felt that the best way to work towards it was by fastening onto established political groupings that seemed likely to help to move towards it. Historical nations could qualify here, in spite of exclusiveness in their past behaviour. Many already possessed state machines and institutions waiting to be commandeered in the name of progress. Some of these could be shown, by virtue of their current interests, to be in a natural vanguard position for championing the new world system.

This was the context in which fathers of nationalist thought like Mazzini emerged. Many were fundamentally liberal thinkers, who viewed the world as potentially a single community. But they also saw the need for a transitional, trustee role for national groupings, in effectively bringing this about.

This concession was crucial. By focusing on the nation, it set a level of group identity and mobilization that humanist *élites* and fraternalist masses could agree, from their different perspectives, in giving some special validity to. Once the nation had become accepted as an appropriate vehicle for promoting universal human rights – both internally through the fostering of democratic citizenship, and externally as supporter of good causes in the world at large – then the way was open for a more favourable interpretation of communalist demands originating among the national masses.

The granting of conditional validity to national solidarity made it possible for state *élites* to give some official sanction to popular communalism. It also gave the masses themselves a definite level of collective identity at which to pitch their main allegiance – on an implicit understanding that communal claims lodged at this level would be rewarded.

Right from the outset the new bourgeois régimes showed a readiness to adopt the nation – that segment of humanity over which they already exercised some actual control – as a useful vehicle. Whatever its imperfections, in a still divided world, it seemed the most likely instrument to assist in the implementation of humanist ideals. The rationale was that as these values proved their efficacy, and nations wedded to them spread the example, a truly universal identity would come into being. Intervening loyalties like that of the nation itself would gradually fade away.

In the meantime, the nation dedicated to individual rights would remain an indispensable adjunct to those rights. One of the most crucial of all individual liberties has been, accordingly, the right to have a nationality. It is through this that the free citizen can share democratically in the control and protection of all other rights.

This was proposed in the American Declaration of Independence, then affirmed decisively in the French Declaration of the Rights of Man. It has been periodically reaffirmed since, from the 1848 German Declaration of Rights, through to the U.N. Charter in the mid-twentieth century.

The progressive nationalist formula is not entirely satisfactory. Most conventional liberals are happy enough to tolerate 'the nation' so long as it is bound in an instrumental role, as trustee to humanity. Having assigned it to an inferior place in their own scheme of things, as servant to a higher cause, they are then content to let it alone to get on with its tasks.

This conception of the relationship, however, is fraught with problems for more anxious, philosophical souls. The worry is that once you have decided to work through the nation, then you are putting human rights at the mercy of forces of a very different hue. Humanist morality is officially supreme in modern society. Furtherance of human rights is the final touchstone in public morality and the ultimate source of political legitimacy. But if pursuance of humanist goals is entrusted to nations, these then have to be granted proximate legitimacy in order to get on with the job. Paradoxically, enemies of freedom may end up being given a very elastic licence by it.

The rights of nations are conceived initially by humanists as attaching to groups of free citizens. These can, however, shade under doctrines of necessity into the rights of nations *per se*. It is important to ensure the survival of those states committed to upholding humanist values. They need some power in order to discharge their higher obligations. But they may come to demand temporal precedence over the nominally superior freedoms of their individual members. The instrument that is strong enough to be effective may usurp control. Herein lies one of the most fundamental dilemmas of liberal conscience. It is the point of departure for any number of obsessive intellectual expeditions to chart the frontiers between nice nationalisms and nasty ones.

This brings us back to consensualist theories. The best way for progressive thinkers to allay the anxieties raised by the accommodation with nationalism lies in concocting accounts which play down the strength and autonomy of the forces they have compromised themselves with. Communalism that appears to dance to libertarian tunes creates few ideological dilemmas. Theoreticians are unlikely to meet much resistance in this. The concealment of the force of communalism is something which sophisticated nationalists are happy to go along with, for reasons of their own.

COMMUNALISM AND CLASS

There are two main procedures for giving a universalist gloss to fraternal collectivist action. All consensualists use the first. Quite a few go on to the second.

The first consists of emphasizing the inclusive aspects of group mobilization. Actions of a particular community are phrased, following Mazzini, as the first rumblings in an outbreak of fraternal solidarity that will spread to all of humanity and reshape the whole world. This treatment can be given both to the 'liberative' expansion of a powerful nation – like revolutionary France – or to the reactive nationalism of a bottled up minority. For example, French Canadians resisting anglophone domination like to present themselves as chipping away at the foundations of a global imperialism. Their victory will be an inspiration to all other submerged nations, and provide them with an important ally.

Such movements are dependent for their progressive credibility on this inclusive complexion. If their exclusive side becomes exposed they are in trouble. Trudeau's rebuttal of Lévesque (see chapter 3) drew everyone's attention to French Canadians' own chauvinist tendencies. It implied that if Quebec ever became an autonomous state they would be equally oppressive themselves. This revelation badly punctured the separatists' universalist pretensions.

The further layer of disguise is achieved by aligning these inclusive tendencies of collective mobilization with the class axis of solidarity. The root source of fraternal sentiments is held to be shared position in the division of productive labour. This renders collectivist actions even more reconcilable with libertarian precepts and makes their exclusivity even harder to detect.

All accounts using these devices turn their backs on the particularistic character of group solidarities. By doing so they ignore vast areas of collective behaviour. In particular, they neglect what is surely one of the commonest of available collectivist strategies in the modern world – i.e. the mobilization of a dominant national community, defining itself along ethnic or tribal lines, in order to exercise monopolistic control over a national state apparatus (Parkin, 1979, ch. 3). This surely is the very essence of successful fraternal action. But it is not often considered as such.

Communalism of this sort would in fact appear to be a much better medium for practising fraternalist morality than is class. The lower orders in a national majority can expect immediate and definite material rewards from a communalist alliance with their political masters.

The main consideration here is that the majority masses do actually have at their disposal something that the *élite* wants, and which they can trade for special privileges and treatment. That is political acquiescence. The political *élite* needs a popular mandate. The majority masses desire material security and benefits. A real exchange is possible. Here is a good foundation for exercising fraternal solidarity.

The operation of this is evident in democratic politics, where the masses can confer their nationalist legitimacy on *élites* through their votes. Electoral support steers the political class into communalist policies. A national *élite*, including some individuals who may not themselves belong to the majority community, is thereby co-opted by the electorate into a tacit alliance against minorities and the hostile outside world.

None of this applies to the class version of fraternal action. The masses, when conceived as a working class, lose their fraternal foothold in the existing state. On the contrary, everything still has to be fought for. Ruling *élites* are enemies, not brothers. Deals with them are treachery. Before any morally acceptable redistribution can take place, the state – perhaps, in principle, all states – must be captured and recast in new moulds.

The returns on class action are therefore very speculative. It all requires great acts of faith. Can you be sure that revolution is feasible?

Proletarian uprisings in the past have resulted in the formation of new *élites*, resting on new divisions of labour. How do you know that the changes in human nature that socialism predicts and requires will actually take place? It is a tremendous gamble. Maybe it is better just to settle for a nationalist alliance within the existing system. At least this is likely to work. It does not require any conscious planning – just a modicum of fraternal collusion with those already in positions of power.

Class action might be worthwhile if you could be really convinced of class solidarity. No great changes are possible without it. In the nineteenth century many believed that better-off workers did have genuine common interests with the worse-off. Without solidarity, the immiseration thesis argued, the artisans and aristocracy of labour would find their own circumstances reduced. But this has not happened. Differentials have survived, even sharpened. The prospects for true solidarity were never very good. Now few in the workforce take them seriously.

The rhetoric of class action lays great store by solidarity. But it is not very evident in actual behaviour. Class fraternalism, although its organizers dare not admit it, is subject to the segmentary and relativist logic governing all group-based strategies. Real material interests tend to unite small segments much more powerfully than large. As you move higher up the pyramid of mobilization, so fraternal solidarity becomes increasingly just an earnest aspiration.

Within a framework of class identity, material interests tend to activate the closure of groups in a position to operate a monopoly, rather than to promote wider unity. Workers who find themselves strongly placed in the market show little inclination to support weaker brethren. Identity of productive role does not entail identity of interests. Those selling the same services are competitors as much as colleagues. Solidarity can provide some insurance against set-backs in the future. But beyond that the call for it is experienced by better-off workers chiefly as a moral demand – by which they are not moved very far. It is no coincidence that union branches are often known as chapels. The class-in-itself is still light years and many prayers away from becoming a class-for-itself.

Class action and popular nationalism

So class fraternalism cannot compete with that operating along a communal axis. The strong members of a communal fraternity, that is members of a national *élite*, have a real interest in looking after the weak. Consequently the weak – the masses – have every incentive to exercise their fraternal claims in this dimension, rather than that of class.

Such an alliance within a national majority does of course have class aspects. In particular it gives an *élite* a means of securing class privileges for themselves, by diverting the ethnocentric masses away from class revolt. However, for these masses themselves it is the communalist content and nature of the alliance which makes it worthwhile. Exclusivity increases the benefits available for sharing out. The broader the fraternity, the thinner the pay-offs. Majority consciousness tends to delineate groupings large enough to be dominant, but small enough to enjoy profitable returns.

This behaviour does not follow the rules of class. However, within the confines of a national state, the pressure put on an *élite* by the dominant masses may look extremely like class action. Any accommodation reached is liable to be interpreted by those who can only see things in terms of class as a reformist deal with the bourgeois masters, settling for some concessions here and now rather than holding to a truly revolutionary course. The trade-offs arrived at may be portrayed as embodying 'truce values' (Rex and Tomlinson, 1979) relaxing what is essentially a class war.

What this presentation fails to give due attention to is the positively ethnocentric spirit articulating the cross-class deal. There is, of course, every advantage for all those party to a nationalist compact in conceptualizing the masses' demands as an expression of class struggle. This is a useful myth to cultivate, attracting universalist virtue for everyone involved. But analytically it confuses lines and principles of mobilization. No labourist pacts would be reached without implicit understandings that One Nation – for which read the controlling majority – comes first. In no way do they promote an internationalist unfolding of humanity. The compacts which make liberal democracies viable are narrowly communalist in spirit, and exclusivist in operation. This is the antithesis of true class action.

In reality the only occasion when the class aspect of mobilization becomes dominant for the majority masses, is when a national *élite* betrays them in the communal dimension. Popular fraternalism shifts into the class dimension when an *élite* fails to respond to calls for patriotism, and allows itself instead to become the instrument of alien imperialism. The socialist revolutions that have occurred in places like

China, Cuba, Algeria and so on represent the withdrawal of nationalist legitimacy from establishments collaborating with foreign powers – respectively Japan, the US, and France. If Mrs Thatcher sells off many more British assets to American stags she may yet save the Labour Party, and even Clause Four.

Even in these circumstances the nationalist side of popular fraternalism remains strong. Members of the erstwhile ruling class who line up against the colonizers are allowed to participate in revolution. Indeed, they usually end up playing leading roles in it. So whether a nationalist compact holds, or temporarily fails, the *élite* stays governed by popular communalism.

Thus the optimal fraternal strategy in modern societies is for the masses to use their weight of numbers to impose a nationalist pact on their betters – while allowing the values held by these betters to impart a universalist appearance to it. Everywhere from France to Fiji the ethnic groups with the political muscle to control a state machine use it to turn themselves into an aristocracy of labour (Lepervanche, 1977).

The constructive ambiguity of progressive nationalism

The idea that nations can serve as instruments for the creation of a new humanist world order is replete with ambiguity. This is the key to its success. It is not a unitary doctrine. It represents more of an interpenetration of ideologies, which permits the relative importance of the contrasting principles it embodies to remain unclear. Hardline advocates of either persuasion can see their own position as the commanding one.

Synthesis of values opens the way to a qualified approval of nationalism by humanists. This is essential to their ability to hold onto faith in a world where communalism is so pervasive. Liberal accounts of modern states give a voluntarist interpretation of it. Groups and group loyalties are accorded conditional legitimacy, as task forces for building the new Jerusalem. As long as nationalisms can be regarded plausibly as steps towards a wider union of peoples, humanist ideals can survive.

This perspective, however, expresses only the aspirations and direct interests of small, privileged *élites*. It is not adequate to secure a general acceptance of humanism, and its long-term retention as the central theme in national creeds and constitutions. Broader endorsement is dependent on a communalist interpretation of universalism. In this, humanist precepts proclaimed by political *élites* are regarded as having the instrumental role – as smokescreens for nationalist enterprises. Such viewpoints are not aired officially. This would be self-defeating. But they are the key to a proper understanding of the nationalist compacts made within majority communities.

For communalists, paying lip service to universal goals is effectively a means of cementing a communal alliance with the *élite*. By acknowledging the superiority of the official creed, they are submitting to humanist leadership, and at the same time helping the *élite* to keep up appearances in the international arena. This makes it easier for that *élite* to participate in a fraternal appropriation of state resources.

The *élite* indicates its acceptance of membership of this 'national' community by actively using its offices to promote that group's sectional fortunes, and to sanctify them with a humanist cover. Only if it does this will the masses extend nationalist legitimacy, and cross-class co-operation, to it. As the willingness of liberal régimes to compromise themselves in this way with popular collectivism became demonstrated, the industrial masses lost their revolutionary momentum, and became safely incorporated to a patriotic and docile role in the state.

It is important to notice that neither component of progressive nationalism is politically viable by itself. Communalist principles giving ordinary citizens security could not operate alone. They need the cover and moderating influence of humanism for their effective realization. But equally, and to a degree which seriously undermines official accounts of their status, ruling liberal mandates are dependent for their own success on communalist usage. It is this reliance on nationalist applications and vetting which is so understated in conventional accounts of the emergence of the liberal system. The worriers in humanist ranks were right all along.

Nationalist foundations of the humanist world order

It is not contentious to observe that the adoption of humanist creeds owes a good deal to a confluence of its vision with the needs of ascendant groupings. Most people would agree with it to some extent. But such admissions are generally kept within consensualist bounds by phrasing the matter in terms of class. Even where nations are regarded as corporate actors in the drama, as in Wallerstein's analyses, they are not treated as autonomous entities pursuing their own interests, so much as passive vessels for the impersonal forces of Capital.

Many authorities are eager to show how rising *élites* grasped at the ideas of the enlightenment to promote their own positions. But they fail to examine how these class interests have themselves been underlain by, and have served the interests of, ascendant nations. This is an important omission. The greatest significance of humanist values in mediating shifts of power surely lies at the international level. There, their ability to inform a secular system of supra-national morality was crucial in restructuring the polity of nations. It was the key factor in wresting the centre of power away from the Catholic states at the heart of the feudal order.

Throughout the later middle ages, the mainly Protestant nations on the north Atlantic seaboard had been gradually increasing their global influence, through the promotion of trade and manufacturing. But they remained ideologically bound by codes emanating from Catholic neighbours to the south and east. This held them back from converting this influence into dominion and hegemony. Growing northern power had opened up some discrepancy in the international system between the capacity of states to stand up for established principles, and their own advantages in doing so. But there was no acceptable alternative ideology for regulating conduct between nations. So it was a gap the feudal states might reasonably hope to contain.

Doctrines of natural human rights and the democratic 'general will' helped to unblock the path of the rising northern powers. They provided just such a new philosophy around which they could adjust and re-balance the international order in their own favour. Assertion of the primacy of individual rights, as a principle setting objectives above the state itself, and on the pursuit of which a state's own legitimacy could be held to depend, offered a new yardstick for national behaviour. In absolute terms it was no less universal than existing conventions of Divine ordination. It was, therefore, every bit as good a basis for co-operation within a community of nations. From the point of view of the new Protestant powers, however, it had a supreme advantage. It did all these things in an idiom of mutual vigilance and intervention on behalf of individual freedoms. This was heavily loaded against feudal régimes. As such it constituted a highly convenient vehicle for grasping the guardianship of world order.

With the benefit of historical hindsight, it is not difficult to discern the shift in emphasis from Divine Right to the Rights of Man as facilitating a broad transfer of hegemony to the Protestant North. This perhaps completed the work of the Reformation, by enabling these nations to define for themselves the grounds on which they were prepared to engage in force.

This process is not accorded much prominence in popular consciousness of the emergence of the modern world. Most people seem only aware of the transfers of power between *élites* inside particular states, through which it was itself affected. In part this is no doubt because, as such a drawn out affair, it is less tangible and dramatic. But more pertinently, I think, it is because it is not so consistent with the new ruling ideology of humanism itself. Post-feudal *élites*, whether actually holding political power or not, have had a stake in representing themselves as above traditional nationalism. On the whole they prefer to collude in ignoring the nationalist dynamic underlying historical movements.

In so far as popular accounts point to certain groups having used enlightenment values to invest their own private ventures with progressive legitimacy, this is done, as we have seen, in class terms, with the third estate indicated as culprits. This judgment is fair as far as it goes. The bourgeoisie undoubtedly did succeed in putting humanist ideas to work for class purposes. But what this line of reasoning plays down is that these groups, at any rate in those rising states pioneering the adoption of humanism, were only in a position to do this because they were genuine 'national' classes. Their interests were widely felt to coincide with those of the national community as a whole.

It was certainly the commercial classes who found the legal restrictions of feudalism most irksome, and who all along provided much of the impetus for the humanist alternative. But trade was making a growing contribution to national power and prosperity. This meant that they were not operating simply in their class interest in identifying themselves as leading servants of the common weal. They were actually instrumental in securing collective advantages for the states in which they sought domestic authority.

This national role is obscured, in part, because from the earliest days a universalist image was useful to them. The true basis of their claim to *élite* status was mercantilist. But humbug had a contribution to make even then. The cosmopolitan dimension of their activities and personal interests meant that they were better placed than other powerful groups, like the landed classes, to avoid narrow identification with local communities. They could, without undue contradiction, transcend old nationalism. This enabled them to place the states they represented in the vanguard of the movement building the new internationalist Jerusalem.

It was their appearance as a new 'world class' that allowed bourgeois *élites* to mobilize their nations behind them in the displacement of feudal establishments. No other groups could put together such strong combinations of nationalist and internationalist political credentials. As the old guards lost their grip under the challenge of natural rights, it was the bourgeoisie who were assembling in the wings to take over leadership. A tentative start was made with the Restoration Settlement and Bill of Rights in England. Later, advantage was taken of revolution in America and France to secure more decisive break-throughs. The bourgeoisie in the most commercially advanced nations rode on a tide of anti-feudal sentiment, to break their way into political establishments.

They lost no time in finding ways of enhancing their private interests at the same time. This set off new class conflicts within the humanist movement itself. But it is a mistake again to become too preoccupied with the class aspect of this. The entrenchment of *élite* privileges by the bourgeoisie was more than just of domestic significance. It was only possible at all in the context of their successful representation of national interests on the world stage. It is even arguable that the class opposition that the bourgeoisie generated was itself helpful at the international level. It occasioned a massive shift of political debate into humanist territory. This was a key factor in establishing the new social order, through which the broad transfer of hegemony to the ascendant nations was achieved.

The political success of the French bourgeoisie revealed the capacity of humanist values to serve élitist purposes. As a result the revolutionary current of the enlightenment became divided. Humanists not sharing in the spoils of office were quick to point to the continuation of social inequality. They accused those co-opted to government of allying themselves with remnants of the old régime, and of using the state machine, through such devices as the retention of private property, to promote their sectional interests.

A few of these critics took the anarchist road of concluding that the state itself was indefensible. But the majority chose the opposite line. They held that full self-realization of the individual was in fact only feasible within a stronger state, dedicated to substantive equality for its citizens, and prepared to use public force to uphold this. Without a base of guaranteed material equality, formal individual rights were a worthless charade.

This division of the movement into liberal and socialist camps did not weaken its challenge to feudalism. More likely it reinforced the political hand of the liberals. For its result was to project them into the centre. While their main rivals struggled to formulate a more complex, and paradoxical, statist variant of humanism, liberals were able to define themselves as champions of the true libertarian core of the enlightenment. They responded to clamourings for a more centralized state with the contention that genuinely universal freedoms were in fact maximized by keeping some independence of civil society from political control. The Jacobin terror of 1793 armed them with an example of the dangers of ostensibly benevolent centralism. They argued that freedom was necessarily more fundamental than equality. The only type of equality consistent with responsible citizenship was that of the opportunity to improve oneself in the service of humanity.

In this way a characteristically liberal version of the open society was forged. It proposed that people must be as free as possible to decide for themselves just how they might serve the community. This doctrine proved most expedient to the bourgeoisie, helping them to secure their position at both national and international levels. The strong insistence on freedom of the individual enabled them to map out a middle and moderating course between feudal and revolutionary elements, both in their home nations and in the world scene. As owners of productive resources, the bourgeoisie had much in common with traditional agrarian interests. Although spurning explicit conservatism, they were reliable allies in the name of property rights when it came to putting down jacquerie. At the same time they shared with the emerging industrial masses a hostility to feudal authoritarianism, and could offer a universalistic and socially inclusive alternative to it.

By being able to balance out pressures from extreme forces on either side, liberals quickly took command of the strategic central ground, exemplified in Britain by Palmerstonian constitutional monarchy. This position allowed them to exercise a large measure of political leadership even before capturing decisive control of the state machinery, or acquiring ascendancy in civil society.

This liberal emphasis on the individual has been the lynch-pin in maintaining a secular international morality and order. Following the Congress of Vienna, governments sympathetic to liberal morality moved into a central and balancing role in European national affairs and co-operated in rebuilding the international system in their own favour. Success in using humanist terms to promote national power, and boost national prestige, was critical for securing Liberal rule in Britain. In turn, the effectiveness of liberal slogans in concealing these nationalist aims eased the process of laying them down as new core values for national political legitimation.

As the centre of gravity in political discourse settled down decisively inside the humanist domain, the way was paved for the emergence of non-liberal adaptations of humanist terms. The most important of them are by socialist governments. These draw on statist humanism to express their opposition to dominant liberal powers in the world system. There are many problems with 'socialist humanism' – which I touch on in chapter 12. These make it inappropriate as a hegemonic ideology.

The key to the viability of the modern world system as a whole still seems to be the fundamental liberal attachment to the supremacy of individual rights. This is the version of humanism which carries greatest conviction in foreswearing particularist intentions. It is necessarily the one adopted by those states seriously aspiring to play the role of policeman to the rest of humanity.

The moderating role of humanist codes

Concern for human rights appears to govern the workings of the modern world system. But it is the interests of nations dominating the system that have guided the formulation of this ruling ideology itself. Universalist creeds rest on nationalist ambitions.

This is no less true of those elements of humanist thinking which condemn nationalism and give specific attention to the needs of minorities. These seem especially amenable to influence by national strategic considerations. Consequently they serve as agents for the very thing which they repudiate. The ways in which anti-imperialist doctrines phrase the rights of submerged communities to liberation are themselves supportive of the supreme imperial powers of the moment. This is elaborated on in the next chapter.

Before going into this, I should make it clear that I am not arguing that humanist ideas are impotent. Universalist ideology is an essential ingredient in any system. The point is, I think, that it only plays a qualifying, not a controlling role. Moral crusades are not likely to achieve their declared aims. But they still serve to direct communalist force into integrative activities.

The power of communalism

The partisan use of humanist prescriptions helps to stabilize the international system by providing goals through which the possessors of force can to some extent actually harmonize their own interests with those of humanity as a whole. Moral values are exploited by the powerful in their quest for dominion. But the successful exercise of power is to some degree dependent on, and hence can be moderated by, the higher values it claims to be serving.

Great powers can generally get support for those definitions of international morality which best suit their own circumstances. They may occasionally override such etiquettes altogether by reference to the need to retain a balance of power – applying the doctrine of necessity, or instrumental priority, at the international level. They are protectors of the world order. So they may with some justice define their own national security as being globally important.

However, if the partiality of all this becomes too blatant, openings are provided for rival powers to mobilize opinion against them within the community of nations. Their claim to moral leadership can be forfeited. Contests for world domination which are channelled into defence of universal values become partially constrained by the logic of the ideologies they call on.

Provided that the values appealed to have integrative implications or potentialities, which has probably been the case with concern for human rights and those specifically of oppressed minorities, then even a self-serving, nationalistic subversion of them may in the last analysis have universalizing consequences. Communalist usage gives libertarian values a home they might not otherwise find. Then, of necessity, communalism is itself tamed and harnessed by the clothes it has chosen to dress up in.

CHAPTER 11
MINORITY RIGHTS AND NATIONAL STRATEGIES

At the international level, communalism is often hidden beneath a veneer of concern for oppressed groups. Appeals are ostensibly made to 'minority rights'. This championing of the weak is supposed to operate as a check on the behaviour of nationalistic majorities. But more often it adds a further item to the armouries of the most successful among them.

The minority rights weapon
The evolution of democratic government carries a clear promise of the emancipation of oppressed communities, through the removal of legal impediments and admission to full citizenship in the modernized nation. But the package of formal rights granted is no guarantee of equal participation in national affairs. So it has not been difficult to conclude that a generalized pursuit of human rights may not be the most effective way of securing the rights of the members of minority groups.

As humanist states have multiplied, there has accordingly grown up within the general edifice of enlightened speculation a division of thought devoted specifically to exploring the failure of governments to assure minorities of their natural rights, and with devising redress and remedies for this. This area of inquiry exists as a critical mirroring of the basic doctrines of progressive nationalism. The main body of theory attempts to set up criteria whereby a nation can assert its stewardship on behalf of human rights. These critiques deploy the same terms to set limits to such claims. Hence the various formulae adduced by minority rights analysts display the same range of constructions as found in the generative principles of progressive nationalism itself. At the libertarian pole of emphasis, we find calls for the enforcement and reaffirmation of personal rights which are reluctant to accord any meaning to the idea of minority group as such, beyond serving as a short-hand term for identifying categories of individuals likely to share some experience of deprivation. At the opposite end of the spectrum there are demands for the granting of corporate rights of self-control and determination to self-conscious groups. These express a virtual moral equivalence of minorities with sovereign nations.

Between these poles are found a host of mixed or looser presentations, which conceive national minorities partly as entities in themselves, and partly as abstract concepts to be used pragmatically in directing special assistance to the most underprivileged citizens.

What unites these various proposals is that all have a very different political value and application from the positions they mirror. Minority rights provisions are reserve principles. They are only to be called on when the chances of achieving equal rights through existing constitutional machinery seem poor.

Liberals only accept the granting of special attention to the needs of certain categories of citizens in the short term. Beyond this it poses a threat to the overriding goal of individual freedom. In the same way, at the other end of the spectrum, notions about the collective right of minorities to self-determination define only second-string corporate identities. These may only be invoked when the trusteeship of an existing nation has clearly failed them. To give the self-determination principle any greater weight than this is to open Pandora's box and discover an artifice derogatory of the sovereignty of all nations – including those set up through the secession of disgruntled minorities.

This secondary or reserve aspect of minority rights formulations is extremely significant. It gives them a distinctly aggressive potential. They are principles qualifying rather than establishing claims to sovereignty, moral considerations rather than codifiable legal entitlements. They have an in-built uncertainty of application. So they can only with great difficulty be organized into a constructive commentary on the performance of a régime.

Their main thrust is always towards sowing doubts about whether an existing nation has the necessary institutions, or exists at the right level of communal identity, to be sanctified by the approval of its peer nations as an authentic instrument of natural rights for its citizens. The rights of minorities may be considered inferior to those of a progressive nation. They are, however, superior to those of a regressive one. Sustained attention to them serves as a clear condemnation of host states. As such it is a potent means of unsettling them. It encourages fifth columns within and it weakens the rationale for non-inter-ference in their affairs by other states.

All this furnishes powerful states with a convenient idiom for chas-tizing their weaker neighbours and protégés. Churchillian maxims setting the treatment of minorities as the test of true civilization serve as preludes to a humanist declaration of Holy War. The transition to a secular code of international morality has created a whole new genre of nationalistic historiography. Alleged injustices to minorities have become the major reason cited in the modern world both by aggressors for their build up to war, and by victors explaining their punitive carve-up of conquered territories.

Great care is needed in the use of this minority rights weapon. It is double-edged and capable of inflicting serious self-injury. In practice what determines where and how it is exercised is the relative power of the states involved. But there is always some danger of it being turned back on its wielder unless its application is carefully phrased to limit its reference. Accordingly, during the period in which fur-therance of minority rights has been admissible as an account of international behaviour, the precise terms in which this is presented, and the academic tablets paraded in their defence, have undergone a number of significant mutations. These reflect shifts in dominance in world affairs between different states, who have put their weight behind versions suiting their own foreign policy requirements.

Changing rules in the great game

There have been four main stages in the use of the minority rights weapon. In each of them the prevailing definition of the concept has reflected the distinctive strategic interests of the dominant powers of the time. The first of these opens at the end of the eighteenth century, with the pioneering use of humanist dicta by the French to dress up their imperial adventures. It continues with Britain's borrowing of the idiom to impart a humanitarian guise to its own growing economic empire. In these early days it was possible to take a utopian line, in which the collective rights of national minorities did not appear to need separate consideration from individual human rights in general. The enlightened mission of the leading nation was not seriously opposed by similar claims from others. All natural rights could be encompassed within a single and undivided formula.

This utopian era was followed by a longish phase from the middle of the nineteenth century to the first world war. During this period ever more régimes found it expedient to appeal to humanist precepts for their legitimation. Consequently arguments were required for blocking the progressive claims of competing nationalisms. It was during this stage that explicit consideration of 'minority rights' and tactical calls for the self-determination of definable minorities moved into increasing salience. Theories and positions relating to group rights proliferated near the end of this period. This was a measure of Britain's growing inability to hold a balance of power around its own universalizing programme.

The third and fourth periods, from Versailles to the second world war, and from Yalta to the present, mark stages in the rise of the United States. Between the wars this emerging superpower used the machinery of the League of Nations to impose on Europe a formalized implementation of the rights of internal minorities. This broke all but one of the remaining continental empires there. It also had the effect of creating a burden of local vigilance for America's liberal competitors. The US in the meantime was free from the military abstinence imposed on its allies, and was able to build up its power in the rest of the world at their expense.

The minority guarantees ended in fiasco for Europe. They were succeeded after the second world war by a switch of American attention to the rights of colonial minorities. Both America and Russia had rediscovered problems of their own with internal minorities. They were, therefore, able to co-operate in setting up the United Nations as a replacement, with revamped objectives, for the ill-fated League. The way forward in the United Nations was defined as requiring above all an attack on overseas imperialism. This has been an important factor in discrediting any lingering French and British claims to a significant share with the US in the task of policing the world. It has helped to bring America's European allies into vassal status on her.

THE UTOPIAN PERIOD

Some time elapsed after the first humanist democracy emerged, before the development of arguments specifically concerned with the rights of ethnic minorities inside such states. As long as progressive nationalism was opposed only to autocratic systems, there was little occasion to consider its own inherent limitations or contradictions. For nearly the first quarter of a century of its use as a diplomatic weapon, humanism was a rebel doctrine, seriously advocated by a single major power. After that its most powerful exponent for the rest of the nineteenth century was a state open to little opposition in humanist terms. The new values were called on to justify action on behalf of minorities in other states. But there was no need to distinguish clearly and systematically between national, minority and purely individual emancipation.

We have to thank the French for taking the initiative in projecting a consensual secular morality, asserting the harmony of natural individual and group freedoms, into the international arena. Natural liberty as embodied in the English Bill of Rights was conceived as the right of a citizen against a particular Crown. This democratic principle was taken up during the eighteenth century by the independence movement in America, as the basis for claims to self-determination. But it remained limited in its application. Then patriotic French volunteers under Lafayette, seeking a charter for their attacks on a rival and ascendant empire, acted across national boundaries to give support to the colonies' claims. In doing so they gave birth to a new and all-embracing notion of liberty.

At first sight the French seem unlikely pioneers for the use of natural rights as a guiding principle in international relations. They lay, after all, within the Catholic fold of old Europe. However, they were on its exposed northern flank, and engaged in long-standing rivalry with the British. France contained powerful elements which, although not Protestant, were convinced that their own parasitic and Teutonic despotism was holding them back in the competition with the English. There were many in the community well disposed to champion secularism, if it could help them to leap-frog ahead of the British.

Success in using democratic principles externally in support of America encouraged forward-looking groups to deploy the same ideas for the undoing of their own autocracy and its feudal alliances. France became committed to a declaration of universal rights, and through this to a radical and trans-national version of human rights far in advance of the English position.

Through universalizing human rights, the French Revolution also universalized the French nation. She now became the self-chosen instrument of history, and found herself standing in the front line of attack on the old régime in the rest of Europe. Many French people, having read their Tom Paine, duly overestimated hostility to the Crown in Britain. They anticipated English help in disposing of their monarchy. But the Britain of Pitt saw no advantage in backing the rebel in the system. Formally it sided with Feudalism, so that all the other great powers ganged up against France. This isolation created some strategic problems for the French. But it meant that they were able to command a virtual monopoly of humanist virtue. So they enjoyed considerable licence in enlightened circles for defining their militarily expansionist response to encirclement as a crusade for the emancipation of all humanity.

They began with a pre-emptive strike in the name of democracy against the Austrian Empire, which was poised to attack France in support of Monarchy. Then they quickly set up a ring of puppet states – the so-called 'sister republics' – at the expense of autocratic neighbours, and to the arguable benefit of previously contained minorities. The isolation of France in its stand for an alternative world order imparted a messianic dimension to its own national adventures. Anti-clericalism, sovereignty of the people, and liberation of the world's downtrodden, all came together harmoniously in the unfolding vision of the heroic French nation, the First International nation, struggling to free the world from its own past (Carr 1968). Setbacks would soon occur to this mission. France was, however, assured as the focus of allegiance for the freest of spirits, and as sanctuary to revelatory sects and tractarian cabals, for at least the next generation.

The outward thrust of the new French Empire proved short-lived against the resistance of the allied monarchs. France was eventually contained by the Congress of Vienna. This sapped the unity of purpose on which the inclusive vision was dependent. At home, loss of communal glory alienated the masses. And the phenomenon of Bonapartism clouded the pure currents of democratic ideology. A traditionalist reaction ensued. Patriots asked whether the secular society was not after all an alien transplant, to be rejected by a healthy political body. Formerly sympathetic elements outside France began to ask how truly universal a movement tied to French fortunes could be. In the end the capacity of the new ideology to inform a new international system was thrown into some doubt.

Albion's hour

Outside France there were several groups willing to champion humanist values. Most, however, were not in a position to create a convincing and consensual focus for them. As France slipped into political instability, reformist movements in neighbouring states, which had previously tied their aspirations to French expansionism and sororal tutelage, now started to copy the French in a different way. They reacted against French domination and looked for alternative humanist programmes centred on their own nations. This process is epitomized in the careers of such liberals as Fichte, now mainly remembered as a father of modern German nationalism. In his youth Fichte had subscribed to a voluntarist cosmopolitanism. Idealists were deemed to owe allegiance to whichever nation – at the time France – seemed most able to grasp the helm and steer humanity out of darkness. But as he grew older he sensed the anomic emptiness of unbridled individualism, and saw the imperialist licence it gave to stronger nations expounding it. He therefore embarked on the romantic venture of patriotically discovering and fostering the progressive potential in his own fatherland. A generation of free spirits like him, particularly in Germany and Italy, reached middle age and gave priority to unifying and strengthening their own hereditary communities as the best means of moving towards a genuinely international order. The universal goal sought by democratic nationalism soon began to appear subordinate to the plurality of national instruments rising up to promote it.

This shift to competing versions of progressive nationalism was eventually to generate the debate about minority rights. For it stimulated doctrines for qualifying the claims of national adversaries. But this further stage of development might not have occurred at all, if the plurality of nationalist visions had been the only legacy of the French experiment. Tying the notion of progress explicitly to particular communities renders it a highly contentious concept – as the drift of European continental politics in the second half of the nineteenth century later showed. If there had not been a power in a position to carry forward the universal aspects of the French programme, and to secure the devotion to a higher cause that was required for upholding confidence in a world order, the new morality might have remained merely an oppositional, divisive and deviant idiom.

The individualistic and supra-national core of humanism was, however, exactly what Britain now needed to consolidate its claim to global hegemony. As the bogie of French domination subsided, Britain was able to become correspondingly more appreciative of the new ethic. It was widely revered among aspiring *élites* throughout Europe. Moreover, English radicals could patriotically claim to have fathered it anyway.

Without making any ostentatious proclamations, British governments modified their position. They detached themselves from the spirit of Vienna and took up a mediating role, between the feudalistic Quadruple Alliance and the Constitutional *bloc* in the West. This role, rationalized by the Palmerstonian conventions of constitutional monarchy, was to serve throughout the long summer of Victorian tranquillity as the basis for exercising the balance of power in Europe. From the 1830s onwards it was increasingly evident that it was the British after all who were the principal beneficiaries of the new morality. Indeed its very survival was intimately linked with its usefulness to British ruling *élites*. Following the Reform Act bringing her up to date constitutionally with France and America, Britain had settled down as the first truly stable liberal nation. Appeals to humanist values, both in domestic politics and foreign affairs, had the centralizing effect of maximizing support for governmental actions. They were, therefore, highly appropriate as a means of consolidating and expressing her dominant role.

This usage transformed humanism from a language of revolution, into one of hegemony. But this did not reduce the utopian quality of the vision. On the contrary, for a while it enhanced it. The French brand of universalism had been put together in relation to direct political expansion by the vanguard nation. It needed to give a specific endorsement to that nation's leading position. This was liable at any time to encounter resistance in other nations.

British universalism was different. It developed in connection with an economic empire, and was channelled into a Cobdenite philosophy of *laissez faire*. In this the metropolitical centre was barely visible as a corporate actor. So an untroubled, simplistic devotion to purely individual rights was easily sustained. Uttering Manchester School invocations, to exorcize the ghosts of reactive nationalism and to cast a fog over London's control of commodity markets and the Gold Standard, the British patrolled the high seas in pursuance of individual freedom and enterprise. They enlarged their own markets at the expense of rival empires like France and Spain. Meanwhile at an ideological level they peddled a de-mercantilized prospectus of affluence for all humanity, in which it really did seem for a while as if there might not have to be any losers.

This application proved much more successful than that of the French. A strong commitment to individual freedom created a climate highly favourable to the discreet extension of empire. Britain portrayed her own citizens as participants just like any others in a universal game governed by impersonal rules. In this way she was able to build up a gentlemanly image for sporting evenhandedness and proper regard for impartial law. This greatly inhibited resistance to the encroachments of her realm.

At the same time an unobtrusive notion of instrumentality became available in the background. Britain was the obvious centre of gravity in the free trade universe. She was, *de facto*, the leading internationalist power. As such she enjoyed some implicit licence to elevate national interests to universal significance, whenever the rule of impartiality might need to be waived.

Later in the nineteenth century, as Britain began to lose economic supremacy, this doctrine of necessity was filled out into a philosophy of liberal imperialism. But for as long as adherence to free trade served her dominion, Britain had a clear interest in assuming a detachment from the fierce debates about national rights which raged in Europe. Her continental rivals tied themselves up in interminable disputations over how to recognize the relative merits of competing nationalisms – a wrangling which gave renewed lease to some feudal monarchies eager to demonstrate their own capacity to reintegrate societies split by democratic fraternalism. Meanwhile Britain quietly exercised a balance of power by staying outside and above the issues.

This umpiring role naturally involved a good deal of siding with underdogs against bullies and overlords. Britain became the main champion of the weak in Europe, as well as refuge for its exiles. This started with Canning's objection in 1822 to the non-representation in Vienna of the smaller powers, and was confirmed in 1839 with ratification of Belgian independence. It was, however, conducted in a pragmatic way, and kept at a libertarian level of defending individuals' freedoms against tyranny. Little attention was paid to rules for determining the relative rights of national majorities and minorities in a general sense. Hence it did not make any challenge to the messianic conviction that nationalism, however troublesome it might be proving in its death throes, was a bankrupt idea whose force was very nearly spent.

VEHICLES IN COLLISION: 1848–1918

The Germans have never been national where the interests of nationality and the interests of progress coincided; they were always national where nationality came into conflict with progress.

(Friedrich Engels, quoted by Davis, 1967, p. 70)

And when the chosen people grew more strong,
The righteous cause at length became the wrong.

(John Dryden; Absalom and Achitophel)

The contradictions between individual and group self-determination remained latent and masked so long as only a few nations, opposed only to despotic régimes, embraced humanist values. But as these precepts became more widely adopted in the conduct of foreign relations, they inevitably began to lose their utopian aura. The more national vehicles there were on the same democratic road, the less room each had to manœuvre and move forward without coming into collision with others. Gradually all participants operating on that route felt the need to argue for inalienable and inherited franchises for carrying particular groups of passengers, in order to justify their claims on space and retain a licence to travel.

Concern with the specificities of national situations eventually came to outweigh and obscure the higher purposes of the journey for many. This did not happen overnight. Communities divided or oppressed by others can openly emphasize their special needs without necessarily forfeiting progressive legitimacy. All they must do is allow powerful states acting as arbiters of international morality to clientize them, by incorporating the fulfilment of their petty needs to the patron's own grand design. Leaders of minority and nationalist movements are usually prepared to subsume their emancipation to a higher vision put forward by a vanguard state. So long as they are, even exclusivist pronouncements among their supporters draw on the moral force exuding from that broader programme.

Such credentials are, however, conditional and restricting. They trap client groups into dependency for their legitimacy on a patron nation. This creates difficulties when formerly submerged communities become strong enough to realize their collective aims, and seek political independence. In order to detach themselves from the moral imperialism which has supported them in their struggles, they may feel impelled to throw overboard the universal values to which they have previously paid tribute. They then, like the Boers and Israelis in recent decades, face condemnation, as reactionary communalists and bullies, from their former allies.

The convulsions of 1848–9 signalled an important turning point in Europe in this respect. Appeals to humanist ideology became more frequent and successful. Divided nations and national minorities subject to feudal autocracies increasingly looked to it for support in destabilizing those despotisms under which they laboured. For a while nationalist agitators throughout the continent basked together in universalist virtue, in the presumption that their assorted causes would soon gell into a single revolution. But as independent national governments were set up, middle-class politicians found a role for themselves as brokers in forging nationalist alliances between patriotic masses and traditional ruling classes. Nationalist movements suddenly lost their internationalism.

Reformists discovered they were patriots first. Most were eager to secure a leading position in the new order for their own democratic nations. They were profoundly and mutually suspicious of the imperialist plots concealed beneath the universalist sloganizing of erstwhile foreign allies. The die was cast for a new phenomenon of democratic nationalism. Demands for individual self-determination yielded place to those for group rights. Movements successful in achieving some political autonomy subordinated libertarian ideals to the strengthening of their national instruments.

The German disaster

This process of entrapment in a more openly communalist development of humanism is clearly shown by the Germans. They had adopted liberalism relatively late. As a result they became steered, as newcomers, into a more exclusive definition of their interests. This seriously hindered their contention for international leadership, in spite of their economic and military might.

Germans had been wrong-footed by the French Revolution – and this perhaps was an element in the French design. The Austrian branch was identified by French radicalism as the main adversary, and heartland of reaction. It was, therefore, hardly in a position to espouse these values itself. Prussians might have been more inclined to respond favourably to the new philosophy. They were commercially more advanced and religiously liberated. But they were caught in cross-pressures and equivocal. Anyway they would probably have been unwilling to appear mere followers and imitators of French initiatives.

Early Liberal ventures among Germans succumbed rather easily. Not until humanism was becoming championed diplomatically by Britain did many of them seriously consider the advantages of phrasing their own collective interests in its terms. By this time they were too late. They had already become outsiders, seeking admission to a new order formulated in the interests of its pioneering advocates. They were aware that they could no longer afford to stay outside the system, but also fearful of incurring dependency on humanism's existing exponents and interpreters. Their labours consequently acquired from an early stage a protectionist and defensive quality.

Many German intellectuals at the turn of the century had been beguiled by French idealism into neglect of the German masses. Later on their over-literal endorsement of British *laissez faire* had exposed young German industry to economic penetration and clientization. So it was a central requirement of emerging German democratic nationalism that it allowed Germans to escape from these imperialist applications. They had to assert their own right to interpret the new moral order for themselves. This meant de-mythologizing French and British humbug, in order to demonstrate their own specific genius, embodied in German culture, for contributing to the development of democracy.

German revival and modernization thus took place around the idea of a beleaguered national community seeking democratic unity in order to express its true collective purpose. National consciousness was cumulatively sharpened by a succession of political and cultural impulses. The Hegelian notion of liberty realizing itself through the state prepared the way for prioritizing the instrument through which human rights were implemented. This then became invested by Herder with tribally specific signs of grace. Finally it was sanctified by Schmoller as resistance to the veiled mercantilism in *laissez faire*.

This communal reaction succeeded in mobilizing Germans to assert their collective identity and will. But the further that the realistic strand in German political thought intensified, and the shift took place – as in the historiography of von Treitschke, Ratzenhofer and Oppenheimer – towards openly indicating communalism as the real motive force in society, then the more that this mobilization itself became prey to the relativist, fractious tendencies inherent in this mode of consciousness. The quest for national unity led into a celebration of force and tribal exclusiveness. Engel's patriotic lament was not entirely pertinent to the early part of the nineteenth century. But it undoubtedly acquired validity during the hundred years following its delivery. What is more, the union that was achieved under Bismarck represented a precarious balancing of rivalrous fraternal calculations. This made it infinitely more fragile than 'western' national identities in which belief in a universalizing mission smothers communal speculation.

No amount of nationalist rhetoric could overcome the fact that pan-Germanic consciousness encompassed a major and self-wounding contest between different limbs of the Teutonic body. The shared concept of unification in reality carried quite different implications. For Prussians, democratic national unity was in part a device for replacing Austrians as the senior partners in the confraternal Bund. Prussia insisted on common culture as the proper basis for political community. This had the effect of putting the Hapsburg Empire on the spot. For by implication it threatened Prussian support for the right to self-determination of non-German elements of the imperial population.

It was in an attempt to escape from this fraternally-imposed quandary that Schwarzenberg was pushed into the unfortunate policy of forced acculturation for minorities. This did more than anything to impede Austrian bids to achieve liberal respectability. It provoked uprisings which – attracting verbal support from Palmerston – both weakened Austrian hold on empire, and helped renew western stereotypes about Teutonic bullies.

Western liberal powers exploited these internal difficulties to block German international advances. They refined the idea of liberalism in ways which accommodated their own overseas empires while condemning the continental variety available to Germans. Under the economic competition of renascent Germany and a rising America, even Britain was no longer able to remain quite so aloof from nationalist competitions. From the 1870s it was obliged to become noticeably more particularistic in the definition and defence of its own global programme. But the maritime and distant character of British Empire, as too of Dutch, French and the remaining Iberian possessions, made it easier to dress them up as liberating ventures. Their backward subjects were prisoners of ignorance, poverty and oppression in their own lands. They lacked modern science and government. All were such obvious beneficiaries of the colonial encounter, that their only chance of being seen as progressive themselves lay in submitting to junior partnership in humanity's great stride forwards.

No such dispensation was possible in Eastern Europe. There, neighbouring communities boxed in by their continental geography, and aroused by the appeals of secular nationalism, had only each other to impose their rule and values on. Bismarck, after unifying Germany under Prussian charge, found that he could keep his western flank safe by allowing western neighbours to indulge in their own progressive games of liberal imperialism. This freed him to concentrate in the East on the more urgent but less presentable task of containing the Slav pressure which pan-Germanism had itself helped to provoke. His choice, if any real choice existed, made it virtually impossible for Germany to compete in liberal terms. It contained her in a deviant role where she created little challenge to the moral supremacy of Britain. While western powers enjoyed a respite from continental wars in the last quarter of the century, playing competitive but not perilous roles overseas as stewards of human destiny, the eastern powers became ever more bogged down in zero-sum imperialism. The only way in which they could express their collective wills was through reciprocal conquest and subjugation.

In the East neighbouring peoples whose cultures were very much on a par resorted to social Darwinism in their attempts to justify bellicosity. These were no match for the Whig fairy tales about caucus races in which everyone is a winner. So in the final decades of the century the western nations piled up a monopoly of political virtue. Slavs and Germans, and those caught between, slugged it out in an escalation of communal consciousness and mutual accusations of minority oppression. Liberal nations in the West contrived meanwhile to appear domestically homogenous and individualistic. By successfully expanding overseas, they remained immune themselves to damage from the minority rights weapon.

This moral polarization might have been averted if Germany had been able to find a new universalist idiom for its dominance. As the revived nation failed to break into the western liberal club, many progressive Germans were turning in fact to an alternative humanism, socialism, in the quest for a programme at once patriotic and idealistic. Early socialist theories had been worked out in the embers of the French Empire. The First International still tended to assume France as the cockpit of progress. But as more nationalisms flowered the centre of attention moved. Marx himself came to see the Germans, in particular Prussia, as having a civilizing role against neighbouring nations. The main debates in the organization were increasingly between himself and Bakunin, who took an equally patriotic line of regarding the Slavs as the true bearers of the torch of progress, with Russia as the chosen centre of revolution, and Moscow the new Rome.

Collision of German with Slav

With the fall of Paris, and proclamation of the new German Empire, the First International dissolved. It was followed by a new one revolving around German fortunes, and dominated by the German Social Democrats whose definition of working-class internationalism clearly favoured Greater Prussian interests and expansion. But as I suggested in chapter four, in so far as the doctrines developing within socialism lent themselves to nationalistic usage, it was the Russians who actually had more to gain from this.

Late nineteenth century Germany was in an expansionary capitalist phase. It was unlikely to be able to produce a régime hostile to private property. Contemporary Russia, on the other hand, was a state in decline. It had gradually been losing its internal cohesion ever since the Decembrist revolt, and was vulnerable to German imperialism. After the 1860s the Russian establishment had shored up its crumbling feudal mandate by experimenting with the secular fraternalism of pan-Slavism. This stiffened resistance to German encroachments in central Europe, and was a handy device for interfering in the Ottoman empire. But it entailed a movement away from universalism, and even further weakening of the Russian hold over non-Slav minorities in its own empire. Forward looking Russians were urgently seeking a cause which could reverse this internal decline and collapse. The adoption of socialism was highly appropriate to this objective.

The battle between Slav and German communalisms permeated deeply into the socialist movement itself. Mutual suspicions latent in the First International became a major undercurrent of nationalism in the Second, and played a significant role in structuring the doctrinal positions taken in it. The basic problem for the Russians was that Germany seemed poised to expand at Russia's expense, whether by capitalist or socialist means. Lenin feared constantly that in a crisis the German Social Democrats would support the Kaiser against Russian comrades. In the event most did.

His contributions to the development of Marxist thought have to be seen as attempting to hedge against this possibility. Giving greater analytic emphasis to colonialism and the rights of minorities expressed an opposition to western penetration. Simultaneously it constructed a universalist programme for salvaging the Russian empire. It set up Moscow as the defender of oppressed minorities, to which its own non-Slav dependencies, instead of pursuing regressive secessionism, could look for principled support and sympathy.

Minority rights and national strategies

The universalist guise of this programme does not necessarily refute the charge often made against Lenin by Mensheviks, that he was at heart a disciple of Bakunin rather than Marx (Carr, 1980, p. 52). Socialism for most Russians has been a means of countering and harnessing nationalist rather than class revolts. Moscow's claim to be the seat of a new universalist church leans heavily on this anti-imperialist posture.

By the turn of the century few national programmes remained in Europe that were not overtly communalized. Perhaps the most important case was Britain, which was no longer strong enough to stand outside the system and keep the peace. In the final years of the Victorian era, British imperial destiny was slipping fast into jingoism. The political class was defensively adopting an Anglo-Saxon self-concept, in a unilateral bid at Atlanticist alignment with the growing power of the US. This failed, however, to prevent it from becoming drawn into the snake-pit of communal feuding in Europe. Eventual slide into the Triple Entente marked the end of omnipotent detachment.

With this displacement of its lintel, the structure of international order was now in jeopardy. Appropriately enough it was movement in the Austro-Hungarian empire, lying along the main fault line between Teutonic and Slav fraternal masses, an area of complex tectonic underpinning and epicentre of communalist rumblings, which actually brought down the weakened edifice.

The Hapsburg empire had clung on for several decades after adopting the ingenious 'Dual Monarchy' formula. This involved meeting the demand for autonomy of its largest minority, the Hungarians. Through this device Austria was able to distance itself from the continuing oppression of most of the smaller minorities, who became subject to Hungarian rule instead. But it provided no real solution to the problem. Germanic forced assimilation of the 1860s, which had brought down western anger on Austrian heads, was followed in the Hungarian part of the empire in the 1880s by a no less offensive Magyarization. This drove Serbs into the arms of Russia.

In the end Austria failed to achieve its Actonian goal of liberal pluralist stewardship. No institutional fabric was found that was strong enough to resolve the basic problem of lying across the Teuton-Slav fissure. It was, fittingly, division within the Hapsburg royal house over how to handle this problem, and the external intercessions it licenced, which finally brought them down. The occasion for war was provided by the assassination of the Hapsburg heir Franz Ferdinand.

He was at the time engaged in plans to try to re-subdue the Hungarians, in order to create a liberal, pluralist régime in which Austria, once again, was guardian of all groups' freedoms. His assassination played into the hand of Austrian hawks, who pressed Francis Joseph to launch a penal attack on Serbia.

The US, grown prosperous and strong in peaceful isolation, and now united in ideology following Yankee victory in the South, grasped its long-awaited opportunity. After their European rivals had exhausted each other in the great war, America was ready to intervene to create a new balance of power, and to set about re-drafting the liberal covenant in a way that would undermine all competing claims to global primacy.

DISMANTLING THE OLD WORLD: 1918–40

The American is just beginning to take stock of his world importance, but is not yet fully cognizant of it.

(Leon Trotsky, 1924, p. 145)

The tangle of contending communal claims which had grown up and choked each other in the late nineteenth century was cleared away in the conflagration of the Great War. This left light and space for a revived strain of liberal optimism to take root. Much of the intellectual spade-work for the new order was done by Fabians like Wells and Murray. But it was the Americans who conspicuously officiated at the ceremonial planting of the new stock at Versailles. There was a good deal of Wilsonian whiggery declaring an end to nationalism, and vesting the protection of order henceforth in a 'concert of powers'. Behind all this was the United States as a great power in a traditional sense. Americans had decisively intervened to restore peace. They now held sway.

The US enjoyed great economic and military power. In addition Americans were currently endowed – as had been the British a century earlier – with considerable moral assets for leading the reconstruction of the liberal order and stemming the tide of nationalism in Europe. These derived partly from their previous detachment from European affairs, and relatively clean hands. But they arose principally because their country appeared to be more truly geared up to cope with the future than was the stagnating world of western Europe.

The US had become the main refuge for minorities displaced by wars and tyranny in the old world. It was, moreover, in the process of refashioning these disparate fragments into a new and vibrant nation. This could hardly fail to excite approval in Europe. Turn of the century liberal opinion had become more receptive to claims by submerged minorities to self-determination, especially when this was at the expense of hostile states. In principle, though, it still preferred pluralistic evolution, in which political unity was held never to depend on – though it might easily precede – cultural unity. In these terms post-bellum America, whose own melting-pot seemed to be working so well, was a living exemplar of pluralistic assimilation. European generations weary of communal strife could look to it with hope.

Paradoxically it was perhaps this very weight of her own pluralist credibility which then made it possible for the US to depart so far from basic liberal tenets. In the moment of liberal triumph, America turned the weapons of the vanquished states against themselves, in a communalist application of minority rights. Prompted by Wilson, the peace conference held that part of the reason why the defeated had fallen was that, unlike America, they had failed to discover appropriate ways of adapting to cultural diversity. It was, therefore, fitting that defeat should lead to dismemberment. Many new nations were then created in Central Europe in the name of self-determination. The League of Nations was instituted with the task of guaranteeing the rights of those minorities in the region which still remained subject to an alien majority.

This great experiment was not launched without misgivings among the allies. France was frankly not impressed by the specific proposals, and was somewhat sceptical of the notion of internationalism embodied in the procedures of the League. But Lloyd-George, heir to Gladstone's idealism, shared passionately in Wilson's aims. The British ruling class in general, many of whose ancient families had been bailed out by American affines, still basked in an illusion of pan-Anglo-Saxonism. This made them more than willing to go along with their Atlantic cousins' schemes. The US was able to mollify French opinion through the addition of punitive damages against Germany. So the liberal allies concurred in endorsing the right of internal minorities to receive external guarantees against their masters, as the best hope they could offer for bringing peace to Europe.

In retrospect, the whole idea of carrying out a successful crusade against aggressive nationalism by supporting the claims of smaller communities seems farcical. Opinion in the US itself remained cautious – not least because the war and its immediate aftermath had exposed limitations in America's own internal cohesion, and was raising questions about the efficacy of the melting-pot. Congress did not ratify Wilson's commitment to the League. This conveniently left the European allies nurturing the newborn internationalism and Britain in particular committed to League pacifism, while Americans were free to go off and achieve naval supremacy.

More fundamental than this setback, however, was the fact that the provisions of Versailles carried liberals deeply into communalist territory. Here they encountered just the sort of hazards that their concentration on overseas empires had previously enabled them to avoid, and which the Germans were old hands at dealing with.

Deliberations at Versailles had fluffed the identification of the roots of nationalism, which surely include secular democracy itself. Blame was heaped instead on the residues of feudal autocracy, and remaining imperial houses were cheerfully swept away. The Romanovs, Hapsburgs, Ottomans and Hohenzollerns were all unseated. The conference followed this faulty diagnosis by producing recipes for the containment of communalism which, in reality, probably stimulated it further.

The witch's broomstick of self-determination

Adoption of a programme of self-determination and formalized protection of minorities at Versailles created several problems. An immediate one which arose concerned how to locate suitable corporate candidates for exercising nationhood or enjoying protected status. Liberal voluntarism holds to a subjective definition of the nation. It sees membership as ideally representing the outcome of free individual acts of association and identification. But a peace conference cannot wait while new nations evolve voluntarily. When it came to it the only way of reaching workable definitions for coping with central European problems was by resorting to the indigenous 'Germanic' procedure. This entailed classifying populations according to their cultural attributes – the so-called 'objective test'. Cobban has demonstrated that this warped the whole project. The Minority Treaties were originally intended to assure individual members of minority groups of their rights. In the event, however, they lent themselves to the assertion of group rights over those of individuals (1969, pp. 57–67).

A further set of problems, which proved more significant as time passed, was that once the propriety of communal claims had been upheld by leading world powers, the potential grievances to be countenanced were endless. Versailles had been moved by a spirit of consensualist internationalism. Those participating in it rather assumed that once oppressed groups had been listed and then liberated or given League protection, that mutual national condemnation – the concert of moral power – would be sufficient to ensure just treatment and prevent the proliferation of new feuds and claims. However, the fragmentation of multi-national states into smaller national entities proved to be a witch's broomstick. Occasions for complaints multiplied rather than faded away.

The self-determination exercise was conducted punitively, with an implicit object of breaking up Germanic domains. This had unfortunate consequences. For it meant that several of the new minorities that were created, and who would now look to the League for protection, were in fact German groups, living outside the Teutonic heartland. At Versailles their former subjects had been promoted into lordship over them. Now it was their turn to accumulate communal grudges. (Robinson *et al.*, 1943)

The League had no independent force of its own, and was found to be powerless to uphold the rights of such groups. Aggrieved German minorities then naturally turned for support to the German fatherland. This was the commonly agreed rogue in the system. It had little international prestige left to forfeit, and was for a long time itself excluded from League membership. Not surprisingly it was not very amenable to moral pressures, emanating from other signatories, to hold back from intervention.

The adoption, therefore, of a communalist device by the liberal powers worked in Europe to the benefit of those communities best versed in their use. The only minorities to get tangible support were irredentist Teutons. The treaties system itself became readily subverted to neo-pan-Germanist designs, and even provided a 'liberal' precept for German resumption of hostile action against neighbouring states (Barnett, 1972).

No eternal peace came out of Versailles. What it did in reality was to impose a period of artificial pacifism on western Europe, which facilitated the rise of new global powers. Russia and Japan both benefited. Above all, though, it was America, which was not itself subject to the penance and self-denial that it had persuaded others to undertake, that really surged ahead.

Versailles gave the US a welcome breathing-space to put its own house in order, before assuming the mantle of supreme world power, and while its liberal rivals for this role became further weakened by the system it had created for them. This preparatory lull was extremely valuable for the Americans – and not just because of the undisputed licence it gave them in the west to build up its armaments. Action in the great war had opened up officially ignored communal divisions in American society between groups tracing ancestry in different parts of the old world. An urgent programme of Americanization and administrative centralization was launched in the 1920s to supplement the traditional alchemy of the melting pot. Social scientists were schooled in consensual theories in order to labour patriotically for the more perfect union that the new world role demanded.

Even more ominously perhaps, returning black servicemen had found themselves comparing the freedoms they had fought for in Europe with their own renewed segregation under Jim Crow. Their resistance to re-submission sparked off a revival of the Ku Klux Klan, and this seriously damaged national pluralist pretensions. It was a matter of some relief in progressive circles that the US had not after all become a signatory to the League of Nations. And when Comintern took up the self-determination weapon against the US on behalf of blacks, American enthusiasm for the rights of internal minorities plummetted.

In order to improve the national image, new initiatives and directions were needed. At home the New Deal was formulated as a fresh route to national unity. But the most significant changes occurred in foreign policy. To divert attention from internal minorities, America geared itself increasingly to attacks on external forms of imperialism, of which the US was itself virtually innocent. This soon became the basis for its claim to moral authority in the world. Trotsky's prophetic warning to Britain began to take on a sharper reality.

> The basic world antagonism occurs along the line of conflict of interests between the United States and Britain. . . . Britain's bases are bound up with her colonial rule and are vulnerable for just this reason. America will find allies and helpers all over the world – the strongest power always finds them – and together with these allies, America will find the necessary bases.
>
> If, at the present time, the United States binds Canada and Australia to herself through the slogan of defending the white race against the yellow – and in this way justifies her right to

naval supremacy – then, in the next stage, which may come very soon, these virtuous Presbyterians may announce that, in the last analysis, the yellow-skinned peoples are likewise created in God's image and are consequently entitled to replace the colonial rule of Britain by the economic domination of America. In a war against Britain the United States would be in a highly favourable position, since it could from the very first day issue a summons to the Indians, the Egyptians and other colonial peoples to rise up, and would assist them with arms and supplies.

(1924, pp. 145, 151)

Meanwhile Russia was likewise using this period to draw back from doctrinaire support for the rights of internal minorities. It, too, was refocusing its attack on overseas liberal imperialism, defined broadly to include American economic domination. We have seen how, on the eve of revolution and imperial dissolution in 1917, the Bolsheviks had successfully bid for support from non-Russian dependencies by allowing the right of oppressed minorities to secession. This declaration, however, had then been rapidly exploited by German armies, before Germany's own defeat. Once domestic power had been secured the party quickly hedged this proclamation on nationalities with specifications about the type of régimes – i.e. Bolshevik – that it would tolerate on Russian borders. Then it set about re-incorporating lost territories, in the name of fraternal proletarianism, into a new continental empire of its own.

A new style of minority control was worked out under Stalin. This drew heavily on a strategy of cultural autonomy similar to that which Otto Bauer had proposed for Austria-Hungary. Stalin had at the time correctly diagnosed it as a device for inhibiting real independence and institutionalizing majority supremacy. So he faced a problem in keeping the party a credible focus of universalist aspiration. In order to surmount this, Moscow, like America, was driven to providing support overseas, to colonial resistance to ailing liberal empires.

The odds were now stacking against Western Europe. A rebuilt Germany was soon to resume hostilities against its neighbours, in the name of liberating down-trodden brothers. Liberal Europe would find that its two main allies against Germany, to both East and West, were now committed to the abolition of that very type of imperialism of which it was itself guilty.

THE POSTWAR ERA – A GOLDEN AGE OF DECOLONIZATION

The second world war offered America its first real chance, nearly two centuries after escaping from British rule, to assume undisputed dominance in world affairs. This war not only again pushed back America's main ascendant opponent, Germany; it helped to finish off rivalrous allies as well. By entering late into the war, and again defining it as not really her own concern, America saved her energy for the decisive final stages of conflict and the critical period of post-war reconstruction. By this time the allies had become reduced to proxy warrior states, impotent to prevent the US dictating the rules of the game. They were still – Britain at any rate – apparently unable to see that with Germany partitioned and disarmed, Japan pacified and vassalized, and Russia still too underdeveloped to pose an immediate challenge, it was they who stood in the way of total US supremacy and who would need to be moved aside (Louis, 1978).

A principal means of effecting this was a reforging of the minority rights weapon. It was all the neater because it could be disguised as a constructive and non-aggressive act. Failure of the minorities treaties, which the US was conveniently not party to, justified a complete shift of emphasis in progressive thinking to the problem of colonial minorities. This was a much safer course to follow. There was far less conflict here with fundamental liberal shibboleths about individual human rights. In supporting decolonization there was no need to attack democratic states. The liberal European empires could be revealed by America as heirs to older and discredited feudalistic notions. A crusade for colonial independence led by the first anti-colonial nation was easily held out as restoring sovereignty to territories subjugated by anti-democratic forces. Now at last these were to be given an opportunity, with American backing, to develop their own democracy – in place of European bondage and their own previous, primordial barbarisms.

Russia was a willing accomplice in this redefinition of oppression. At Yalta, partly no doubt in response to Churchill's patrician arrogance, Stalin and Roosevelt achieved a close anti-imperialist accord. This became the basis of a new international idealism, which was institutionalized, while American and Russian interests briefly coincided, in the machinery of the United Nations.

The driving impetus of the UN has been the desire of colonial dependencies to achieve nationhood and participate fully in inter-national deliberations. All this is now unpalatable to the American Right. But it was American sponsorship of the concept which set the apparatus in motion. At the end of the war, the UN served the US and USSR well as a device for undermining the liberal empires. The two superpowers colluded in expanding their own spheres of influence, and populating the world with client states. America augmented its economic empire, concealed behind nominally 'multi-national' enterprises. Russia has cocooned itself inside the pan-Slav domain, stretching from Baltic to Aegean, for which it had striven so long.

In the last couple of decades several factors have combined to reduce the usefulness of the anti-colonialism weapon for the US. In a sense it all boils down to the fact that the weapon was too effective. Successful decolonization of European empires largely eliminated that particular bugbear, and in doing so created conditions for the revival of internal minority issues. Migration to the metropolitan centres of the old empires produced ethnic and racial tension within European democ-racies. At the same time, the removal of imperial overlords has allowed communal tensions to assume prominence in formerly dependent ter-ritories. All over the world the minority problems that have char-acterized the 1960s and 1970s have been ones to which America – along with her old anti-imperial partner Russia – could not pretend to hold any magic answer.

America's use of the decolonization weapon led to a change in its nature, and a turning back on its wielder. It was perhaps a mistake for America to play host to its anti-imperial instrument – the United Nations. For this proved to be a Trojan Horse. When leaders of liberated African nations began to receive diplomatic honour in New York and Washington, the long-suppressed pride of Black Americans was reawakened. As a result American society teetered for several years on the edge of instability.

However, the country was too powerful to be subjected to any forceful intervention on behalf of blacks from outside. So it was able to weather the immediate storm of Negro discontent by means of a 'second reconstruction' in the 1960s. This undid Jim Crow, and consolidated individual rights of members of minorities; all without significantly threatening the dominant position of the Anglo-Saxon majority.

Thus, as chapter 8 shows, the civil rights episode in the longer run produced a revival of the American ethnic hierarchy, around the slogan of individual freedom. By the time of Nixon's presidency, doctrines of minority self-determination had very little utility left for America, in any form. The European empires had long been dismantled, and the ex-colonial world, through the UN, had found a collective voice which was increasingly attacking the US itself as the main imperialist power. Under the reappraisal carried out by the New Right in America, anti-colonialism itself was disavowed, reinterpreted as anti-American, and conceived as a Fabian-Bolshevik plot. In its brief and lonely supremacy over the last twenty or so years, America has largely abandoned concern for rights of oppressed groups. It has retreated to bedrock liberalism by making a stand for basic human rights. This defuses the communalism of its own internal minorities which was stimulated by the civil rights movement. At the same time it provides a stick to beat the USSR into recognition of American pre-eminence.

Even this, however, has failed to halt the decline in American moral influence. With the possible exception of Carter, her leaders have shown such blatant double-standards in the pursuit of human rights, that clients and allies have been seriously antagonized. Over-free use of Kissinger's rule that the highest good is the security of the nation leading the defence of liberal values has eroded much of the support for America's leadership which formerly existed.

Meanwhile a revived western Europe has been moving back onto the centre of the stage as a potential new focus for humanity's aspirations. As the contending superpowers outbid each other in reducing global affairs to their own states' interests, Europe, revolving around a Germany virtually untainted by third world memories of domination, finds itself in a strong position now to exercise positive moral leadership by mediating between the super-powers. This can be done by giving attention to genuinely global issues, like protecting the environment, where substantive and genuinely integrative political initiatives are possible. Relative military weakness is not necessarily a handicap here. The over-kill capacity of the contemporary super-powers is a contributory factor in their decline in moral appeal.

Thus the minority rights weapon played a very significant role in the re-ordering of international relations after the second world war. But it is currently lacking both sharpness of definition and whole-hearted advocates. This may be because we are at a point where the partisans for the industrial blocs of the northern hemisphere – Japan, the EEC, Russia and America – are having to adopt more divergent approaches in their competition to woo and control the territories lying to their south. On the other hand we may be moving into a period when novel global prospects and dangers are now throwing up an entirely new universal morality, of One Worldism or Spaceship Earthism. This would require a new set of international rules, a Green ideology, in which arguments referring to natural human rights would play an altogether less prominent part.

For whatever reason, it does seem clearer now than it has been at any time this century that downtrodden communities, whether colonial subjects or ethnic enclaves, are not about to inherit the earth. States may yet be destabilized by the call to minority self-determination. America herself seems a ready candidate here. She may well, if her global influence weakens, and isolationist tendencies accelerate, fall prey to deepening internal divisions. Her backyard Latin American neighbours would be only too pleased to mount pressure on behalf of the growing Hispanic community. But minorities themselves, ever the pawns of great power politics, can have little to gain from all this.

CHAPTER 12
DISCRIMINATION AND THE LIBERAL SOCIAL ORDER

Holding the triangle
Conventional 'liberal dilemma' thinking has it that so long as a discrepancy exists between universalist creeds and ethnocentric behaviour, a responsible *élite* will have serious problems in holding a national society together. This account is sound statecraft. But the truth is more complex. For the hybrid and equivocal language of progressive nationalism in fact constitutes a valuable resource for *élites*. In nations capable of resisting foreign sanctions, ruling classes turn the existence of competing claims on them to their own advantage. They can draw selectively from a pool of alternative precepts. This enables them to play off contending groups against each other, in classic divide and rule, and so evade representations from any of them.

This opportunity for speaking with a forked tongue is one of a modern *élite*'s most important props. Majoritarian masses are endowed with the brute force of the mob to back up their demands. Oppressed minorities may call on external allies to support their claims. Neither challenge to a régime can be ignored. A national *élite* possesses little physical power of its own. But it does have the strategic advantage of occupying a position of *Tertius Gaudens*, the third party which interposes itself in a dyadic conflict and allies with both antagonists. By mediating between a national majority and minorities the *élite* can take control of the situation, and resolve it into a comparatively stable triad. Its own position is enhanced by the conflict which it serves to contain. By using the claims issuing from each side of the national triad to check those from the other, a ruling establishment gets the chance to demonstrate its own capacity to ride over deep social divisions and to exercise unifying leadership. This is illustrated in figure 1.

Triads generated by these integrative labours are not so clear and symmetrical as in Simmel's original concept. This makes them difficult

228

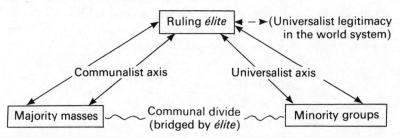

(Note: the arrows to and from the ruling *élite* are to indicate that each axis allows legitimacy both to the authority of the *élite*, and to demands made upon it.)

Figure 1: The national triad

to express diagrammatically. The universalist component has refractions and ramifications outside any single state. It is better to think of national *élites* as forming triangulation points in a more complex grid or field of forces, rather than just sitting at the apex of discrete pyramids. A modern ruling class occupies a political moment at the intersection of two axes of legitimation. It inhabits both of these terrains and can slip at will between them. In this way members of the *élite* can outmanœuvre the unidimensional beings populating their states and superimpose themselves upon them. The more important of these interlocking dimensions is the international. We can best understand the differing success of *élites* in actually reconciling the demands on them, by looking at their positions in the world power system.

The greater the military and economic strength of a state, the more easily its ruling class can close off its own triad from external interference. This leaves it freer to move between ideological dimensions without being exposed for double standards. It is among the great powers at the hub of the liberal world order that *élites* are best equipped to turn the existence of ethnic and racial discrimination to their own advantage, and have most to gain from pronouncing on its dire consequences. Meanwhile it is among weaker and vassal states that the most frequent punishments for duplicity are exacted.

Several aspects of this are considered in turn here. First a look is taken at the different ability of states to keep up the appearance of an open society, to secure international toleration and support. This leads to an exploration of the way in which the need to maintain decorum strengthens the hand of ruling classes against the common people. Popular class action has greater difficulty than that of a ruling class, in preserving a universalist guise. The final section argues that this is a key factor in sustaining the supremacy of liberalism – and the inferiority of workers' states – in the humanist world order.

KEEPING AN ORDERLY HOUSE

A precondition for closing off a national triangle from outside attention is the maintenance of a clean national image. It is in the interests of ruling classes to be vigilant in schooling their populations in the arts of universal citizenship. States whose ordinary members can help to actualize libertarian fictions by conceptualizing not just their own behaviour in voluntarist terms, but that of their political opponents as well, make poor targets for outside criticism.

Great powers have most chance of success. States that have carved out a leading position for themselves in global affairs can offer their members many more opportunities for individual fulfilment and self-expression. Pacemaker nations are accordingly governed by *élites* who can attach themselves wholeheartedly to the universal programme their state stands for. They know that their collective '*élite*' position in the world enables them to pass on enough benefits down the line to buy off potential dissidents below who might otherwise spoil the show for them.

The chief threat to a nation's image comes from the beliefs and behaviour of its lower orders. But these classes are venal. Once they have been introduced to the pleasures of forming an international aristocracy of labour, and sharing the burden of carrying the torch of civilization to the darker corners of the globe, they soon learn to conduct domestic disputes with their masters in terms which are compatible with the nation's dignified proclamations. There is little call for narrowly chauvinistic ideas among citizens of great powers. It is at the metropolitan hearts of flourishing empires that the concept of politics as a contest between rational associations of free individuals reaches its fullest implementation.

Much the same can be said about the co-option of ethnic minorities to a sanitized account of their position in society. Second-class status can be borne in dignity and silence if you are nevertheless well off compared with the rest of the world. When you know that you cannot hope to get a better deal elsewhere, you might as well stay and enjoy the party. Celts found their terms of incorporation to the British Union tolerable so long as it entitled them to join in a profitable imperial adventure.

In the same way Catalans and Basques knuckled under to Castilian supremacy, as Ukrainians still do to renewed Russian hegemony.

Loyalty does not go unrewarded. If its minorities are willing to lend patriotic support to the progressive mission they are engaged on, the majority will be more inclined to extend them the nationalist legitimacy they need in order to feel that they are on the road to acceptance as equal citizens.

Thus, more powerful nations have the least cause to worry about whether they can meet the tests of international opinion. They are also the best placed to promulgate tough-minded versions of libertarian dogma, thereby creating problems for their international competitors, without alienating their own citizenry in the process. Might is ever right. It is always the dominant power of the age which comes nearest to pure voluntarism – extolling the idea of citizenship of the whole world, and urging that the only valid object of loyalty below humanity as a whole is the most enlightened nation of the day. Ruling groups in strong states need only to perform tacit nationalist acts in order to keep popular trust. As long as benefits continue to be won and distributed among the dominant masses, *élites* are free to support an ideology declaring the priority of individual rights over those of the group.

However, as we are witnessing in post-imperial Britain, this heady individualism can turn into a liability when power has been snatched away by a rival (Kaldor, 1978). Facilities needed by the ruling class for rewarding fair play soon start to drain away. The lower you slip in the power league, the more formidable is the task of maintaining an integrative vision. Governments of states that are having difficulty in winning resources, or even in holding onto those that the nation does already possess, have a hard ride. Second rate powers may just about manage. But below that, a liberal creed does pose real dilemmas for the political classes. Populist majority opinion requires displays of special commitment. If no material benefits are forthcoming, words and assurances are needed instead. So there is strong pressure to slide towards overt nationalism.

In these circumstances the *élites* most likely to try to resist popular pressure and make a rearguard stand for individual liberty, are those lumpenbourgeois (Frank, 1972) cliques heading puppet states propped up by foreign liberal bankers. Such régimes, like the Batistas of old Havana, and until very recently the Marcos family in Manila, are actually vulnerable on almost every flank. They are divorced from and fearful of the ordinary people. And they are highly dependent on their metropolitan paymasters for assurances of support against the enemies of freedom.

This is a familiar scenario throughout Latin America – the original Third World – where problems of combining formal autonomy with 'dependencia' are the common heritage of most nations. There is little chance of stability. The desire for internal security leads to the development of a repressive political apparatus. This in turn makes a mockery of the values uttered in order to qualify for the protection of foreign allies and patrons.

Legitimacy bondage of this sort usually wins only temporary respite. It involves visibly anti-nationalist collaboration with foreign forces – undertaken in the hope of keeping witnesses to their liberalism at the court of international opinion. But this alienates the masses and fuels their discontents even further. Eventually it leads to populist attempts to purge the country of imperialist stooges and compradors. These moves then have to be met by a tightening of repression. Even the government's own supporters, main allies and patron state cannot stomach this indefinitely. American disenchantment was the death warrant for 'liberal' régimes in Persia and Ethiopia. After Moi, as they are saying in Nairobi, the deluge.

Right wing despotisms tied to liberal ideologies are prone to instability. The discrepancy at the base of the national triangle stretches out until the political class can no longer contain it. Then the régime falls prey to – or perhaps comes to alternate with – a Peronist style of popular dictatorship which is unashamedly nationalist and protectionist. The new Iran is an extreme instance of this. Deep chasms are opened between dominant and dominated communities. The country becomes fair game to disparaging commentators in more privileged nations.

The socialist alternative

This instability may be reduced by the adoption of a statist variant of humanism, in which the idea of individual liberty is played down. Socialist ideas permit more direct admission of communalist claims from the masses. And they do it without entirely giving way to exclusive nationalism. This is because the blame for a nation's ills can be placed at the feet of foreign powers – often its former liberal guardians. National mobilization is part of a wider human struggle.

Early liberalism was able to approve of nationalism as a legitimate reaction to feudal imperialism. In the same way today, socialism can universalize it as a response to liberal domination and neo-colonialism. Under socialist leadership, a weakened nation can pull back somewhat from class and communal warfare, by uniting around an anti-imperialist explanation for its impotence and internal divisions. Such a mobilization may at the same time be able to avoid outright xenophobia or withdrawal from the world community. It subsumes local upheavals to a new and hopeful vision of international proletarianism. Worldwide co-operation to eliminate capitalism will finally purge humanity of the curse of strife.

Adoption of this alternative universalism does not completely resolve the dilemmas of the governing class. Dependence on new foreign patrons, albeit now conceptualized in fraternal terms, still creates problems. Moreover, the stronger-arm tactics against dissidents which statism justifies is a mixed benefit. But this type of system is probably the best that a vulnerable state can hope to find for achieving stability. It gives explicit recognition to the needs of its 'own' people. This reduces the distance between rulers and the majority of those ruled – a gulf which in a weak nation can easily become unbridgeable.

However, the value of the alternative mandate in defensive circumstances points to its limitations in other contexts. Socialism openly declares that the state has a special obligation for the welfare of loyal citizens. This version of humanism draws only the thinnest of veils across the communalism which informs and drives official policies. It tends towards a fascist conception of the state and nation as a higher personality with its own morality.

This severely compromises socialism's utility as a doctrine for more powerful nations. Fraternalist statism is an excellent idiom for rallying transnational support for resistance to oppression and imperial penetration. But it is less successful in expressing plausible bids to world hegemony. It falls way behind liberalism in articulating believably supranational objectives and programmes, free from the control of particular national communities. This point is taken further at the end of this chapter.

Rites of compurgation and dissociation

... where we are all a little scared of being thought to be illiberal, and where none want to appear prejudiced, the accusation of racial prejudice becomes as potentially powerful a weapon as the exploitation of prejudice itself.

(John Garrard, 1971, p. 7)

The political classes in modern nations need to play down the significance of ethnocentric behaviour among their populations. But this does not mean that they would eliminate discrimination altogether if it was in their power to do so. On the contrary, they have a stake in the perpetuation of a dual standard. It is a convenient basis for maintaining a moral gradient within society in their own favour, whether they are fully aware of it or not.

Élite citizens cannot afford to discriminate themselves. But there are several things they do, either consciously or by default, which help others to get away with it. They can simply overlook exclusive practices by the masses. Or they can deny the importance of particular events which might be seen as having the effect of excluding minorities. And they may pursue policies of 'colour blindness', 'benign indifference' etc. which are ostensibly enlightened, but leave the field clear for bigotry.

There is some risk of personal and institutional discredit in this complicity in nationalist exclusion. But in political terms it is a good investment. Any fraternal support given to ethnocentrism helps to maintain a fund of popular legitimacy for the *élite* itself, within the majority. At the same time it provides them with moral hostages against their more obviously offending compatriots in the majority.

A strategy of tacit collusion in discrimination by a ruling class has parallels with the customs of compurgation found in stateless societies. The central institution of any system of compurgation (Gellner, 1958 and 1969) is a collective oath, declaring a colleague innocent of charges made against him by an external agency. Where a group is prepared to stand by an individual in this way then that is, typically, the end of the matter as far as the plaintiffs are concerned. No reprisals can be taken. The collectivity containing the alleged offender is deemed to be pledging joint responsibility for his behaviour.

This sort of juridical system is not concerned with establishing objective truth. What it does is to mobilize group solidarity, to help prevent incidents arising. Group members are never very happy to support colleagues they know to be guilty. Perjury risks divine retribution against the whole community. All group members are constrained to think twice before committing acts which may lead to it.

Compurgation is not, therefore, a licence for anarchy. The more often that a group is called on to put itself out on behalf of wayward members, the more indebted these miscreants become to the blameless brothers who swear a false oath for them. In the end, persistent offenders risk expulsion. By thus mediating its individual members' responsibilities in the outside world, a group sustains an internal hierarchy of authority and power.

This is the sort of exercise that a modern political *élite* is involved in when it provides cover for offensive xenophobia among its citizens. Declarations of their innocence will be forthcoming only so long as guilty elements submit to the state's official creed defining them as deviants and bringers-of-trouble-for-all. The very act of taking their side against a critical world community is simultaneously an occasion for collecting hostages against their future submission to authority inside the nation. Through ritual displays of solidarity, the political *élite* can steer the vulgar mob it is obliged to identify with into acquiescing in its own moral inferiority. Ethnic and racial discrimination is a perfect stick for beating the masses. There is little room for disputing who the principal culprits are. Masters and bosses may sometimes chivalrously acknowledge formal liability. This is part of their fraternal roster – as perhaps in the recent case at British Leyland where the employers were penalized for restrictions set up following pressure by the unions (Ollerearnshaw, 1983). But admissions of liability for actions manifestly carried out under duress do not claim – and certainly do not manage – to take away the ultimate responsibility from the lower orders. It is they who are overwhelmingly visible as the initiators of moves to discriminate against minorities (Bonacich, 1979).

It is at the lower reaches of the social scale (Turner and Singleton, 1978) that exclusive communalist values have most attraction. Members of the majority in menial and relatively insecure positions constitute a front line. They are the ones who compete directly with marginal groups who are fighting to up-grade their position in the nation. Accordingly it is these poor whites who have the most to gain from adopting a nationalist rhetoric and practice, in which entitlement to rewards and privileges is limited by hereditary identification with the state and nation. This is the level in society where, through the calling up of fraternal loyalties in attempts to control the state machine at the expense of weaker communities, a 'national majority' comes nearest to defining itself as a self-conscious and concrete body.

As it takes shape, however, it becomes trapped into breaking the universalist rules. In this way a manifestly deviant stratum is created, which can be repudiated whenever the *élite* needs to make sacrifices in order to keep up its own universalist credit.

The key clause in any compurgatory pact is that support and cover from innocent co-jurors – the clean-nosed *élite* – is only conditional. To retain it the malefactors – the lower orders – must remain aware of their moral indebtedness, and make continuing efforts to mend their ways. The mob must not forget this. If it seems to be getting the upper hand in any way, a ruling class can always activate the dormant threat of abandonment, and transfer official credence to minority protests instead.

The racist smear

It is interesting to see how the resulting processes of dissociation are then handled. A progressive establishment dare not damage the image of the whole nation. So when clamping down on deviants and insur-rectionaries it is important to keep a social distance between per-petrators of discrimination and 'respectable citizenry' as a whole.

A consensualist ideology really pays its way here, by allowing the official gaze to be averted from fundamental conflicts of interest between communities. It is no use to a ruling class to take the view that discrimination is entirely understandable in certain quarters, but is too negative and divisive to be tolerated. What the articulate classes prefer to do is to attribute its practitioners with views that are quite unreasonable and untenable. With a little help from anti-racist cam-paigners on the Left, who are waging permanent battles of their own along this same front, stereotypes are spun which mystify communalist exclusion into the irrational reflex of a pathologically inadequate personality. A favourite ploy at the moment is to lump together all types of rejection of outsiders as 'racist'. Racial prejudices are the least amenable to rational, scientific justification in contemporary society. No right-thinking person could countenance such foolishness. It can therefore be dismissed as an unpatriotic and unrepresentative deviation.

This mystification of discrimination serves entrenched interests much more effectively than a realistic account could. It preserves the steep gradient of moral virtue at the heart of their structures of social control. To start with it reinforces the tendency of minorities to regard the incumbent *élite* as their best source of patronage. The harassment carried out by poor whites does in truth suit the higher classes rather well. It holds back minorities from reaching positions where they would start to compete directly with the *élite* itself. It also maintains the overall supremacy of the majority community, which the ruling *élite* both shares in, and can exploit against the masses. There is no need (Cox, 1948, p. 542) to display prejudice yourself, if you can get others to do it for you. The lower orders are the ones engaged in the front line communal battle. Minorities, therefore, can be induced to regard them as the genuine enemy, and are willing to follow the *élite* into crusades against periodic outbreaks of popular bigotry.

Receiving this support from national minorities in turn helps the governing *élite* to convert a potentially embarrassing domestic situation into an occasion for gathering external sympathy. A secure régime will open its national triangle a little, by ritually offering trouble-making citizens up for international execration. This pre-empts intervention. Through grasping the nettle of intolerance amongst its own, and permitting authoritative figures like Kerner or Scarman to endorse criticisms of majority behaviour, an establishment shows itself willing to play by the book. Correction faced in a constructive spirit is no censure.

A policy of disavowal may even summon up some measure of 'class' collaboration. Cosmopolitan régimes in different states tacitly invite like-minded elements to join in condemning their unruly masses. Mutual commiserations are welcomed. Where a national confession is carried out in a properly contrite manner, with due reaffirmation of liberal oaths, then the ruling régime will normally be allowed by its peers in the world community the right to preside over the cleaning up of its own house.

The greater virtue enjoyed by the *élite* is useful in fending off the challenge to their personal pre-eminence within the nation. Members of privileged strata break plenty of rules themselves. Notably they use ostensibly impartial public offices and procedures to do little favours for friends and relatives. But they are insulated from direct conflict with minorities. So they are untainted by the much greater sins of communal exploitation. Their own peccadilloes go unremarked, and they are not hindered by them from constructing individualist careers in the image of the libertarian ideal-type.

By contrast, moral disability is what belonging to the lower orders in an open society is all about. Strength of numbers gives power, but not honour. The more successful the masses are in uniting communally to cut out weaker groups' claims on national resources, the greater the moral handicap they incur on their other front, in the class struggle against their superiors in the establishment (Parkin, 1979, pp. 91–2 and Meisel, 1958, p. 374). Claims to public goods made in the formal political arena are vetted in terms of scrupulously universalist criteria. Lower classes can only lodge modest demands, because they are beholden to their betters who act as co-jurors in witness to their good character and behaviour. This does not rule out individual transactions and challenges. Ambitious members of the working class are allowed to aspire to improve their personal standing. Provided they are willing to cut loose from their origins, they do not pose a class threat, and are usually permitted to pursue meritocratic claims. This is not so for political combinations acting to augment the overall share in the national cake enjoyed by ordinary people. These run the risk of being smeared as gangs of bullies. They should not presume to press universalist demands *vis-à-vis* the establishment while they are cheating on their other flank. Hard hats are everywhere known as poor losers. There is nothing quite so good at taking the progressive steam out of working-class movements as the observation (Boggs, 1970) that the social benefits their members enjoy have been won on the backs of an oppressed and voiceless underclass.

A lower-class community may become so polluted by its communalist leanings that wholesale repudiation is necessary (Hannerz, 1974). It becomes transformed into an 'honorary minority' inside its own state – tied to a destiny narrower than befits an enlightened nation as a whole. When this happens the group may hardly be able to exercise its democratic power at all. The White Trash of Dixie come to mind. They are reviled and ignored at every opportunity by more respectable compatriots, and reduced to filibuster and recalcitrance in order to make the smallest point.

Such a process is all the more likely where a majority already contains lines of communal differentiation, so that an *élite* can shunt a sector of it into a 'minority' position by refusing to identify with it. Oriental Jews in Israel are a current example of this. They are now numerically superior to, and can out-vote, their European co-religionists. However, they have been hustled by the Ashkenazi *élite* into the dirty work of standing as super-patriotic buffers against Arab minorities and neighbours. The atrocities they commit in the name of Zionism bring about much wailing and wringing of hands among the diaspora community in the West (Timerman, 1982) who supply and succour the national *élite*.

These various devices go a long way towards helping sustain liberal ruling classes. Post-enlightenment societies have set themselves against hereditary privileges. But ways can be found to stage-manage self-recruitment. The existing upper classes retain a virtual monopoly of the personal rectitude now needed by democratic leaders. Tenure is perpetuated.

MASQUERADES OF CLASS ACTION

One cannot see why the strong state-socialist communities should disdain to squeeze tribute out of the weaker communities for their own partners where they could do so, just as happened everywhere during early history.

(Weber, in Gerth and Mills, 1957, p. 169)

... so long as the goal of the German workers consists in setting up a national State, no matter how free or how much of a people's State they imagine it to be, ... they will ever continue to sacrifice the liberty of the people to the greatness of the State, Socialism to politics, and justice and international brotherhood to patriotism.

(Bakunin, quoted by Davis, 1967, p. 101)

Liberal *élites* in secure states are true *élites*. Their sectional interests do actually coincide with the needs of the 'progressive nations' they lead. Challenges to them are therefore usually self-defeating. Even when the masses try to universalize their opposition, they are likely to end up playing into *élite* hands, and to trap themselves into confirming their own inferiority.

Probably the best way for communalist action to dodge an ethnocentric tag is by phrasing its demands in terms of universal class. In this idiom all the oppressed, regardless of their roots and origins, are held to possess overriding common interests, pointing to a shared destiny. This mirroring of establishment consensualism displays a similar commitment to the goals embodied in the ruling mandate. So it cannot just be shrugged off by rulers. At the same time it provides some chance for the masses to show the limitations in the *élite*'s own programme for realizing these agreed ends.

In particular, class action exposes the least presentable ingredient in the ruling strategy, that is the element of equivocation which is called for when stringing along a diversity of interest groups. Modern statecraft requires a constant shifting of support between the majority masses and minorities, involving a transfer of emphasis between the major dyadic alliances – the nationalist and internationalist axes –

making up the sides of the national political triangle. The underlying tactic in united class action is a direct response to this alternation. Class mobilization attempts to resist *élite* domination, by drawing the attention of the exploited partners in each of these dimensions to the divide and rule by which they are both betrayed.

It is the act of discovering this hypocrisy which appears to put many on the socialist road in the first place. Gramsci's conversion from Sardinian loyalist arose out of seeing for himself how the Piedmontese proletariat and 'immigrant' southern Italian peasantry were played off against each other by unscrupulous bosses. The only way to beat this manipulation is to set up a competing alliance along the base of the triangle. Action along this class axis will break the mystique and hold off the ruling establishment. (See figure 2.)

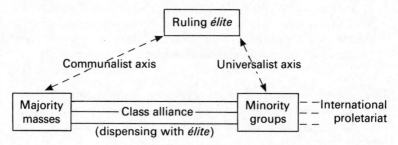

(Note: Existing *élite*'s alliances, along both the internationalist and nationalist axes, are brought into question. This is indicated by broken lines of arrows.)

Figure 2: The strategy of class action

This class alliance is, however, problematic. It is unfortunately more artificial and fragile than those it attempts to replace. The groups harnessed together in common faith and cause do undoubtedly share many experiences and predicaments. But they include direct competitors in nationalist terms. There remains more dividing than uniting these. Consensualists of the Left try to minimize the problems by treating communalism as a delusion willed onto the masses to confuse and disunite them. But it cannot really be spirited away like this. The rift between majority and minorities amounts to considerably more than a slight fracturing of the class.

I argued in chapter 10 that a nationalist alliance is a source of proven, tangible benefits for the majority masses. Class action cannot hope to match them. The prospects its advocates hold out are altogether too speculative and hypothetical. It is probably true, as class theorists claim, that an alliance by the masses with their rulers is exploitable by the latter to its own class advantage. But it is not a one-way traffic. Popular nationalists use the alliance too, to exercise a corporate title to the concrete goods controlled by a state. This gives it an immediate and materialist appeal. Programmes of class redistribution patently lack this – except of course in so far as they refer back to property nationalized (*sic*) by the state on behalf of the masses. (Palley, 1978)

Furthermore, a group mobilizing along a nationalist axis calls on a more enduring sort of commitment than associations, like class, can muster. This gives it organizational advantages. Associations only exist in relation to specific calculations of benefit. They are purely contingent, and need explicit co-ordination. A national community, however, even when it does not have a very active or clear conception of itself as a group, appeals to a wider and deeper set of interests. Consequently it has the durability to infiltrate an association and commandeer the organization to its own ends. Many nationalist régimes and politicians have passed their youth in, and drawn some supports from, movements seeking to bring about international revolution. They have given little back afterwards towards the fulfilment of a new world order.

Socialist parties, accordingly, are often required to mount witch-hunts to flush such tendencies out. But if they were too scrupulous they might find few members left. For even where mass action does appear to be articulating itself in terms of class, it may still contain a veiled communalist impulse which is the chief source of its strength and direction.

Class as a tactical cover

In this respect it must not be overlooked that the moral inferiority of communalism is, ironically, a tactical advantage to its practitioners – whether they are aware of it or not. The point is that it encourages them to dissemble. Groups whose common interests lie along a communal axis have an incentive to adopt a mantle of class rhetoric. For this carries them into a morally more acceptable realm, where they will find less resistance. They may even be able to confuse communal opponents into thinking that a truce has been called. The more participants who convince themselves that this is actually what they are doing, the more effective the whole show is.

This resource is not available to class protagonists. Nationalist moves are morally upgraded by being mystified as 'class'. Class warriors have little comparable opportunity to fool their antagonists as a shift into communalism is morally isolating and politically defeating.

This can be illustrated by looking at the familiar example of late nineteenth century Russia. The Pan-Slav movement was not an effective mobilizing principle, either overtly on behalf of the Slav fraternity, or indirectly as a medium and cover for the Russian masses to extract class benefits from the Russian state. It failed because it provoked communal resistance among national minorities and neighbouring states. This speeded up dissolution of the old empire on which traditional Russian privileges were based.

On the other hand, whatever direct success it might be judged to have had in banishing class distinctions and divisions, the Bolshevik movement served well the ends of nationalism. It gave prominence to Russian penitence for past chauvinism, and emphasized their need to unite with former dependents to sweep out old ways and usher in the consensual revolution. As a result the movement succeeded in calming minority fears, and enabled Great Russians to refurbish their traditional dominance in a new guise.

Whenever class protests appear to be successfully mobilizing 'the people', we must ask whether there may not be a hard core of communal interests guiding them. Political demands are easier to support when phrased in universalist terms. So mass movements which work best are those couched in the language of class. But the measurable gains and losses resulting from such action are generally more discernible in the communal dimension. The most incisive analyses, from Gumplowitz to modern ethnopolitics, are those which turn socialist accounts on their head. It is universal proletarian solidarity that serves as the ideological artefact. 'Class consciousness' is revealed as an integrative dream, which is fostered by aspirant *élites*, and works on behalf of dominant majorities.

Socialist illusions are more useful to governing *élites* than to the oppositional movements conjuring them up. Even those establishments which rely on some disunion between minorities and the masses for their ruling strategy can benefit from stimulating class cohesion as well. No modern ruling class needs to fabricate communal rifts in order to control its lower orders. Fracturing is endemic within popular fraternal consciousness. *Élite* interests are better served by the opposite strategy, a consensualist playing-down of nationalism. A united class opposition faces tremendous difficulties overcoming communal divisions. If an *élite* can steer all major protest into such a movement it may aggravate dissenters' problems, and so stifle serious challenges to itself.

In this way the rhetoric of class solidarity becomes a tactical extension of the nationalist alliance. Where protest is channelled into a democratic class movement, minority individuals involved are subjected to nationalist suspicions and vetting by the rank and file, and the movement will in the long run serve the interests of the dominant national community. *Élite* denial of the significance and power of communalism is thus in part a means of delivering minorities into the hands of the masses. Class mobilization harnesses minority dissent to majority causes. It appoints the masses themselves (Parkin, 1979) as stewards for the representation of minority grievances.

Moreover, this division of the spoils of patronage is carried out in a way which enhances the *élite*'s progressive reputation. By allowing united and universalized opposition, it demonstrates its own merit as keeper of an open and tidy house. This ensures at the same time that most of the troubles arising out of communal divisions in the nation are locked within oppositional movements. They become a drain on their coherence and energy, rather than on the whole nation's. If the strains inside these movements do become too great to conceal, it is their consensualist pretensions which are given the lie, and the leadership and good sense of the rulers that is confirmed.

The looking-glass world of socialism

Class traitors figure prominently in the leadership of class organizations. This is perhaps because, whatever their motives, such people can draw on integrative skills learned in their original circumstances, to smooth over awkward splits in the movement. Socialist programmes only seem able to hold together and stay on the tracks when they are generating their own replica 'triangles', topped by self-consciously governing groups prepared to treat their followers' prejudices with scorn and contempt in order to ride over communal and other rifts.

Socialists must be internationalists even if their working classes are not; socialists must also understand the nationalism of the masses, but only in the way in which a doctor understands the weakness or the illness of his patient. Socialists should be aware of that nationalism, but, like nurses, they should wash their hands twenty times over whenever they approach an area of the labour movement infected by it.

(Deutscher, 1972, pp. 110–11)

The internationalist vanguards performing this delicate function are much further away in their view of the world from those whom they would lead, than from the establishment they condemn. It is hardly surprising that their ranks include many of its own repentant, rebellious or anxious children.

The First Internationalist himself was a renegade capitalist who hoped – or maybe it was feared – that his class of origin had had its day. His political initiative lay in forging an alliance between workers in different nations. He achieved this by showing them how to exorcize their mutual suspicions, through projecting them onto machinating employers. This was a design which entailed a reapplication of bourgeois values and insights to workers' situations. Marx dubbed liberal internationalists' willingness to hire cheap foreign labour a 'nationalist' ploy to set groups of fellow workers against each other. In doing so he neatly contrived a looking-glass world in which workers could see themselves as the unifying force, and the bosses as divisive. It was this reversal of conventional liberal morality that produced the confidence among underdogs to try to turn the political tables on their masters.

The comfortable illusion of proletarian unity is maintained most easily in the tranquillity of opposition. Here selectivity can be exercised in finding safe issues on which to take a strong stand. The finest battles are those where support for a faultlessly universal principle coincides exactly with the material interests of the national majority.

Take the affair at Grunwicks. In the year immediately preceding this, British unions had taken a good deal of flack for alleged malpractices in relation to immigrants. The TUC accordingly had pledged a drive against racism. The Grunwick dispute, where immigrant workers were being denied the right to enjoy the benefits of union membership, proved most timely. It presented a splendid opportunity to realize this pledge by transforming it, in true looking-glass fashion, into a holy war against the exploitation of sweated labour by evil bosses.

It is hard to detect much genuine solidarity with immigrant workers underneath the picketing in support of the strike. The coachloads of white, male unionists who came into London each day had little to lose by their action. Their principled stand is bound to look to outsiders more like a privileged stand. They could use the issue, whatever its outcome, to reassert their own supremacy in the labour movement. It is significant that willingness to swallow the union line about what the picket was all about – or even better the ability to say that you were there – is still taken as an acid test of good intentions towards the movement as a whole.

The union version of the campaign encourages a highly inflated view of white unionists, who are presented as acting out of the purest motives. The keynote of this account is that white workers were doing their vulnerable black brothers – or in this instance mainly sisters – a favour by encouraging them to risk their livelihoods.

This is obviously humbug. Support for the strike carried minimal risks for white workers. Local unionized workers stood to gain if the strike was successful, for the company would become less competitive or forced into closure. Black strikers, whose jobs were actually in jeopardy, could not expect to find as much fraternalism in the dole queue as on the picket line. The likely pay-offs were extremely one-sided.

Another salient aspect of the affair is that it was black scabs who were breaching the picket lines. It was, therefore, the class treachery of outsiders that the bosses were in league with, and which was forcing the white lads to have their outing to London. So alongside the idealization of the chivalrous white unionist, the campaign reinforced the view that blacklegs were actually black, and blacks were blacklegs.

Leaders in a class movement cannot always choose ground to fight where they can obscure their membership's true motives. Opportunities become fewer, the more frequently that their principles are appealed to for drawing up state policies and priorities. The closer that power is approached, from legalization of unions, through 'organized' capitalism in which raw market forces are moderated by political controls, towards a full workers' state, the more explicit the client status of minority members in the movement is bound to become.

Roosevelt's New Deal was the nearest a US government has yet moved to implementing a class-based programme of reform. But it was at the same time a setback to the Democrats' hopes of capturing the black vote. For it brought home to negroes that the poor whites would expect at least as many benefits from any 'universal' class action as they received (Sitkoff, 1978). The long road of workers' control, opening out so invitingly from Tolpuddle, travels on through Detroit and Broken Hill before leading inexorably down towards Pretoria.

Absorption into a concerted class attack on privilege does not help minorities in breaking out from oppression. Their predominantly lowly position in the economic division of labour is not their only, or even their basic problem. An alliance with members of the majority sharing this objective location can only be partial and artificial; a fact which is a source of recurring divisions and weakness in class movements themselves. Governments are rarely toppled by class action, unless they consistently fail to protect vital national interests on the world scene.

Workers' states which do nevertheless get set up are even less capable than protest parties of concealing the ethnocentrism of their membership. Under socialism, oppositional classes are not supposed to exist. Groups dissenting from official policies do not have a legitimate universalist medium of protest available to them, within which minorities could be cosmetically concealed. The writings of Solzhenitsyn demonstrate that even criticisms of a régime from within a dominant community are liable to be tinged with nationalistic references. This makes it considerably harder for rulers to close off their national political triangles from outside scrutiny and condemnation.

Within a secure liberal state, by contrast, the availability of a class axis for pooling dissent strengthens the base of a stable triad. Overlapping conflicts and alliances give rulers more room for balancing and containing societal tensions. A moderate amount of class conflict is not a sign of impending collapse. On the contrary, it is a further manifestation of the vitality of the liberal system permitting it, and of which it must be seen as a valuable component.

The relative absence of class development is hardly a matter for self-congratulation. This is evident in a society like the US, which, during the height of its world influence has remained more divided along ethnic than class lines. It is a pointer to trouble after the power of the nation starts to ebb. When the ruling ideology is no longer able to deny the extent and depth of protective communalism within the realm, the union of its constituent parts may rapidly turn out to be looser and more precarious than imagined.

The supremacy of liberalism

Discrimination is generally taken to indicate the failure of liberal order. In practice, though, it sustains the pre-eminence of liberal régimes, which are better equipped to capitalize on ambiguity than their socialist opponents. Liberalism's built-in advantage is that it keeps nationalism on a tighter rein. Liberals have a minimalist conception of the state, as a self-denying instrument for realizing personal freedoms. The 'nation' is discreetly allowed some room. But ideologically it is firmly subordinated to the superior dictates of individual rights. So it need cause no embarrassment.

Socialists are on much stickier ground. Anyone following a collectivist route to the open society is bound to get bogged down in disputes about the exact relationship between individual and group interests. Much grassroots socialism is simply nationalist. What its followers are primarily seeking is a fraternal stake in the durable, valuable resources a centralized state can control on their behalf. The appointed exponents of socialist visions may vigorously underline their own libertarian goals. But the mere fact of demanding greater moral value for organized groups carries for them a risk of becoming submerged in the untutored communalism of the masses they court. Nationalism painted red shows up all too clearly as nationalism (Bell, 1978).

This is an ever-present handicap for labourist movements. The contradictions which arise call for a degree of casuistry which can satisfy few opponents, while repelling many potential believers. Socialist theoreticians are driven to a sharper denunciation of communalism than is needed by liberals. They must all the time rebut suspicions that their programmes are covers for nationalist ventures. This is a real difficulty for them. In the course of conducting endless purges against ethnocentrism among their own followers, socialist thinkers are likely to alienate many of their natural constituents. By striving to impress on them the spurious quality of national consciousness, they drive them instead into the arms of parties that can afford to take a more relaxed view of the nation.

Liberal movements are not slow to take advantage of socialist quandaries in this area. This is especially true in contests within strong states, where liberals already hold most cards, and need but one trump to carry off the prize of long-term electoral dominance.

Liberal régimes are formally hostile to collectivism in all its forms. This stance helps them to win collective benefits from their citizens in the outside world, with less fear of appearing communalistic in the process. They need only admit communalist demands tacitly. This is enough to undercut revolutionary opponents. They can make a compact with popular sentiments, without needing to do anything which will offend the respectable classes. It was through Disraeli's cross-class courting of the popular nationalist vote that the Tories recovered their role as the British party of government. They have kept this vote ever since, both despite and in a sense because of the fact that their formal platform has remained impeccably individualistic. Martin Barker (1981) is way off track when digging for the foundations of British communalism in Tory philosophy. Its real origin is closer to home. Only deviant Tories, making an open bid for the patriotic working-class vote, consort with such notions.

Socialism as supportive opposition

In the humanist world, liberalism works best as a ruling doctrine for the genuinely powerful. Similarly, socialism is most appropriate in defensive situations. For workers' movements stand their best chance of being seen to stay within the bounds of enlightened discourse when they are engaged in protest against a ruling liberal establishment. Domestically this means that they benefit from having a liberal régime successfully siphoning off communalist undercurrents. At the global level it means that socialist régimes keep on the tracks because liberal states provide targets which disparate national formations can transcend their differences by opposing. Only in these circumstances are they able to avoid being swept out themselves into the great and turbulent sea of fascism.

It is hard for socialists to maintain universalist purity outside this role. Those nations capable of great power stature that have adopted socialist systems have done so at moments of national dislocation. Resistance to foreign penetration has temporarily taken priority over the search for hegemonic visions. Their revolutions have been locally grounded, and have tended to happen on the fringes of the international proletarian movements of their age – and at times when these organizations have been weak. The Second International was moribund in 1917 when the Bolshevik coup took place. Similarly the Chinese revolution started after Comintern had been disbanded.

Socialist revolutions occur where existing *élites* have forfeited popular legitimacy, through failure to keep trust with the masses. This leaves the way open for more sympathetic leadership to denounce the old guard as dupes and accomplices of alien adventurers. New régimes then tap directly into the communalist sentiments for which the discredited rulers had formerly contrived cover, channelling it into their own new moulds.

These new accommodations with the people are achieved at the price of doctrinal compromise. We have seen that Lenin, the pioneering architect of mass socialist mobilization, needed to shift the emphasis away from de-nationalized class struggle, onto national reaction to imperialism, in order to sell cosmopolitan Marxism to patriotic Russians. His judicious revision was successful in papering over the fissure between westernizers and Slavophiles while the reconstitution of Russian society was set in motion. Its admission of corporatist chauvinism was rejected by orthodox non-Russian Marxists. It was, however, rapidly institutionalized under Stalin, and has become a legacy which the Soviets could well do without. It confines them to a negative role in world affairs.

Russia is now seen as a 'state-capitalist' pioneer that nationalized proletarian consciousness, and weakened faith in world revolution. It is able to command universalist respect only through attacking western imperialism, and offering cover, advice and assistance to nations seeking freedom from their yokes. Instead of being free to use its vast resources to formulate an independent and positive global strategy, which would mark it out as a truly forward-looking power, it has become stuck as permanent leader of opposition to the West. It has little real influence beyond its ring of satellites, and is obliged to respond mainly to initiatives taken elsewhere. With the passage of time it is turning into a museum for spent and obsolete idealism.

The difficulties of labour movements in relation to communalism work to confirm liberal supremacy. Socialists' continual efforts to uphold their universalist credibility help keep the central political debate firmly within the humanist arena. Liberals, with their more consistent and less sophisticated doctrines, and their secret nationalist card, can expect to win most encounters here.

Doctrines at the collectivist end of the humanist spectrum seem doomed to operate merely as sparring partners. They supply liberals with constructive opposition, rather than posing a serious challenge. The strivings by socialists to preserve a dignified interpretation of lower-class collectivism tend to corroborate the claims of a liberal ruling *élite* to be running a tidy house. By denying that popular consciousness has xenophobic roots, they launder practices which could embarrass the nation and unsettle its rulers. Labourist oppositions in liberal states play a patriotic and stabilizing role.

Socialist régimes get no such support. They do not admit class opposition. So they tend to force their own dissenters into openly communalist positions. This makes it all the harder for these governments to uphold a universalist face themselves. Their ideological apparatus, whatever its other qualities, seems to have little ability, except in a defensive context, to bind diverse groups into a consensual and humanistic whole.

CONCLUSION
THE ROLE FOR SOCIAL THEORY

Virtually all contemporary accounts of race and ethnic relations are built on the bland, consensualist premises outlined in the first chapter. Equal participation of minorities is seen as a public good (Banton, 1985), which majorities and minorities alike have an interest in bringing about.

The materials presented in this book challenge this orthodoxy. It should be evident from them that public declarations of concern for minorities are self-serving. They express a commitment to abolish ethnic hierarchies. But their underlying effect is to protect them, by offering an acceptable face to the rest of the world. This outcome may not be planned. But the logic of it is indisputable. Indeed, the more plausible that any attempts at denial are, the more certain the outcome seems to be.

In view of this it is facile to suggest that there are no real divergencies of interest between minorities and their hosts. Most national majorities have extensive resources – including their cosmetic creeds – for keeping subjugated groups in productive servility. Moreover, they can do this at minimal risk to themselves. The opportunities for communal exploitation are very one-sided. This indicates a sharp basic conflict of interests.

I suspect that many commentators on community relations would privately agree with this assessment. Consensualist models are popular not because they produce convincing analyses. They are adopted for tactical reasons. Race and ethnic relations constitutes an area of particular strategic difficulty for social theorists. Many of them feel that the best hope for improving the position of oppressed groups lies in publicly putting on an optimistic face. This is an understandable position, but I do not think it is the one that is most appropriate to the circumstances.

THEORY AS EXHORTATION

This is a variant on an old quandary – sociology's original sin of entanglement with its subject matter. Social theorists are participants in the processes they study. Their own persons and wills exist simultaneously as subject and object. The same applies to some extent to the people and groups who are being investigated. In so far as they are aware of a theory and understand it, they can react as fellow subjects. Because of this overlapping of roles, social theories have a tendency towards being either self-fulfilling or self-defeating. If a theory convinces people, those who want it to be right will adjust their own behaviour to conform with its predictions. Equally, any who do not regard its prognoses as desirable will do what they can to frustrate it.

The activity of theorizing, therefore, has an inherently strategic dimension. This tempts many commentators into wish-fulfilment. If you can convince yourself that something is going to happen, you may get others to believe it too; and this may actually help bring it about (Dunn, in Lloyd, 1982). Parallel anxieties also exist. Maybe your writings will unleash forces you have not taken full account of. Or, in publicizing how society works, you may inadvertently destroy myths on which its whole operation depends. What if, by looking too closely at what goes on behind the scenes, you let loose demons you cannot control, or betray vital secrets?

> What is the sociologist to do if he believes that his ideas might be used in some quarters for ends that are unacceptable to him? Press on regardless, keep quiet, or what? Or should the 'truth' be established 'pragmatically' anyway? Should those who produce ideas relate them to their social consequences and the responses they will elicit in others?
>
> (Bryant, 1976, p. 27)

These are, I believe, the sorts of considerations which maintain the popularity of consensualist positions on race and ethnicity. Most commentators are only prepared to utter those pronouncements which they think are likely directly to encourage progressive forces, by showing that history is on their side.

Nobody wants to publish accounts which might harm their objects of study, and turn strained communal relations into bloody ones. A diagnosis of deeply conflicting interests might be refashioned by hostile elements into threats or intimidations against weaker factions. Pettigrew was probably just being more honest than most when he concluded – and for me confounded – his review of the prospects for minorities in America by openly confessing an underlying objective of conjuring up confidence in a good cause.

> The entire analysis of this book is predicated on the ... optimistic view that American society will muddle through. To assume otherwise ... is to risk contributing to the problem by engaging in a self-fulfilling prophecy.
>
> (1971, pp. 320–1)

Now clearly there is nothing wrong in principle with the exhortatory use of social theory to help bring about a desirable social objective. Theory does not exist for its own sake, but to help inform and transform action. As long as the objects of social analysis can intercept and react to theories being formulated about them, and interaction occurs between behaviour in the 'real' world and codes adopted by specialists for understanding it, there will be opportunities to issue predictions which help to coax nature into imitating art.

There are, however, limits to this usage. Theory can only retain its strategic power while it provides a credible account of what is going on. We must have reasonable grounds for supposing that an intended bluff will succeed. Otherwise the exercise runs a high risk of proving counterproductive. Theoretical suicide (Friedrichs, 1970) will occur.

Consensualist accounts of race and ethnicity are not good risks in this sense. There would be no harm in them, and arguably some benefit, if their authors themselves genuinely had confidence in their own pronouncements, and were able to reconcile their prognoses with what we can see happening around us. But this is not usually the case. A good proportion of pundits making a stand for integration are clearly not doing so because they are sure that it will or could come to pass. They are simply fearful that unless they can trick or shame people into changing their ways, things will get worse.

Their theories are not applied as gentle pressure to speed the transition to a new and progressive order. They are wielded as rough and ready cudgels with which they hope against reason to be able to knock a little moral sensibility into an uncaring world. The bluff is hollow. It debases the currency of social theory, without actually redeeming the world by causing anyone to behave more acceptably. Far from it in fact. An idealistic strategy in this area, involving as it does a serious discounting of the stake that majorities have in oppression, is probably harmful to its declared aims. For the parties it most needs to influence are those most resistant to it. Communities that enjoy reasonable power to control their own lives can and will define their world-views and interests for themselves. There is little to prevent a national majority in a free and democratic state from realizing its powers. These include the ability to impose its will on weaker communities, and to ignore the idealist bluff of committed theorists seeking to divert or restrain them from this. Such groups do not need intellectual classes to structure their consciousness for them. Although they will pay for it in terms of their own 'honour', they are adept at filtering out unwelcome ideas that their moral betters attempt to instill in them. (Willis, 1977)

The bluff takes in the wrong people. Those who are likely to give credence to the consensualist message of hope and universal brotherhood are to be found mainly within demoralized and sub-merged minority groups, lacking a strong and autonomous collective life. It is among such communities, whose members have the most to look forward to from the opening of a new frontier, but possess the least power to bring it into being, that the word finds its most ardent adherents.

The net effect of consensualist bluff must be to leave communalist elements it is aimed at uncowed and undismayed. Meanwhile minorities with a desperate need to believe in its prophecies are lulled into a false and precarious confidence. By suggesting that a host nation will somehow manage to fulfil the promises implied in its humanist creed, theorists recruit themselves as agents for the Janus-faced ruling class. It is this, and the patriotic programme it stands by, which is the real beneficiary of these theoretical labours, whatever their authors' own intentions may be.

Theory as flattery

This strategic deployment of theory draws community relations ana-lysts into *élite* perspectives. Here the primary task of understanding what is going on quickly becomes overlaid by the work of informing, drafting and monitoring viable and rounded social policies. As a result of the immersion in broader issues that this entails, their orientation to minority needs is liable to become decidedly partial.

This is noticeable on two levels. First, and in a general sense, they become party to a Platonic conspiracy. Those who convince themselves that it is their solemn duty to protect the moral order may feel justified in resorting to deceit and bluster if these seem likely to secure it.

More specifically, many also align themselves with a particular faction among those in contention for political power. No desirable social change can take place unless there is a régime or movement capable of seeing it through. Accordingly many commentators permit their enterprises to become governed by the needs of public policy debates and intrigues. It is difficult to find a widely held theoretical model which has not become cast in the heat of some combat as someone's manifesto. Its key objective becomes to assert the progressive character of that body which it projects as the true guardian of a just social order – liberal employers, anti-racist labour combinations, pro bono lawyers and bureaucrats, revolutionary internationalists and so on – and of the reactionary nature of all who would stand in their way.

All too often this leads towards a methodological dualism. The social world is seen as populated by two quite distinct species, the redeemed and the damned. Each answers to its own pattern of motivation. Each requires quite different epistemological emphasis. Such dichotomizations are unacceptably partial. Morally they are distasteful celebrations of the supposed virtue of their authors and associates. Analytically they permit only limited conceptions of the problems which minorities actually face.

The embattled theorist is not the best disposed to see the situation in the round. That is why so few seem able to acknowledge that all sections of the majority can derive benefits from discrimination, and that the various stances taken by different elements may fit together to mutual benefit as part of an effective package of exclusion.

This is perhaps the central weakness of consensualist accounts. For if one thing stands out from the preceding analysis, it is that the apparently disparate behaviour of national majorities makes much more sense if considered as ultimately interlocking expressions of 'progressive' nationalism.

As we have seen, for example, outright discrimination is largely self-defeating in modern society. It virtually invites foreign powers to intervene on behalf of subjugated groups. Certainly it is much less potent than the imposition of an immobilizing ambiguity in preventing minorities from breaking out of subservient positions in the nation. It follows that discriminators benefit from the existence of an active and

vocal progressive lobby. Liberals help their supremacist co-major-
itarians to hang on to a system much closer to their declared objectives
than they could possibly hope to achieve through their own vulgar
efforts alone.

Similarly, on the principle of *cui bono*, I have argued at various
points that universalists in the majority benefit indirectly in a variety
of ways from the chauvinist behaviour of others. Their pious denials
or neglect of the power of communalism, or of any advantages accruing
to them from other peoples' illiberalism, may sometimes be another
way of playing up to it. They are part of a humbugging strategy
of dissociation, which attempts to remove from non-participating
beneficiaries of exclusion any suspicion of collusion. All the blame for
continuing ethnic inequalities can then be thrust on to those sectors of
the majority occupying the front line, who are obliged to be more
overt because they do not enjoy the same opportunities to conceal the
true nature of their interests.

Most commentators fail to acknowledge these interplays between
different stances towards minorities. Consequently they end up by
fortifying, and giving licence to, progressive smokescreens behind
which communalism can easily hide. They may mean well in emphasizing the harmonious nature of the whole nation's interests. Nevertheless, they smooth the way for further discrimination. Herein lies the
dilemma that contemporary theorists have constructed for themselves.
The more they try to reassure minorities by playing down the obstacles
they must face, the more they become part of, and give additional force
to, that ambiguity which comprehensively envelopes and restrains
minorities. In attempting to steer clear of the fast waters of theoretical
self-fulfilment, those who preach the imminence of integration may
instead beach their followers in the shallows of self-defeat.

In the process they reveal that the notion of social theory as a moral
force is empty flattery. The consensualist strategy flatters first of all
political activists and leaders by endorsing bland official scenarios of
how the world works. It flatters sociologists by inflating their capacity
to stand as heroes of progressive morality. Above all its flatters minorities by issuing false prospectuses which encourage them to believe
that their moment of liberation is nigh.

This is surely a gross betrayal. Nothing is more likely to dismay and
demoralize the groups we claim to care about than the realization,
which must come eventually, that in place of the candid and clear-
headed account they deserve all we are offering is pious aspiration.

Lewis Killian noted this astringently in relation to the loss of heart among Negroes in the US:

> If Negroes were naïve in expecting that white Americans would follow the law of the land, they were certainly encouraged in this belief by the optimism of social scientists and by the repentence of the churches.
>
> (1968, p. 54)

An exhortatory strategy in community relations seems virtually certain to back-fire in this way. Even tough-minded variants, like Miles and Phizaclea (1979), which appear to be hoping to frighten the British majority into better behaviour by predictions of black insurrections, are merely mischievous. They invite black youth into a confrontation they cannot possibly win.

What we really need are approaches which place the risks of self-defeat by idealist formulae on an equal footing with those of self-fulfilment by more realistic accounts. Only these can produce an adequate diagnosis of the difficulties that minority groups experience.

TAKING THE PRESSURE OFF

If we seriously want to help minorities, we need to redress the current theoretical balance by taking greater account of unsavoury facts of life such as the resilience of majority communalism.

I am not advocating an abandonment of progressive ideals and goals. This would help no one. Minorities need the prospect of fuller participation, to give them a real stake in the national system. And some of them will, in fact, whether by individual assimilation or the fading of group boundaries, eventually shed their disabilities and escape from confinement. Host states equally need to retain an inte-grative vision. Their stability and international reputation depend on a level of striving to implement their universalist creeds.

National hosts and their clients are thus together servants of the same moral imperatives. However, it is the latter who carry the main burden of contradictions arising, and who are required to contain within themselves the consequent stress.

We have seen that the acceptance of ideas about universal justice and brotherhood by modern states rests on motives of collective aggran-disement. National instruments take priority over the libertarian goals to which they are ostensibly devoted. This does not matter all that much for the liberal international system as a whole. Such a state of affairs does at least mean that group ambitions are channelled into constructive contests. The desire of nations to run tidier houses than their neighbours keeps up the general pressure for maintenance of progressive standards in the world community. It ensures that some progress does actually take place.

The problem is that someone has to pay the price for this self-deception. At the moment it is not national majorities. Nor is it engagé sociologists. It is the oppressed groups who are urged to have faith in the future, but who receive only minimal real support.

Certain minority communities, by luck and judicious selection of patrons and allies, may exploit consensualist predictions to improve their own position. But such usages are limited. Many groups are unable to find powerful friends with an interest in supporting them. How long since anyone truly cared about the Kurds? Even where patrons can be found, any changes that ensue are likely to be at the expense of other groups – betraying that even this application of universalist ideals is basically communalist.

It is possible to alter who occupies dominant and subordinate positions. You may also moderate the harshness of treatment by which this stratification is sustained. I will come back to this shortly. What, however, seems beyond our power is to approach the consensual ideal itself, in which groups with the muscle to impose hierarchies of supremacy actually refrain from doing so.

National governments are not going to admit this. It is minorities who are left to face up to the self-serving nature of liberal creeds, and to bear the cost of their declaration. The ungrounded optimism of theorists makes things worse. It necessarily tightens the pressure of ambiguity on minorities, who are left suspended between unattainable dreams and unacceptable realities.

This is where a shift of theoretical strategy would be beneficial. No amount of ingenuity or scholarly application is going to help minorities to escape from captivity. But theorists are in a position to make conditions there more bearable. If they were more sceptical of the calls of conventional idealism, rather than as so often peddling even more fundamentalist versions, they could do much to reduce the sharpness of contradiction to which minorities are subjected.

An exhortatory strategy sets out to maximize the possible benefits available to minorities. It does this by encouraging them to have trust in progressive forces, and to expect and insist on their full, formal entitlements. But vulnerable groups, with limited nationalist legitimacy, are just not in a position to behave in this way. They are bound to be resisted in some way or other. So exhortation just widens the gulf between aspirations and attainment. This breeds disillusion, leading in turn to sullen reactions which help trap minorities even longer on the margins of society. Bland optimism prolongs majority supremacy.

It would be more rewarding for minorities if commentators followed a minimalist strategy instead. The aim here would be to limit the pain caused to them by predictions that might prove to be empty. Theory would be used to caution against expecting too much, too quickly. In this way, any theoretical failures would be pleasant, and integrative, rather than disillusioning and alienating as at present.

A minimalist approach would call for honest and straightforward explorations of such matters as the inherent duplicity in progressive nationalist programmes, and the limited capacity of states to implement fully their humanist creeds. Above all, it would require theorists to treat with more respect those traditional modes of minority accommodation to the demands of majorities, such as taking on client roles.

Acceptance of a junior partnership in the nation runs counter to liberal tastes, as it acquiesces in a degree of inequality. But unpalatable as it may be, clientship does have the merit that it allows the construction of some real common interest with a dominant majority; and this can enhance effective participation in national life.

Loyal clients do not provoke defensive barriers against themselves. Majorities that do not feel their supremacy threatened are better able to extend nationalist legitimacy to subject groups. If these accept their place, there is less need to criminalize and marginalize them. On the contrary, they can be allowed more room to share in the performance of some socially important activities. There is no natural harmony of interests. But tolerable accommodations can be achieved by those willing to work and pay for them.

The pivotal rule of clientship is that minorities can retain the goodwill of sponsoring groups so long as they remember that they are clients, and cannot hope to achieve anything which contradicts that basic relationship. By all means declare a belief in future justice and equality. This is part of the role. But do not expect it to materialize. It only embarrasses and annoys patrons when their protégés make demands which draw attention to shortfall of performance over promises.

The clients that are nice to have around are cheerfully confident for the future. They do not spurn the generous opportunities and concessions that are offered. But nor are they too pushy or impatient for delivery. They are content, while waiting, to enjoy the enduring compensations in minority life, of conviviality, spirituality, community sentiment, and attachment to other worlds lingering on in the collective memory. The clients who get on are not the ones who care about the original injustice. They are those who flatter their masters by presenting as tribute to them those exploits they are allowed to succeed in; who are suspicious of rival patrons who offer quicker advancement or easier solutions; and who avoid demeaning tasks by diligent and productive application to the most honourable and intrinsically interesting occupations that are open to them.

A cautious clientship role is all that is really available for most minorities in the modern world. It is through acceptance of this that vulnerable groups can align their interests most closely with those of their hosts. The most helpful role for social theory at the moment lies in taking this clientship system more seriously, and allying with realist elements in minority communities to help them make advantageous accommodations with their national patrons.

Few commentators seem prepared to do this at the moment. For example the Swann Committee, reporting recently on the educational needs of minorities (DES 1985), noted that Asian groups, who incline towards making the best of the school system as it stands, showed reasonable academic results; while Afro-Caribbeans, who take a more confrontational approach, performed less well. But then instead of urging Afro-Caribbeans to consider a more adaptive stance the Committee concluded by endorsing their demands – surely utopian – for a thoroughgoing reform of the educational system. The agony is prolonged.

It is time we withdrew from heroic postures struck in the past to a more cautious role which recognizes the harmful nature of prevailing self-indulgences in this area. Contributing to puffed up accounts of what is possible has caused a lot of avoidable anguish. A redirection of energy, into deflating overblown national or party images, would do much to relax the strain of ambivalence experienced by minorities. It would help minorities to see the real conditions of their existence, and to construct more viable life-plans for themselves. This would be particularly valuable in a country like Britain, where long traditions of championing liberal principles have led minorities into anticipating far more than we have proved capable of delivering.

Frankly, this does not involve telling minorities very much that they do not already know. Most minority individuals over the age of thirty do not need to be told the rules of clientship. So what is really called for is abstention from consensual dream mongering. This abuses the idealism of younger generations, by trapping them into visions of easy progress to the promised land of full equality. It is when these prospects fail to materialize that the pain of ambiguity is sharpest. This is what a minimalist emphasis would help to avoid.

Minority communities which retain some corporate identity and autonomy of spirit already have ways of cautioning against facile optimism. Their members wisely hedge against disappointments in the public domain, by investing more heavily in the private worlds of domesticity and communal affairs. These realms are not intrinsically inferior to the public, 'state' area. They have been devalued by post–enlightenment society. But they are sources of great personal satisfaction to those prepared to look there for them. It is obviously unfortunate, and offensive to progressive sensibilities, if certain groups are confined involuntarily to these areas for their main sources of meaning in life. However, resorting to them is an intelligent reaction for those caught in the privations of minority existence. Unless we can be sure that there really is a more valid response open to them, we should not denigrate or seek to discourage it. Theorists still have much they can learn about society from members of minority groups. We will understand more, and be more useful, if we moralize less.

REFERENCES

Adam, Heribert (1971), *Modernising racial domination* (Berkeley: University of California Press)

Baltzell, E. Digby (1970), 'The immigrants' progress and the theory of the establishment' in E. O. Laumann, P. M. Siegel and R. M. Hodge (eds) *The logic of social hierarchies* (Chicago: Markham Publishing Company)

Banton, Michael (1955), *The coloured quarter* (London: Cape)

Banton, Michael (1985), 'Why inter-racial negotiation is slow', *New Society*, vol. 71, no. 1150, 10 January 1985

Barker, Martin (1981), *The new racism: Conservatives and the ideology of the tribe* (London: Junction Books)

Barnett, Corelli (1972), *The collapse of British power* (London: Eyre Methuen)

Barth, Frederick (1970), *Ethnic groups and boundaries* (London: Allen & Unwin)

Basham, Richard (1978), *Crisis in Black and White* (Boston: Schenkman)

Bell, Coral (1978), 'Why fellow-marxists are bad neighbours', *New Society*, 21–8 December 1978

Berlin, Isaiah (1979), 'Benjamin Disraeli, Karl Marx and the search for identity' in Henry Hardy (ed.) *Against the current* (London: Hogarth Press)

Bermant, Chaim (1978), *The Jews* (London: Weidenfeld & Nicolson)

Bernstein, Deborah and Swirski, Shlomo (1982), 'The rapid economic development of Israel and the emergence of the ethnic division of labour', *British Journal of Sociology*, vol. 31, no. 1, March 1982

Béteille, André (1971), 'Race, caste and ethnic identity', *International Social Science Journal*, vol. 23, no. 4

Bierstedt, Robert (1948), 'The sociology of majorities', *American Sociological Review*, vol. 13, no. 6

Blair, Thomas (1977), *Retreat to the ghetto: the end of a dream?* (New York: Hill & Wang)

Blake, Robert (1966), *Disraeli* (London: Eyre & Spottiswode)

Boggs, James (1970) *Racism and the class struggle* (New York: Monthly Review Press)

Bonacich, Edna (1972), 'A theory of ethnic antagonism: the split labour market', *American Sociological Review*, vol. 37, no. 2

Bonacich, Edna (1979), 'The past, present and future of split labor market theory', *Research in Race and Ethnic Relations*, vol. 1

Borrie, W. D. (1959), *The cultural integration of immigrants* (Paris: Unesco)

Boyson, Rhodes (1978), *Centre forward* (London: Temple Smith)

References

Brauer, Carl M. (1977), *John F. Kennedy and the second reconstruction* (New York: Columbia University Press)

Brotz, Howard (1955), 'The outlines of Jewish Society in London' in M. Freedman (ed.) *A minority in Britain* (London: Vallentine, Mitchell)

Bryant, Christopher G. A. (1976), *Sociology in action* (London: Allen & Unwin)

Bulhan, Hussein Abdilahi (1979), 'Black psyches in captivity and crises', *Race and Class*, vol. XX, no. 3, winter 1979

Cameron, David (1974), *Nationalism, self-determination, and the Quebec question* (Toronto: Macmillan of Canada)

Carlebach, Julius (1978), *Karl Marx and the radical critique of Judaism* (New York: Fairleigh Dickinson)

Carr, E. H. (1968), *Nationalism and after* (London: Macmillan)

Carr, E. H. (1980), *From Napoleon to Stalin and other essays* (London: MacMillan)

Cashmore, Ernest (1982), *Black sportsmen* (London: Routledge & Kegan Paul)

Clark, Ian (1980), *Reform and resistance in the international order* (Cambridge: Cambridge University Press)

Cleaver, Eldridge (1969), *Soul on ice* (London: Jonathan Cape)

Cobban, Alfred (1969), *The nation state and national self-determination* (London: Oxford University Press)

Cox, Oliver Cromwell (1970 ed.), *Caste, class and race* (New York: Monthly Review Press)

Cox, Oliver Cromwell (1976), *Race relations – elements and social dynamics* (Detroit: Wayne State University Press)

Cunningham, Hugh (1981), 'The language of patriotism', *History Workshop Journal*, no. 12

Davis, Horace B. (1967), *Nationalism and socialism* (New York: Monthly Review Press)

Davis, Horace B. (1978), *Toward a Marxist theory of nationalism* (New York: Monthly Review Press)

Dench, Geoff (1975), *Maltese in London* (London: Routledge & Kegan Paul)

DES (Department of Education and Science) (1985), 'Education for all' (HMSO: Cmnd 9453)

Deutscher, Isaac (ed.) (1961), *Stalin: a political biography* (London: Oxford University Press)

Deutscher, Isaac (1968), *The non-Jewish Jew and other essays* (London: Oxford University Press)

Deutscher, Isaac (1972), 'On Internationals and internationalism' in T. Deutscher (ed.) *Marxism in our time* (London: Jonathan Cape)

DuBois, W. E. B. (ed.) (1968), *Souls of black folk* (New York: Fawcett World Library)

Ellison, Ralph (1968), 'The myth of the Flawed White Southerner' in J. M. Burns (ed.) *To heal and to build: the programs of president Lyndon B. Johnson* (New York: McGraw-Hill)

Emerson, Rupert (1960), *From empire to nation* (Cambridge, Mass.: Harvard University Press)

Fanon, Frantz (1967), *Black skins, white masks* (New York: Grove)

References

Fawcett, James (1979), *The international protection of minorities* (London: Minority Rights Group. Report 41)

Fitzgerald, Marian (1984), *Political parties and black people* (London: Runnymede Trust)

Frank, A. G. (1972), *Lumpenbourgeoisie: Lumpendevelopment* (New York: Monthly Review Press)

Franklin, John Hope (1974), *From slavery to freedom* (New York: Knopf)

Freedman, Maurice (1957), 'The structure of Jewish minorities', *Noah Baran Memorial Lecture, British Section, World Jewish Congress*, London, December 1957

Friedrichs, Robert W. (1970), *A sociology of sociology* (New York: Free Press)

Garrard, John (1971), *The English and immigration, 1880–1910* (London: Oxford University Press)

Gartner, Lloyd P. (1960), *The Jewish immigrant in England, 1870–1914* (London: Simon Publications)

Gellner, Ernest (1958), 'How to live in anarchy', *The Listener*, 3 April 1958.

Gellner, Ernest (1969), *Saints of the Atlas* (Chicago: University of Chicago Press)

Gerth, H. H. and Mills, C. W. (eds), (1957), *From Max Weber* (London: Routledge and Kegan Paul)

Gilroy, Paul *et al.* (1982), *The empire strikes back: race and racism in seventies Britain* (London: Hutchinson, for Centre for Contemporary Cultural Studies)

Glazer, Nathan (1957), *American Judaism* (Chicago: University of Chicago Press)

Glazer, Nathan (1976), *Affirmative action: ethnic inequality and public policy* (New York: Basic Books)

Glazer, Nathan (1983), *Ethnic dilemmas, 1964–1982* (Boston: Harvard University Press)

Gordon, Milton (1978), *Human nature, class and ethnicity* (London: Oxford University Press)

Hannerz, Ulf (1974), 'Ethnicity and opportunity in urban America' in Abner Cohen (ed.) *Urban ethnicity* (London: Tavistock)

Hertzberg, Arthur (1982), 'Begin and the Jews', *New York Review of Books*, XXIX. no. 2, 18 February 1982

Hingley, Ronald (1974), *Joseph Stalin: man and legend* (London: Hutchinson)

Holmes, Colin (ed.) (1978), *Immigrants and minorities in British society* (London: Allen & Unwin)

Jarman, T. L. (1970), *Democracy and world conflict: 1868–1970* (London: Blandford Press)

Jay, Martin (1973), *The dialectical imagination* (London: Heinemann Educational)

Joyce, James Avery (1978), *The new politics of human rights* (London: Macmillan)

Kaldor, Mary (1978), *The disintegrating West* (London: Allen & Unwin)

Killian, Lewis M. (1968), *The impossible revolution? Black power and the American Dream* (New York: Random House)

Klineberg, Otto (1961), 'Intergroup relations and international relations' in

References

Muzafer Sherif (ed.) *Intergroup relations and leadership* (New York: Free Press)

Koebner, Richard and Schmidt, Helmut Dan (1964), *Imperialism* (Cambridge: Cambridge University Press)

Kosmin, Barry A. (1980), *Jewish voters in the United Kingdom: the question of a Jewish vote* (London: Institute of Jewish Affairs)

Krickus, Richard (1976), *Pursuing the American Dream: white ethnics and the new populism* (Bloomington: Indiana University Press)

Lambert, John R. (1970), *Crime, police and race relations: a study in Birmingham* (London: Oxford University Press)

Lea, John and Young, Jock (1984), *What is to be done about Law and Order?* (Harmondsworth: Penguin)

Lee, Rose Hum (1960), *The Chinese in the U.S.A.* (Hong Kong: University of Hong Kong Press)

Leggett, George (1981), *The Cheka: Lenin's political police* (London: Oxford University Press)

Lehman-Wilzig, Sam N. (1978), 'The House of Rothschild, prototype of the transnational organisation', *Jewish Social Studies*, vol. XL, no. 3–4, Summer–Fall 1978

Lepervanche, Marie de (1977), 'Exclusion, exploitation and extermination', *Mankind*, vol. 11, no. 2

Levine, Robert H. and Campbell, Donald T. (1972), *Ethnocentrism: theories of conflict, ethnic attitudes and group behaviour* (New York: John Wiley)

Lloyd, Christopher (ed.), (1982), *Social theory and political practice* (London: Oxford University Press)

Louis, William Roger (1978), *Imperialism at bay: the United States and the decolonisation of the British Empire, 1941–45* (London: Oxford University Press)

Lunn, Kenneth (ed.), (1980), *Hosts, immigrants and minorities* (Folkestone: Dawson)

McAdam, Doug (1983), 'Tactical innovation and the pace of insurgency', *American Sociological Review*, vol. 48, no. 6, December 1983

MacDonald, Ian (1977), *Race relations – the new law* (London: Butterworth)

McGrath, Peter (1979), 'Defenders of the faith', *New Society*, 25 January 1979

MacIver, Robert M. (1948), *The more perfect union* (New York: Macmillan)

McNaught, Kenneth (ed.) (1976), *The Pelican history of Canada* (Harmondsworth: Penguin)

Mandel, Bernard (1955), *Labour, slave and free* (New York: Associated Authors)

Maurois, André (1927), *Disraeli: a picture of the Victorian age*, trans. Hamish Miles (London: Bodley Head)

Meisel, James H. (1958), *The myth of the ruling class* (Ann Arbor: University of Michigan Press)

Miles, Robert and Phizaclea, Annie (eds) (1979), *Racism and political action in Britain* (London: Routledge & Kegan Paul)

Minogue, Kenneth (1967), *Nationalism* (London: B. T. Batsford)

Moore, Sally F. (1972), 'Legal liability and evolutionary interpretation: some aspects of strict liability, self-help and collective responsibility' in Max Gluckman (ed.) *The allocation of responsibility* (Manchester: Manchester University Press)

Mullard, Chris (1973), *Black Britain* (London: Allen & Unwin)

Nairn, Tom (1975), 'The modern Janus', *New Left Review*, no. 94 November–December 1975

Novak, Michael (1971), *The rise of the unmeltable ethnics* (New York: Macmillan)

Ollerearnshaw, Susan (1983), 'The promotion of employment equality in Britain' in Ken Young and Nathan Glazer *Ethnic pluralism and public policy* (London: Heinemann Educational)

Owen, David (1978), *Human rights* (London: Jonathan Cape)

Palley, Claire (1978), 'Constitutional law and minorities' (London: Minority Rights Group. Report 36)

Parkes, James (1938), *The Jew in the medieval community* (London: The Soncino Press)

Parkin, Frank (1979), *Marxism and class theory: a bourgeois critique* (London: Tavistock)

Parsons, Talcott (1942), 'The sociology of modern anti-semitism' in Isacque Graebner and Stewart Henderson Britt *Jews in a gentile world* (New York: Macmillan)

Parsons, Talcott (1960), 'A new deal for the American Negro' in *Sociological theory and modern society* (New York: The Free Press)

Payne, Robert (1966), *The rise and fall of Stalin* (London: W. H. Allan)

Pettigrew, Thomas (1971), *Racially separate or together* (New York: McGraw-Hill)

Piven, F. F. and Cloward R. A. (1979), *Poor people's movements* (New York: Vintage Books)

Radawanski, George (1978), *Trudeau* (Toronto: Macmillan of Canada)

Rainwater, Lee and Yancey, William (1967), *The Moynihan Report and the politics of controversy* (Cambridge: M.I.T. Press)

Rex, John (1974), *Sociology and the demystification of the modern world* (London: Routledge and Kegan Paul)

Rex, John (1979), 'Black militancy and class conflict' in Robert Miles and Annie Phizaclea (eds.) *Racism and political action* (London: Routledge & Kegan Paul)

Rex, John and Tomlinson, Sally (1979), *Colonial immigrants in a British city* (London: Routledge & Kegan Paul)

Robinson, Cedric (1979), 'The emergence and limitations of European radicalism', *Race and Class* vol. XXI, no. 2, Autumn 1979

Robinson, Jacob et al. (1943), *Were the Minorities Treaties a failure?* (New York: Antin Press Inc.)

Robinson, Jacob (1944), 'The Soviet solution of the minorities problem' in R. M. MacIver (ed.) *Group relations and group antagonisms* (New York: Harper & Row)

Rose, Arnold (ed.) (1964), *The Negro in America* (New York: Harper & Row)

Rose, E. J. B. et al. (eds) (1969), *Colour and citizenship: a report on British race relations* (London: Oxford University Press)

References

Rose, Peter I. (1977), *Strangers in their midst. Small-town Jews and their neighbours* (Merrick, New York: Richmond Publishing Company)

Rothman, Stanley (1974), 'A confusion of perspectives' in Peter Rose and Stanley Rothman (eds) *Through different eyes* (New York: Oxford University Press)

Rothman, Stanley and Licther, Robert S. (1982), *Roots of radicalism: Jews, Christians and the New Left* (New York: Oxford University Press)

Rothschild, Joseph (1981), *Ethnopolitics: a conceptual framework* (New York: Columbia University Press)

Roucek, Joseph S. and Eisenberg, Bernard (eds) (1982), *America's ethnic politics* (Westport, Conn.: Greenwood Press)

Schlesinger, Arthur M. Jr. (1965), *A thousand days. John F. Kennedy in the White House* (Boston: Houghton Mifflin Company)

Schrag, Peter (1972), *The vanishing American* (London: Gollancz)

Sellin, Thorsten (1938), *Culture conflict and crime* (New York: Social Science Research Council)

Shannon, Richard (1976), *The crisis of imperialism* (London: Paladin)

Sitkoff, Harvard (1978), *A new deal for Blacks* (New York: Oxford University Press)

Sivanandan, A. (1976), 'Race, class and the state: the black experience in Britain', *Race and Class* vol. XVII, no. 4, April 1976

Sivanandan, A. (1981), 'From resistance to rebellion: Asian and Afro-Caribbean struggles in Britain', *Race and Class* vol. XXIII, no. 2/3, Autumn 1981/Winter 1982

Smith, Anthony D. (1983), 'Nationalism and classical social theory', *British Journal of Sociology* vol. 34, no. 1, March 1983

Stein, Howard F. and Hill, Robert F. (1977), *The ethnic imperative* (Pennsylvania: Pennsylvania State University Press)

Steiner, George (1978), Review of Leslek Kolakowski *Main currents of Marxism*, *Sunday Times* 26 November 1978

Stewart, Robert 1971, *The politics of protection* (Cambridge: Cambridge University Press)

Stone, Julius (1933), *Regional guarantees of minority rights* (New York: Macmillan)

Stonequist, Everett V. (1942), 'The marginal character of Jews' in Isacque Graebner and Stewart Henderson Britt *Jews in a gentile world* (New York: Macmillan)

Svensson, Frances (1979), 'Liberal democracy and group rights', *Political Studies* vol. XXVII no. 3 (September 1979)

Szajkowski, Zosa (1974), *Jews, wars and communism* volume 2 (New York: Ktav Publishing House Inc.)

Timerman, Jacobo (1982), *The longest war* (London: Chatto & Windus)

Tinker, Hugh (1977), *Race, conflict and the international order* (London: Macmillan)

Trotsky, Leon (1924), 'Anglo-American rivalry and the growth of militarism', speech of 28 July 1924, printed in *Collected writings and speeches on Britain* vol. 1, R. Chappell and A. Clinton, (eds) (1974) (Clapham: Plough Press)

References

Trotsky, Leon (1947), *Stalin* ed. and trans. Charles Malamuth (London: Hollis & Carter)

Trotsky, Leon (1975), *Social democracy and the wars of intervention in Russia, 1918–21* (First published Moscow, 1922) (London: New Park Publications)

Trudeau, Pierre Elliott (1968), *Federalism and the French Canadians* (Toronto: Macmillan)

Turner, Jonathan H. and Singleton, Royce (1978), 'A theory of ethnic oppression', *Social Forces* vol. 56

Van den Berghe, Pierre L. (1975), *Man in society: a biosocial view* (New York: Elsevier Scientific Publishing Company)

Van den Berghe, Pierre L. (1981), *The ethnic phenomenon* (New York: Elsevier)

Wagley, Charles and Harris, Marvin (1958), *Minorities in the New World* (New York: Columbia University Press)

Wallman, Sandra (ed.) (1979), *Ethnicity at work* (London: Macmillan)

Watson, James L. (1977), *Between two cultures: migrants and minorities in Britain* (Oxford: Basil Blackwell)

Webster, Nesta H. (1931), *The surrender of an empire* (London: Boswell)

Weiss, Richard (1979), 'Ethnicity and reform', *Journal of American History* vol. 66, December 1979

White, Theodore (1965), *The making of the president, 1964* (London: Jonathan Cape)

Williams, Robert J. and Kershaw, David A. (1979), 'Kennedy and Congress: the struggle for the New Frontier', *Political Studies* vol. XXVII, no. 3, September 1979

Williams, Robin M. Jr. (1948), *The reduction of intergroup tension* (New York: Social Science Research Council)

Willis, P. (1977), *Learning to labour* (Farnborough: Saxon House)

Wills, Garry (1982), *The Kennedy imprisonment* (New York: Atlantic-Little, Brown)

Wirth, Louis (ed.) (1956), *The ghetto* (Chicago: University of Chicago Press)

Worsley, Peter (1967), *The third world* (London: Weidenfeld & Nicolson)

York, Alan (1981), 'American Jewish leaders from the periphery', *Jewish Journal of Sociology* vol. XXIII, no. 1, June 1981

Young, Jock (1983), 'Striking back against the empire', *Critical Social Policy* vol. VII, no. 1, Autumn 1983

Young, Michael (1958), *The rise of the meritocracy* (Harmondsworth: Penguin)

INDEX

Acton, John Dalhberg, 17, 18, 73
affirmative action in US, 143–4
Africa, 44, 163
Algeria, 141, 194
Aliens Act, 1905, 150, 167
ambivalence: rationality of, 155; response to dualism (q.v.), 8
American Declaration of Independence, 189
American Federation of Labor, 166
Americanization programme, 92, 222
Asquith, Herbert Henry, 137
Attlee, Clement, 140
Australia, aboriginal culture, 166
Austria: bastion of feudalism, 207, 212; communal destabilization of, 214–18

Bakke case, 146
Bakunin, Mikhail, 215–17, 239
Balfour, Arthur James, 152
Baltzell, Digby, 48, 171
Bangladesh, 34
Banton, Michael, 131
Barker, Martin, 21, 248
Basham, Richard, 74–5
Basques, 29, 231
Bauer, Otto, 82, 89, 223
'Beaconsfieldism', 110
Begin, Menachim, 147
Belgium: as plural society, 138; ratification of independence, 210
Benn, Tony, 151
Bentinck, Lord George, 103–5
Berlin, Isaiah, 105
Bermant, Chaim, 60, 159, 160
Bevan, Nye, 27

Bierstedt, Robert, 164
Bill of Rights, 198, 206
Bismarck, Otto Eduard von, 213–15
'Black Cabineteers', 152
black crime, 25, 123–5
Black Hand, 132
Black Parents Movement, 130
black sections in Labour Party, 139, 152
Blair, Thomas, 15, 154
Boas, Franz, 157, 166
Bolsheviks: coup, 248; strategy on minorities, 62, 80–9, 223, 226, 242
Bonaparte, Napoleon, 55
Bonapartist integration, 9, 54–5, 67–9, 88, 106–7
Bourassa, Henri, 72
Boyson, Rhodes, 108
Brauer, Carl, 99
Brent Labour Party, 152
Bretons, 29
British Leyland, 235
British North America Act, 71, 76
Broken Hill, 246
Brotz, Howard, 119
Bryant, Christopher, 252
buffer institutions, 139–40
Bulhan, Hussein, 163

Campaign against Racial Discrimination (CARD), 139
Canada: Charter of Rights, 71, 77; French nationalism in 70–7; Official Languages Act, 75; Royal Commission on Bilingualism and Biculturalism, 71, 75
Carter, Jimmy, 148, 226

Catalans, 43, 231
Caucasian Bureau, 87
Chartists, 102, 138
Cheka, 56
China, 194, 248
Chinese: enterprise of, 49; in the US, 120
Churchill, Winston, 204, 224
Civil Rights Act, 1957, 93, 96
Civil Rights Act, 1964, 99, 143, 146
civil rights movement, 151, 162, 225
class: humanist veil for communalism, 27–31, 183, 193, 239–46; mechanical solidarity of, 48; nationalist feet, 21–5, 62, 190–200; segmentary tendency, 192–4, 240, 243; in the US, 28–9, 246; voluntary nature of bond, 23, 184; in workers' states, 232–3, 246–50
Clause Four, 194
Cleaver, Eldridge, 56
clientship role of minorities: accommodation to dualism, 9, 45–6; avoidance of competition, 49–52; benefits of, 259–60; dangers in, 52–3; dispersed by party system, 135–6; economic, 46–53; ideological, 58–64; at international level, 42–5; political, 53–8, 135–55 *passim*; in trade union movement, 245
Cloward, R. A., 141
Cobban, Alfred, 220
collective responsibility and social control, 113–17; *see also* compurgation
collectivism, *see* communalism; fraternalism
Comintern, 222, 248
'Commentary', 147
Commonwealth Immigrants Act, 1962, 150
communalism: contrasted with class, 22–6, 190–200; fractious nature, 187; fraternalist morality, 180–8; nationalist form of, 190–4; need for humanist cover, 27–31, 177–8, 183–4, 195, 200, 241; power of, 177–201

Community Relations Commission (CRC), 139
complementary legitimation, 95, 101
compurgation, 234–6
Congress of Vienna, 199, 207, 209–10
consensualism: limitations of, 32, 256; reason for popularity, 251–3; in theories of community relations, 16–20, 222; utopian aspect, 59, 258
Conservative Party, *see* Tory Party
Constitutional Bloc, 209
Constitutional Monarchy, 199, 209
Council for Racial Equality (CRE), 139
Cox, Oliver Cromwell, 44
crime: group responsibility for, 113–34; lure of, 123; as service occupation, 51–2; *see also* black crime
Crossman diaries, 149
Cuba, 194
culture: differing evaluations of, 157–60; as justification for imperialism, 214; objective test of, 157–73, 220; pluralist, 158, 164–5, 219
Cyprus, 34

decolonization: of Africa, 163; and capitalism, 24; and US expansionism, 34–5, 40, 57, 92, 224–6
Democratic Party: and black vote, 151, 245; on civil rights, 91–100, 143–8; minority caucasus in, 139
Detroit, 246
discrimination: liberal dilemma, 15–18; mystification as racism, 236; stability of social order and, 228–50 *passim*
Disraeli, Benjamin, 9, 61, 101–10, 248
Divine Right, 180, 196
D'Silva, Everard E., 126
dual labour market, 46
'Dual Monarchy', 217
dualism: importance of acknowledging, 31–41; methodological, 255; minority accommodation to, 45–6; of minority identity, 172–3; of modern state, 15–41 *passim*; need to reduce, 257–9; in treatment of

minorities, 5–6, 12, 21, 31, 121–2, 154, 157
Du Bois, W. E. B., 172
duplicity of national majority, 7, 16, 19, 31–2, 178–9

Eisenhower, Dwight D., 93
Emerson, Rupert, 15
Engels, Friedrich, 210, 213
Ethiopia, 34, 44, 54, 232
ethnic honour, 126–34
ethnopolitics, 25–31, 159, 242

Fabianism, 218, 226
factionalism in minority groups, 6–7, 135–55 *passim*
Fanon, Frantz, 74, 161
Ferdinand, Archduke Franz, 217
feudalism: challenge from humanism, 196–9, 207; as closed society, 180; made scapegoat for communalism, 220, 224
Fichte, Johann Gottlieb, 208
First International, 207, 215–16
France: adoption of humanism, 198, 204–9; revolution in, 198, 206, 212; as universal state, 40; at Versaille conference, 219
Franklin, John Hope, 56, 99
fraternalism: logic of, 184–95; source of popular legitimacy, 38, 182–3
Freedman, Maurice, 119
French Canadians, 69–77 *passim*, 190
French Declaration of the Rights of Man, 189, 206

Gandhi, 'Mahatma', 140
Garrard, John, 166, 233
Gartner, Lloyd, 167, 168
Gaulle, Charles de, 71, 141
Geertz, Clifford, 20
Georgia: nationalisms in, 83, 90; Stalin's dilemma, 87–9
German Declaration of Rights, 189
Germany: Black Americans and, 56; irredentism, 43, 221–2; national-ism, 208, 212–17; partition of, 186,

224; rising power of, 226; Spar-tacist revolt, 63
Gilroy, Paul, 124
Glazer, Nathan, 145, 166
Gompers, Samuel, 166
Great Britain: adoption of human-ism, 207–10; imperialism of, 108–10, 215, 217; post-imperial decline, 231; as universal state, 40, 101, 209
Greece, 34
Grunwick affair, 244–5
Gumplowitz, Ludwig, 242

halal slaughter, 162
Hapsburgs, 214, 217–18, 220
harmony of natural interests, 7, 259; *see also* consensualism
Harris, Marvin, 18, 19, 32
Hechter, Michael, 159
Héraud, Guy, 159
Herder, Johann Gottfried von, 213
Hingley, Ronald, 86, 88
Hitler Adolf, 159
Hohenzollerns, 220
Holland, 138
Howe, Irving, 162
Huguenots, 50
human rights: 170, 180–90 *passim*, 196–200; *see also* minority rights
humanism: division into liberalism and socialism, 198; and minority rights, 42, 202–4; moderating role of, 200–1; nationalist use of, 208, 210–17; *see also* universalism
Hungary: autonomy in Dual Mon-archy, 217; Socialist Peoples' Re-public, 63

Immigration Act, 1924 (US), 166
immigration: lobbies, 168–9; politics of control, 149
India, 34, 140
individualism: élitist implication, 38, 181; and selfishness, 187; spirit of liberalism, 37, 180–3
international relations, 42–4, 202–27
Iran, 43, 232
Irish Home Rule, 137

Irish in Britain, 102, 133
Israel, 30, 238
Italian Americans, 132

Jacobin terror, 199
Japan, 194, 221, 224, 226
Jewish Board of Guardians, 167–8
Jewish Chronicle, 167
Jews: acculturation of, 159; and class consciousness, 62; enterprise among, 50; humanist visionaries, 59–64; in medieval Europe, 118–19; Mensheviks, 83; place in the Labour Party, 152; in New Right, 147; in Politburo, 63; Russian dissidents, 43
'Jim Crow', 92, 222, 225
Johnson, Lyndon B.: civil rights legislation, 98–9; Great Society, 141–4
Joseph, Emperor Francis, 218
Joseph, Sir Keith, 152

Kennedy, John F., 9, 71, 91–100, 101
Kennedy, Joseph, 94
Kenya constitutional conference, 150
Kerner Report, 35, 237
Khan, Javed, 169
Killian, Lewis, 257
King, Martin Luther, 95
Kissinger, Henry, 147, 226
Klineberg, Otto, 163
'Koba', 83–4
Korea, 186
Ku Klux Klan, 56, 92, 222
Kun, Bela, 63
Kurds, 29, 43, 258

La Rose, John, 130
Labour Party, 27, 28, 108, 137, 138–9, 149, 169, 194
Lambert, John, 133
Lassalle, Ferdinand, 61
Laurier, Wilfred, 70, 72, 74
Lea, John, 25
League of Nations, 205, 219–22
Lenin (Vladimir Ilich Ulyanov): attitude to imperialism, 22, 79–81; as patron of Stalin, 9, 78–90 *passim*;

two-stage policy on self-determination, 81; universalizing Russia, 40, 216, 249
Lesage, Jean, 71
Lévesque, René, 71–2, 75–7, 190
Liberal Party, 106–8, 137, 150, 200
Liberal Party (Canada), 71, 74–6
liberalism: accommodation with nationalism, 183, 188–90, 194–5; facility in concealing nationalism, 230–1, 246–9; minimal conception of state, 37, 199, 247; ruling version of humanism (q.v.), 37–8, 181–2, 200, 209, 230–2, 248–9; western monopoly on, 214–16, 223
Lloyd George, David, 219
Luxemburg, Rosa, 61–4, 89
lynch-law, 127–8

McAdam, Doug, 141
MacDonald, Ian, 153
Macedonians, 186
McGrath, Peter, 165
MacIver, Robert, 16, 33
McLeod, Ian, 150
Macmillan, Harold, 141
Maltese in Britain: criminal activities, 122; experience of collective responsibility, 113–16, 125; subject to dual expectations, 2–6
marginal men, 171–2
Marx, Karl, 17, 60, 63, 215, 244
Maurois, André, 109
Mazzini, Joseph, 188, 190
Mendès-France, Pierre, 141
Mensheviks: in Georgia, 87–8; Jews as, 83
meritocracy, 182
'Midstream', 147
Miles, Robert, 257
Minogue, Kenneth, 15
minority rights: different concepts of, 204–5; guaranteed by League of Nations, 219–22; stages in development of, 205–27; weapon for national majorities, 200, 202–4
Minorities Treaties, 220–1, 224
Moi, President Arap, 232

Montagu, Edwin, 152
Moore, Sally, 114, 118
Mountbatten, Lord Louis, 141
Moynihan, Daniel P., 145
Moynihan Report, 123
Mullard, Chris, 123
Myrdal, Gunnar, 154, 178, 180

NAACP, 139, 155
National Front, 149
National Italian-American League to Combat Defamation, 132
Neil, Ambrozine, 152
New Deal, 36, 93, 222, 245
New Left, 21–5
'New Republic', 147
New Right, 145–8, 225–6
Newham by-election, 152
Nixon, richard, 145–8, 226
Novak, Michael, 160

Office of Minority Business Enterprise, 146
Ogaden, uprising in, 34
Oppenheimer, Franz, 213
Ordzhanikidze, S., 87
Ottomans, 216, 220
Owen, David, 170

Paine, Thomas, 206
Pakistan, 34
Palestine, 197
Palmerston, Lord Henry, 107, 199, 209, 214
Pan-African Congress, 163
pan-Anglo-Saxonism, 217
pan-Germanism, 214–15
pan-Slavism, 225, 242
Parkes, James, 118
Parsons, Talcott, 18, 94
Parti Québecois, 71, 75
Pearson, Lester B., 74
Persia, 232
Pettigrew, Thomas, 253
Phizaclea, Annie, 257
Piven, F. F., 141
Plaid Cymru, 28
Plural society, 138
Podhoretz, Norman, 147

Police Bill, 39
Polish Americans and Polonia, 129
Powell, Enoch, 125
Pretoria, 246
primordialism, 20
Primrose League, 167
progressive nationalism: basis of political compact, 38–41, 183, 193–5, 234–5; competitive adoption of, 208, 210–18; interdependence of parts, 177–9, 195, 236–7, 255–6; synthesis of legitimations in, 38–40, 188–90, 194–5
Protectionist Party, 103–7 *passim*
Prussia, 80, 212–14
'Public Interest', 147
purdah, 162

Quadruple Alliance, 209
Quebec: autonomy movement, 70–7, 190; Bill 101 76; Sovereignty-Association referendum, 76

racism: mystification of nationalism, 236–8; taint of, 41
Radawanski, George, 70, 72
Rainwater, Lee, 124
Rastafarians, 131, 164
Ratzenhofer, Gustav, 213
Reagan, Ronald, 148
'Red Summer' of 1919, 56
Reform Act, 209
Reform Bill, *see* Second Reform Bill
Reformation, 159, 197
Republican Party, 91, 93–4, 143, 145–8
Restoration Settlement, 198
Rex, John, 20
Robinson, Jacob, 83
Romanovs, 220
Roosevelt, Franklin Delano, 93, 95, 152, 224, 245
Roots, tracing of, 161–6
Rose, Arnold, 155, 177
Rose, E. J. B., 165
Rosenbergs, trial of, 56
Rothman, Stanley, 163
Rothschild, Joseph, 25

Rushdie, Salman, 163
Russia: beneficiary of Versailles Treaty, 221; fear of western penetration, 80–2, 216–17; Declaration of the Rights of the Peoples of, 85, dissident Jews in, 43; modernization of Empire, 79–90 *passim*, 223, 242; nationalization of revolution, 63, 89, 249; October revolution, 85–6; as universal state, 40; uprising in 1905, 81; *see also* Bolsheviks; Stalin

Salisbury, Lord Robert, 107, 109
Scarman Report, 35, 237
Schmoller, Gustav, 213
Schrag, Peter, 147
Schwarzenberg, Prince Felix, 214
Scottish nationalism, 185–6
Second International, 61–2, 216, 248
Second Reform Bill, 106–7
self-determination by minorities: stages in formulation, 202–5; Stalin's manoeuvre, 83–9; Versailles implementation, 220–3; *see also* Bolsheviks
Sellin, Thorsten, 121
Serbia, Austrian attack on, 218
Serbs, 186, 217
Silesians, 186
Simmel, Georg, 164, 228
Sivanandan, A., 21, 130
socialism: appeal to minorities, 59–64; difficulty in concealing nationalism, 193–4, 216–17, 233, 241, 246–50; oppositional variant of humanism (q.v.), 198–9, 215, 232–3; sparring partner for liberalism, 242, 246, 248–50
sociobiology, 20–2
Somalia, action in Ogaden, 34
Spain, 43, 160, 209
Spartacist revolt, 63
split labour market, 46
Sri Lanka, 34
Stalin (Joseph Vissarionovich Djugashvili), 9, 54, 62, 78–90, 91, 95, 96, 100, 101, 141, 165, 223, 224, 249

Stanfield, Robert, 75
Steiner, George, 58
Stonequist, Everett, 171
super-patriotism of minorities, 53–8
Swann Report, 260
sweated labour, 50–1
Switzerland, 138
Szajkowski, Zosa, 64

Talmud, 59, 167
Tamils, 34, 186
Tertius Gaudens, *élite* power of, 228
Tocqueville, Alexis de, 164
Tory Party, 103–10, 141, 149, 248
Touré, Sekou, 163
Trades Union Council (TUC), 244
Transcaucasian Federation, 88
Treitschke, Heinrich von, 213
Triple Entente, 217
Trotsky (Lev Davidovich Bronstein), 62–4, 78, 84, 89, 218, 222
Trudeau, Pierre, 9, 69–77, 190
Turkey, 34

Ulster Catholics, 29
underclass, *see* dual labour market
Union Nationale, Quebec, 71
United Nations: charter, 189, 205; instrument of Soviet-American accord, 224–6
United States: anti-imperialist stance, 35, 40, 57, 92, 224–6; dualism of, 15–16, 177–8; ethnic politics within, 91–100, 142–8; as universal state, 40; WASP cultural domination of, 164–5; world leadership, 218–27
universal state, 18, 40
universalizing nationalism, *see* progressive nationalism
universalism: basis of international order, 36–8, 196–8; minorities as upholders of, 58–64; nationalist vetoes on, 200–1; *see also* humanism

Van den Berghe, Pierre, 20
Versailles, Treaty of, 159, 205, 218–21

Victoria, Queen, 109
Vietnam, Black Americans in, 56

Wagley, Charles, 18, 19, 32
Wagner, Richard, 160
Wallerstein, Immanuel, 195
Walloons, 29
Weber, Max, 54, 239
Welsh nationalism, 27–31
White Hand Society, 132
Williams, Robin, 16, 126

Wills, Garry, 91
Wilson, Woodrow, 218–20
Wirth, Louis, 118

Yeats, William Butler, 162
Young, Andrew, 55
'Young England', 106
Young, Jock, 25
Young, Michael, 182

Zangwill, Israel, 152